CW00922954

Advance Praise for *Af*

"Throughout this wonderfully written and fascinating story of talents, ambitions, clashes, failures, and successes I kept thinking, 'Who can ever predict the path that life will turn?' This was a great comfort to me. Again and again it was the serendipitous mix of new 'actors' arriving onto the stage that resulted in the most marvelous artistic and business accomplishments.

To my eyes the invisible Hand of Providence is clearly at work in the way this history unfolded and that this book captured so beautifully."

—Glen Keane, Academy Award® winning Director, Animator, and Disney Legend

"On each page, this inspiring book reveals new details regarding the transition from Walt Disney and his Nine Old Men, to the second renaissance of Traditional Animation. How the veterans who invented 'The Illusion Of Life' passed down their tribal knowledge, and craftsmanship to their apprentices who went on to bring you 'The Little Mermaid,' 'Beauty and the Beast,' and 'The Lion King.' This book also reports on the shift from a boutique family run studio to a corporate powerhouse. Mr. O'Brien is a respected journalist who gleaned, and meticulously fact checked each detail with the folks who were actually there—who shared with him their respect, passion, and love for hand drawn animation, soon perhaps a lost art. A page turner of animation history in a book you can trust, that inspires, and delights."

—Tony Anselmo,
Animator, Voice of Donald Duck, and Disney Legend

"I worked at the studio for forty years and voraciously read many, many books on Disney Studios. I learned more about the man Walt Disney from this book than any other book I've ever read—who he was, not what he did. Neil O'Brien has written an entirely fresh, compelling book full of incredibly well-researched, deep dive personal accounts from the primary players that ran the studio. How could there possibly be this many things I didn't know about the second golden era of animated films—and I was there for the entire run! All written in such an engrossing, intimate way. Kudos to an epic book of animated proportions."

—Mike Gabriel, director of *Pocahontas*
and *The Rescuers Down Under*

After Disney

**TOIL, TROUBLE, AND THE TRANSFORMATION
OF AMERICA'S FAVORITE MEDIA COMPANY**

Neil O'Brien

Post Hill
PRESS

A POST HILL PRESS BOOK
ISBN: 979-8-88845-138-0
ISBN (eBook): 979-8-88845-139-7

After Disney:
Toil, Trouble, and the Transformation of America's Favorite Media Company
© 2025 by Neil O'Brien
All Rights Reserved

Cover design by Cody Corcoran
Cover photo licensed from Associated Press

This book, as well as any other Post Hill Press publications, may be purchased in bulk quantities at a special discounted rate. Contact orders@posthillpress.com for more information.

This is a work of nonfiction. All people, locations, events, and situations are portrayed to the best of the author's memory.

No part of this book may be reproduced, stored in a retrieval system, or transmitted by any means without the written permission of the author and publisher.

Post Hill Press
New York • Nashville
posthillpress.com

Published in the United States of America
1 2 3 4 5 6 7 8 9 10

To Kim, Henry, and Abigail

"Magic is only magic once upon a time."
—Walt Disney

Table of Contents

Timeline of Key Events xi

Prologue: Once Upon a Time... xiii

Chapter 1 1

Chapter 2 17

Chapter 3 27

Chapter 4 35

Chapter 5 44

Chapter 6 51

Chapter 7 62

Chapter 8 74

Chapter 9 85

Chapter 10 100

Chapter 11 115

Chapter 12 121

Chapter 13 135

Chapter 14 144

Chapter 15 157

Chapter 16 173

Chapter 17 183

Chapter 18 197

Chapter 19 214

Epilogue: Ever After 219

Endnotes 233

Author's Note 267

About the Author 271

Timeline of Key Events

December 15, 1966: Walt Disney dies from lung cancer

December 20, 1966: Ron Miller joins Disney's board of directors

December 1967: Roy E. Disney joins Disney's board of directors

1968: Ron Miller is named executive producer, Walt Disney Productions

Fall 1970: California Institute of the Arts (CalArts) opens

December 24, 1970: *The Aristocats* is released

Spring 1971: Disney's animation training program begins

October 1, 1971: Walt Disney World opens

December 20, 1971: Roy O. Disney dies

Fall 1975: CalArts Character Animation program begins

March 4, 1977: Roy E. Disney leaves Walt Disney Productions, remains on board

June 22, 1977: *The Rescuers* is released

November 3, 1977: *Pete's Dragon* is released

December 16, 1978: *The Small One* is released

September 13, 1979: Don Bluth leaves Disney Animation

June 3, 1980: Ron Miller is named president of Walt Disney Productions

July 10, 1981: *The Fox and the Hound* is released

July 9, 1982: *Tron* is released

October 1, 1982: EPCOT Center opens

February 1983: Ron Miller is named CEO of Walt Disney Productions

April 15, 1983: Tokyo Disneyland opens

April 18, 1983: The Disney Channel is launched

February 15, 1984: Touchstone Pictures is founded

March 9, 1984: *Splash* is released

March 9, 1984: Roy E. Disney resigns from Disney's board of directors

September 7, 1984: Ron Miller resigns from Walt Disney Productions, facing pressure from board

September 22, 1984: Michael Eisner is named chairman and CEO of Walt Disney Productions, Frank Wells is named president and chief operating officer

September 28, 1984: *Country* is released

July 24, 1985: *The Black Cauldron* is released

Prologue: Once Upon a Time...

When Walt Disney died of lung cancer on December 15, 1966, Disney Animation almost disappeared with him. The loss of that storied Animation Department would have essentially killed off what is now a multibillion-dollar industry. Most of today's major animation studios have roots in the Disney Animation Department of the 1970s and 1980s, as well as the Character Animation Department at the California Institute of the Arts—established in the mid-'70s as a feeder program for Disney. This era laid the groundwork for the Disney renaissance—a series of animated films beginning with 1989's *The Little Mermaid*—as well as the creation of DreamWorks Animation and Pixar. It was also the breeding ground for major directors like Tim Burton (*Wednesday, Batman*), Brad Bird (*The Incredibles, Ratatouille*) and Henry Selick (*Coraline*). In 2023, the top seven most-streamed films in the U.S. were all animated.[1] Given the medium's current prominence, it seems inconceivable that it all nearly disappeared half a century ago—but looking back at 1966, it seemed equally inconceivable that Walt Disney would ever die.

To those who knew Walt or watched him on television every week, he didn't seem to be slowing down in his sixties. Even as he was aging before their eyes, his ambition was as great as any time in his company's four decades of operation. He would occasionally acknowledge he wouldn't live forever, but few took notice. In 1966, he gave an interview to Australian journalist Margaret Jones in which he mused about Walt Disney Productions "after Disney." The reporter noticed something odd about the comment. Walt seemed to be talking about death, not retirement. Yet Jones admitted in her column that she couldn't fully reconcile the comment. She wrote, "Disney may be near the age when most men start thinking of tending their gardens, but in many ways he is just beginning to reach his peak."[2] Mortality seemed to be incongruous with Walt's boundless vision for the future.

It's believed Walt was unaware of his late-stage cancer throughout 1966 until just a few weeks before he died. The aging mogul was experiencing severe pain; he thought it stemmed from a decades-old polo injury from his early Hollywood days[3]—back when he and his brother Roy played against the likes of fellow moguls Jack Warner and Hal Roach. He seemed to not suspect the polo pain was instead caused by terminal lung cancer brought on by years of heavy smoking.

In early November 1966, Walt went into the hospital for surgery. His health concerns were slipped into TV personality Ed Sullivan's gossip column: "Walt Disney needs throat surgery."[4] The item was eclipsed by headlines of a more prominent patient undergoing throat surgery at the same time, President Lyndon Johnson. Two weeks later, Walt Disney Productions finally issued a public statement acknowledging part of Walt's left lung was removed after a lesion was found. Perhaps because of LBJ's favorable prognosis the prior week—a benign polyp on the president's vocal cords—or because Walt himself was downplaying the severity of his cancer, most newspapers gave Walt a preordained happy ending: "All's Well After Walt Disney's Lung Surgery."[5] Only a few articles included: "[the studio] declined to disclose whether the tumor was malignant."[6]

After the diagnosis, Walt returned to the studio lot in Burbank. He had a drink in his office with one of his closest confidants, producer Bill Anderson.

"They found a spot on my lung," Walt said—as Anderson would later tell an interviewer.

"Oh my God, Walt." Anderson was in disbelief.

"Don't worry now, I'm gonna whip it. They found it, they're gonna go in, take a biopsy and so forth."[7] It wasn't until after Walt's demise that Anderson looked back and realized Walt knew he was dying.

Chapter 1

At 9:30 a.m. on December 15, 1966, at St. Joseph's Hospital directly across the street from his Burbank studio, Walt Disney lost his battle with lung cancer. He had just turned sixty-five a few days earlier. News of his death quickly spread across his empire. Within minutes, Walt Disney Productions VP Donn Tatum called Orbin "Mel" Melton, the president of Disney's theme park design group WED Enterprises, to break the news. The men sat in stunned silence, unable to find any words to convey their grief. Minutes passed before either could hang up. "It is such a tragic thing," Melton wrote later that afternoon. "It seems that he was just on the threshold of building the biggest dream I think a single man has ever dreamed," referring to Walt's plans for Disney World, which included a utopian Experimental Proto-type Community of Tomorrow (EPCOT), as well as other projects like Mineral King, a ski resort, and the further expansion of Disneyland.[8]

Walt's employees were utterly devastated. "The only thing that came close to that, and it didn't really come close, was the assassination of JFK," recalls Floyd Norman, the studio's first Black cartoonist, who got to know Walt well that final year while working in the Story Department on *The Jungle Book*. "That day, we were kind of thunderstruck, wondering what the hell had just happened.... It was a sense of disbelief, the sense of shock. It was watching grown men walk to the parking lot with tears in their eyes. Literally watching people weep at the Disney Studio."

Phones at the Disney Studio were ringing off the hooks with inquiries from around the world. When a French journalist called for confirmation, the studio scrambled to find someone who could translate the press release.[9] They hadn't appreciated that the grief over Walt's death would be felt so widely and so personally. For years, "Uncle Walt" had been a staple in people's homes via Disney's weekly television show. California's then governor-elect Ronald Reagan, who was also one of the TV hosts for Disneyland's 1955 opening, said, "The world is a poorer place now."[10]

Walt's brother and lifelong business partner, Roy O. Disney, took Walt's death as hard as anyone. According to biographer Bob Thomas, Roy believed Walt had a "good chance" of making it—even just hours before he died.[11] It made the sting of death that much harder. It also threw off Roy's plans to retire. He was now seventy-three years old.

The prospect of Walt Disney Productions without its founder and namesake was troubling to investors. In an interview where Walt mused about a world 'after Disney,' he said, "As well as I can, I'm untying the apron strings."[12] But if succession was on Walt's mind, he left little evidence. In the minutes after his death, Disney stock plunged about 5 percent.[13] Rumors were flying about possible takeovers.[14] In a rare move, the New York Stock Exchange temporarily halted trading of Disney stock.[15] It would be among the most uncertain moments in the history of the stock—eclipsed perhaps by a hostile takeover attempt nearly two decades later. Roy had to quickly assemble a statement to reassure investors. It read: "It was Walt's wish that when the time came he would have built an organization with the creative talents to carry on.... We will continue to operate Walt Disney's company in the way that he has established and guided it."[16] When trading resumed, Disney stock rebounded.[17]

Roy's statement laid out the company's future priorities: film and television production, and the expansion of the theme park business. What was missing was any specific reference to the future of animation, once the core of the business. When Walt Disney moved to California in 1923, he operated his modest cartoon studio out of his uncle's garage. His business grew exponentially as his films gained popularity, notably with the introduction of Mickey Mouse in 1928 and the first animated feature *Snow White and the Seven Dwarfs* in 1937. Walt started to branch into hybrid live-action/animation films in the late-1940s (*Song of the South* in 1948, *So Dear to My Heart* in 1949) to help his studio rebound from World War II—but animation was still at the heart of everything. The studio lot in Burbank, built after the success of *Snow White*, was designed around the animation process with an underground corridor connecting the Animation Building, where the characters were drawn, with Ink & Paint, where they were painted and readied for filming. Things began to change in the 1950s after Walt released his first non-animated film, *Treasure Island* (1950). He continued to expand into live-action movies, television, and in 1955, he opened Disneyland.

By 1966, animation was a small part of the larger film and television portfolio, which itself represented less than half of the company's annual income. Around the time of Walt's death, films accounted for under 48 percent of the company's annual income, Disneyland 35 percent, and the rest was largely divided between television, music, and merchandising.[18] Animation was an expensive, time-consuming venture, and success was rarely instantaneous. After more than two decades and three rereleases, the animated film *Bambi* (1942) had finally earned about $8.6 million.[19] By contrast, the Hayley Mills comedy *That Darn Cat!* (1965) earned $9 million in its first release,[20] proving live-action films could be just as popular as animation and made with far less time and expense.

With Walt gone, his brother Roy had to figure out how to keep Walt Disney Productions moving forward, including who should lead the film division. After conferring with Walt's widow Lillian, Roy offered the job to Walt's close aide, producer Bill Anderson.[21] Anderson, a decade younger than Walt, grew up on a ranch in Cache County, Utah and moved to Hollywood in 1929. He abandoned his dreams of becoming either an actor or a lawyer, and instead worked for Firestone in production management.[22] During World War II, he joined Disney to help with production control.[23] In due time, Anderson rose through the ranks, from associate producer to the board of directors—and he was responsible for one of Disney's biggest live action hits, *Swiss Family Robinson* (1960).

In the wake of Walt's untimely passing, Roy offered Anderson the role of Production chief, but it came with an unimaginable request.

"Bill, when you finish the picture that we're working on [*The Jungle Book*], I want you to close up Feature Animation."

Anderson objected, "Roy, that's the most valuable thing we have." He understood animated films differentiated Disney from other studios.

Roy insisted, "Nobody could make feature animation pictures but Walt. I want you to close up Feature Animation."

"Roy, I won't do that unless you write me a memorandum."

There was silence between the two men.

Anderson continued, "I couldn't do what you're asking me to do. You have to write it, because I don't think people would understand." Walt's passing was shock enough. Shutting down Animation so soon after his death would compound the trauma. Anderson needed to make the case to keep animation alive. He invoked Walt.

"We already have an idea of what the next one will be and Walt has been in on it roughly," he said.[24] He was referring to *The Aristocats*, the story of a family of cats set to inherit their owner's fortune. It had originally been conceived by longtime Disney executive Harry Tytle as a live-action project, but he and Walt later agreed it could work better as a cartoon.[25] As early as 1965, *The Aristocats* was announced as the next animated feature after *The Jungle Book*.[26] Anderson was hoping Walt's initial green light was enough to convince Roy.

Anderson said, "He didn't approve [the story] but he did approve it as a project." He decided to push his luck with Roy, "I'll go ahead until I hear from you."[27]

With that, Anderson put the matter back in Roy's hands. If Disney Animation was shutting down, Roy would have to be the one to do it. Anderson knew he bought the Animation Department some time, but he didn't know how much.

With the fate of Disney Animation now in question, *The Aristocats* took on new significance. It would be the first animated film without

Walt's direct involvement. It needed to be a success on its first release. In the decade before Walt's death, Walt Disney Productions released only three full-length animated features: *Sleeping Beauty* (1959), *One Hundred and One Dalmatians* (1961), and *The Sword in the Stone* (1963). *Sleeping Beauty* was particularly expensive due to its larger-than-life 70 mm widescreen format, and when it didn't recoup its costs, the Animation Department was hit with layoffs. *The Aristocats* could not afford to follow that model.

Two weeks after Walt's death—in the week between Christmas and the New Year—Bill Anderson assembled a creative team to discuss *The Aristocats*. The huddle included key members of the Animation Department: Ken Anderson, Larry Clemmons, Vance Gerry, Dick Lucas, and Wolfgang 'Woolie' Reitherman, as well as screenwriters Bill Walsh, Don DaGradi and producer Winston Hibler.[28] This assembled team—responsible for Disney's most treasured films, from *Cinderella* (1950) to *Mary Poppins* (1964)—were trying to sort through the film's characters: who they were, what their names were, what they did and how many.

"You got too damn many cats…" one of the men offered.

"You need a dummy, you need a dopey, you need a cat that gets into trouble—a bad kid," another suggested.

"Certainly they have them in well-bred families as well as—don't look at me!"

They could still crack jokes, despite the seriousness of the assignment. The meeting concludes with the decision to continue building out the personalities and letting the story take shape from there.[29]

What is remarkable about this story meeting is not just the free exchange of ideas, but how little Walt was discussed. Just two weeks after Walt's death, no one mentioned anything along the lines of "Walt would have liked…" or "What would Walt do?" Disney storytelling was so ingrained in, and largely defined by, this group that they weren't entirely paralyzed by Walt's absence; with Walt's ever-expanding portfolio demanding his attention, they had grown accustomed to his absences. When Walt was referenced, it was only to contextualize earlier conversations. For example, when the men started to discuss what era the story takes place, one chimed in, "Walt just said, 'Why don't you make it around the turn of the century sometime?'"[30] The turn of the century coincided with Walt's childhood, and it became an endless source of inspiration. It was the backdrop for films like *Lady and the Tramp, So Dear to My Heart, Summer Magic*, and *Pollyanna*, as well as Disneyland's Main Street, U.S.A. As presented by Disney, this age is conflict free; the bumpiest ride on Main Street is a horse-drawn trolley. It is altogether fitting that the final animated film to receive Walt's blessing would be set during his favorite era.

Producer Harry Tytle is not listed as an attendee of this late December '66 story meeting, but the transcribed conversation shows he may have been there for at least one awkward moment. After much back-and-forth over how to streamline the story, one of the men said, "…Harry, we're not talking about changing the whole story—it's a matter of degrees."[31] Sometime around this meeting, Tytle was moved off the film. He wrote in his memoir, "My grief over Walt's passing was heightened by the pain of losing my project, like offspring adopted from me without my consent."[32]

Given the abrupt nature of Walt's death, Roy Disney formed an executive committee of Walt's lead advisers to take charge of the studio's creative decisions. It consisted of some of those involved in that early meeting shaping *The Aristocats*—Bill Anderson, Bill Walsh, Winston Hibler—as well as Harry Tytle, and director James Algar. None of the Animation Department veterans known as the Nine Old Men were included. The committee was rounded out by two junior members of the Disney family, Walt's son-in-law Ron Miller and Roy's son, Roy Edward Disney. The group reported up to Disney's VP of Marketing, Card Walker.[33] The effectiveness of the committee setup would later be questioned, but in the uncertain period after Walt's demise, it allowed for checks and balances in an era where other studios were gambling away fortunes.

Walt was a once-in-a-lifetime visionary, and his empire was so tied into his persona that it seemed no individual could replace him. However, Walt had hoped his beloved son-in-law could take over Walt

Disney Productions when the time was right. Of Ron Miller, Walt once said, "I have great ambitions for him. He will run the Studio one day."[34] Walt seemed to see more potential in Ron Miller than perhaps anyone else. Five days after Walt's death, Ron Miller was placed on the Disney board. More than a decade later, Walt's dream of Ron taking the helm as president and CEO of Walt Disney Productions would come true.

Ron Miller was born into a working-class family in April 1933, in Los Angeles. His father John was born in Trail, Canada, in 1905, more than a decade after that frontier city's initial gold rush.[35] Ron's mother Stella was originally from Kentucky.[36] Both made their way to California looking for better opportunities. For John, that meant steady employment at the Goodyear plant.[37] For Stella, it meant odd jobs like working at Hoffman's Chocolates[38] and later, as a cheese wrapper at a grocery store.[39] The family lived close to John's job at the Goodyear plant, and growing up, Ron would go see Santa hitch a ride on the company's famous blimp.[40]

John Miller loved the mythology of the West, a mystique reinforced by the movies. When the Millers had a second child in 1936, they named him John Wayne Miller—even though "the Duke" was still a B-picture actor who hadn't yet starred in *Stagecoach*. John Miller instilled in his sons a love of adventure and the outdoors. As an adult, Ron was able to fulfill his childhood dreams of being a cowboy at the Disney family's Diamond D ranch in Wyoming.

As a kid living in the shadow of Hollywood, young Ron loved going to the movies. Though Westerns were the family's favorites, Ron was coming of age as Disney animation was in its prime—with movies like *Pinocchio* and *Snow White*. "I had grown up on Walt Disney," he once said. "I had seen everything he had made."[41]

As he matured, Ron displayed innate charisma and athleticism. He would occasionally be confused for a matinee idol like Rock Hudson. Floyd Norman remembers, "The young Ron Miller, we're talking movie star looks. The women wanted to be with him and all the men wanted to be him." The statement belongs to a different era, but in a way so did Ron. He was the seeming embodiment of a certain kind of idealized

1950s American youth, which *Life Magazine* dubbed "The Luckiest Generation."[42] To put it another way, he was Disney's Prince Charming in the flesh.

In high school, Ron excelled at math and could compute complex problems in his head. Still, he was more of a jock than a star student and he could often be awkwardly quiet. He had a brash high school football coach who helped him get a scholarship to college. The coach called USC, demanding they help pay for Ron's tuition or else he'd make sure Ron got into rival UCLA.[43] It worked. Ron was accepted and attended USC on a football scholarship, just as his hero John Wayne had more than twenty-five years earlier. At USC, Ron majored in commerce and was known as "Mister 88," his jersey number for the USC Trojans.[44] At 6'4", 204 lb., Ron was built for football.[45] His USC teammates included future NFL cornerback Lindon Crow, future Disney executive Dick Nunis, and Al Baldock, who later mentored John Madden.[46]

One of the biggest games of USC's 1953 season was against rival UC-Berkeley on October 24. Seventy-eight thousand fans packed the stadium, including hundreds of USC students who made the trek up to Berkeley.[47] California played a messy game, fumbling the ball more than a half a dozen times.[48] USC took the lead and held it, despite California's attempts at a comeback. The victory was so lopsided that Ron's third-quarter touchdown almost seemed gratuitous to the reporters covering the game.[49] The final score was 32–20, with USC prevailing. As triumphant as that day was for Ron, the next few hours would change his life forever. After the win, Ron's teammate and close friend Tom Nickoloff arranged for a double date with Tom's girlfriend's roommate. Her name was Diane Disney.[50]

Diane Marie Disney was born to Walt and Lillian Disney on December 18, 1933. On the day of Diane's birth, Walt was nervously awaiting word of his daughter's arrival while receiving an award from *Parents' Magazine* for his "distinguished service to children."[51] He was only half listening to the "flowery and heart-throbbing"[52] speech extolling his films because he was keeping an ear out for the possible call that his wife was in labor. Just as Walt began his acceptance speech, an attendant whispered good news in his ear. "This is the biggest moment of my life," Walt told the crowd. "You'll pardon me, I'm sure, if I run away and show this beautiful medal to my wife and…"[53] With that, Walt sped off before the audience knew quite what happened—rushing to the hospital for Diane's birth.

From the start, Walt was smitten with his baby daughter. He laughed at her little hiccups and marveled as he counted her tiny fingers and toes. She was a good-natured baby who "doesn't cry," according to Walt. He would brag about her light-color hair and big brown eyes, which resembled his mother's. "I used to laugh at those poor mutts who thought they'd got the only baby in the world," he told a reporter. "Now I know.… She's the swellest baby you ever saw."[54] After Diane's birth, the Disneys wanted more children. Their hope was to have a large family, but Lillian suffered multiple miscarriages and ultimately they decided to adopt a child.[55] Diane's sister Sharon was welcomed into the family three years later.

Walt was a loving father who loved to entertain his daughters. For Christmas 1939, Santa delivered a cottage in their backyard, which was built to resemble the same Germanic fairy-tale influence as *Snow White*. It had a sloped roof, a bay window with curtains, running water and a white picket fence. When the girls entered the child-size house that Christmas morning, the phone rang. The girls picked up the call and found Santa on the other line, asking how they liked their new place.[56] On weekends, the Disney Studio became the girls' playground, where they were free to ride bicycles along Mickey Avenue or Dopey Drive.

Sometimes Walt's films didn't get the reaction from his daughters that he expected. Walt took five-year-old Diane to a private screening of *Snow White*, and when the evil Queen transformed into the old crone, Diane started crying. She was whisked outside; Walt later used the story to say the film wasn't meant for small children but instead, the child inside every adult.[57] Similarly, when he showed preteen Diane rushes of *Song of the South*, she found some of the scenes to be overly emotional and corny. Walt rarely watched dailies with Diane after that.[58] Still, he

couldn't help sharing all his ideas with his daughters over family dinners—held after he got home from his fourteen-hour workdays.

Diane appeared in one of Walt's early television specials called "One
Hour in Wonderland,"[59] but she never had much desire to join the family business. At USC, Diane was a member of the Kappa Alpha Theta
sorority and formed a close group of friends. The women dubbed their
three-story house "Theta Land."[60] Theta had the distinction of being
the first sorority at USC—dating back to 1887—with the mission of
offering "social, intellectual and moral growth" for its members.[61] Diane
fit in well. She was intellectually curious and studious, and loved the
arts. She was also a dynamo—a small but tough woman, strong-willed
and adventurous. On weekends, Diane and college friends would travel
the West to ski[62] or cheer on the USC Trojans.

That October 1953 night when Ron and Diane met, they did not
hit it off. When they joined their friends at a Bay Area dive bar, Ron
ordered "a shot of bourbon thinking I'm going to get in the mood."[63]
However, the day's excitement caught up with him and he began to
shut down. Diane, turned off, signaled to her friend that the sleepy Ron
seemed to be a "square." Even though Diane thought Ron was nodding
off, he saw her hand motions. Realizing the date was not going well, he
excused himself to the bathroom. He went back to the hotel and fell
asleep without saying goodbye.

The following day, it was time to head back to Los Angeles. Ron saw
Diane at the train station, and he apologized for his sudden disappear-
ance. On the ride home, they ordered beers and got to know each other
better.[64] This second unofficial date proved far more successful, and they
began a whirlwind romance.

Exactly two months later, on Christmas Day, Diane invited Ron to a
family party.[65] Ron was nervous at the prospect of meeting the legendary
Walt Disney. "I could hardly talk. Here's this great guy, who's probably
one of the most talented people in Hollywood back then. The most
celebrated, respected, and everything else." But Walt quickly put Ron at
ease. "He was just as warm and humble as anyone. His Midwestern roots

came right out, and he made me feel comfortable and Lilly made me comfortable, and they accepted me. It was really a great relationship."

Ron and Diane weren't exactly sure why Walt and Lillian took such a keen liking to him. The twenty-one-year-old Ron was "not very articulate" around them, according to Diane.[66] He would also dress extremely casually—walking around barefoot in Bermuda shorts. Nevertheless, to Walt and Lilly, Ron seemed like a godsend. "I think that Diane had been out with so many duds that I was a ray of light," Ron joked.[67] A few weeks after that Christmas brunch, Walt and Lilly started asking Diane when Ron was going to propose.[68]

Ron and Diane's courtship became all-consuming, and they let their academics fall by the wayside. Within six months, Diane was pregnant. They were married on May 9, 1954, at All Saints-By-The-Sea Episcopal Church in Montecito. The best man was Ron's brother, John, and the maid of honor was Diane's sister, Sharon; Ron's USC football teammates were also in attendance.[69] Walt walked Diane down the aisle, and when it was time to answer the minister's question, "Who gives this woman to be married," Diane saw tears on Walt's cheeks.[70] The reception was filled with laughter, love, and a healthy amount of champagne. Walt surprised the couple with a comical cake topper—the bride figurine attired in USC gear and the groom in Bermuda shorts.[71] Walt, Ron, and Diane laughed gleefully at the gag, and those in attendance could see the mutual affection between father and son-in-law.

Now that Ron was part of the family, Walt hired him to drive documents back and forth between the studio in Burbank and the Disneyland construction site in Anaheim.[72] However, Ron's career at Disney was put on hold shortly thereafter—first by the army and then by the NFL. Ron was drafted and stationed at Fort Ord in Carmel, where Ron and Diane's first child, Christopher, was born. Walt had hoped his first grandchild would be named after him, but Ron admits he was "ornery" about the request at that time.[73] (When the couple had their second son—the fifth of seven Miller children—Walt finally got his wish.)

Diane would remember their early days in Fort Ord as some of her happiest. Even though she and Ron lived in small and simple accommodations, Diane was excited to be starting a new life with her husband and their new baby. The simplicity of their home was happily complemented by the natural beauty of Carmel. "It was a wonderful point in her life," said her son Walter Disney Miller. "She always looked back on it fondly."

After leaving the army, Ron joined the LA Rams. As a rookie, Miller looked to have great potential as an offensive end. In an exhibition game, he made an impressive diving catch on a forty-yard pass.[74] However, his football career was plagued with injury. "Walt saw me play a couple games," said Ron. "One game, I fractured my ribs, and the other game I had a concussion."

"You're going to get killed out there," Walt told his son-in-law. "I am too damn old to raise your—my grandchildren. So why don't you come work for me?" Ron also thought Walt was worried that life on the road would not be good for the young family. That—compounded by the Rams four-and-eight losing season[75]—was all Ron needed to change career paths.

Now that Ron was at Disney full time, Walt got Ron into the Directors Guild, and he was made second assistant director on *Old Yeller*. Jobs followed on *Mickey Mouse Club* and *Zorro*. He even directed "Uncle Walt" in an intro for Disney's weekly TV show. "Talk about being nervous," Ron said. His shoot with Walt went about as poorly as one could imagine. The novice director decided to change the blocking, keeping Walt stationary the entire time. But when Walt came in, he wanted to stick to the original plan, which involved a more dynamic movement between two parts of the set: the bookshelf and Walt's desk. Ron hadn't lit those positions so it took half an hour to rework the lighting. When film was finally rolling, a rumbling truck drove by; the noise was so loud it could be heard on the soundproof set. It seemed to happen "on every damn take just as Walt was in the middle of the take." Adding to the gremlins of the day, the teleprompter also went out. Miller later called it "the most frustrating, spooky day I've ever had in my life. You can just feel Walt on edge."[76] It was the last time he directed his father-in-law.

Walt encouraged Ron to give up directing and focus on producing. Producers could focus on multiple projects at a time, and at Walt Disney

Productions, the producer typically exercised more control than the director. Walt also began training Ron on how to run the studio. Father and son-in-law would arrive at the lot early in the morning to watch as employees showed up. As each person drove up, Walt explained who they were and what they did.[77]

Ron was also taken under wing by producer Bill Walsh, who had worked on many of Walt's live-action hits including *Mickey Mouse Club* and *The Absent-Minded Professor*. Bill was twenty years older than Ron and referred to him as "kid." They became good friends. Walsh taught Ron a lot about production, including managing a budget. When projects came along, Ron would try to team up with Bill whenever possible.

As much as Walt loved Ron, he grew frustrated by his son-in-law's shyness, particularly in story meetings. Walt complained about it to Diane and in turn, she told Ron, "Dad thinks you ought to open your mouth."[78] Ron embraced the feedback and started speaking up more. It delighted Walt to see Ron become more assertive and grow into the role of producer. "[Ron] was like a blank notebook," Diane would later say. "Dad could take and mold him in his pattern. Dad was able to give this man I married something that he loved to do that he could be uniquely qualified for…it was almost too good to be true that the situation worked out that way."[79]

Ron appreciated the family bond that developed with Walt and Lilly. "Lilly was a great mother-in-law. They were both great grandparents. They loved my kids." Walt would spoil his grandchildren every Christmas, giving each child the latest Disney merchandise.[80] Walt was often able to outshine Santa with better toys.

"I say this in all honesty," said Ron. "It was just a great relationship. I so admired that man. He's a real person. [His values] were phenomenal."

Ron was also keenly aware of one of Walt's greatest frustrations—the increasing limits placed on him by the Disney brand. Whereas the rest of the film industry was pushing the limits with increasingly mature themes, violence, obscenities and sex, Disney films were reliably "safe" and family friendly. Even though Walt believed deeply in making wholesome entertainment, he also began to feel like he was in a creative straitjacket—one he had tailored for himself. His daughter Diane later said he was "really beginning to get tired of films" by the 1960s.[81] There were exceptions like *Mary Poppins* (1964), which allowed Walt to use all the tricks of his trade: special effects, animation, Audio-Animatronics figures, and music. Even though it became one of the top-grossing movies of all time, Walt saw *Mary Poppins* as a unique achievement—not a template for future films. "We're not making another *Mary Poppins*. We never will," Walt said. "Magic is only magic once upon a time."[82]

At one family movie night at Walt's private screening room, Walt ran Universal's 1962 film *To Kill a Mockingbird*. "What a fine picture, what a great story and a great cast," remembered Ron. "From top to bottom, it's about as perfect a motion picture as you can come up with." Yet as the lights came on, Walt seemed distressed. He was tapping his finger and said, "God, I wish I could make a film like that."

Walt's envy of *Mockingbird* makes particular sense in the context of its young heroine Scout, who is not radically dissimilar from the child protagonists of Walt's films. Yet, thematically, the story was unlike anything Walt had previously tackled. "It had content that he couldn't touch, and he knew it," explained Ron. The film was released at an inflection point in the Civil Rights Movement—in the window between James Meredith's enrollment at Ole Miss and George Wallace's "segregation forever" speech. Even if he tried to make a "message movie" about one of the most urgent issues of the day, Ron said Walt felt the public would reject it coming from him.

"He was sorry he couldn't do it," Ron said. "But he had to live up to his reputation, and he had to protect it. And obviously, he was right. He did what was right."

In the postwar era, Walt had cultivated a noncontroversial family brand, but it had become so inflexible that a then-contested topic like civil rights or even the hint of innuendo was off-limits. In 1962, the same year as *Mockingbird*, Disney released the Technicolor-travelogue comedy *Bon Voyage*. The film looks at the romantic relationships of a happily married American couple and their adult children as they travel abroad. In one section, the father is propositioned by a well-dressed French prostitute. A few moments later, he finds the same woman trying to pick up his wannabe playboy son. These scenes are so vaguely scripted that some viewers may miss what is happening. Still, audiences at the time objected. "That was a disaster," Walt told reporter Bob Thomas. "You should have seen the mail I got over it. I'll never do it again."[83] Walt's takeaway was that "sex is a very private matter for most people. They feel uneasy and uncomfortable when they see it portrayed in public."[84]

Walt had once thrived on being able to surprise movie audiences with something they didn't know they wanted, like *Fantasia*'s two-hour symphony featuring dancing hippos. Now though, his audience wanted to be delighted, but not challenged. The *Mockingbird* screening and Walt's frustrations with the Disney brand would stay with Ron long after Walt was gone.

By 1966, the professional and personal bond between Ron and Walt was as strong as it had ever been. That year, Walt shared an Emmy award nomination with his son-in-law for an episode of his weekly show *The Wonderful World of Color* called "Gallegher." When asked about the joint nomination, Ron downplayed its significance. Still, it shows Walt's commitment to boosting his son-in-law's profile.

On a family trip to Vancouver in the summer of 1966, Walt's physical deterioration was becoming obvious to Ron and the rest of the family. Walt had trouble moving around—needing to pick up his leg to get in and out of a boat.[85] The family assumed it was the polo injury acting up. It wasn't until the exploratory surgery in November that they knew Walt was seriously ill.

As Walt recovered from the surgery, Ron updated him on the studio's latest film, *Follow Me, Boys!*, which was doing solid business at Radio City Music Hall in New York.[86] The film would go on to break house records at the famed theater, as twenty-seven thousand people came to see it paired with the Rockettes' Christmas show the weekend before Walt's death.[87] Walt liked the film a fair bit,[88] but did not expect it to be the last one he'd live to see released.

As Walt was recuperating from surgery, his doctor warned him that he would need to cut back at the studio. His fourteen-hour workdays were no longer possible. Ron believed Walt intended to hand off film production to a creative committee,[89] like the one Roy later assembled, so he could focus on the projects that mattered to him now—specifically, Disney World and EPCOT.

As Walt's health deteriorated, Ron and Diane were a constant presence. He spent his final Thanksgiving at their house, surrounded by his family.[90] Shortly after, he checked back into the hospital for what would be the last two weeks of his life. Ron stopped by regularly. During one visit, Walt introduced him to a nurse as his son. The nurse corrected him, "You mean your son-in-law."

"No," Walt objected. "My son."[91] Ron thought it was the greatest thing ever said to him.[92]

Ron and Diane arrived at St. Joseph's Hospital on the morning of December 15. "As we got off the elevator on the floor, I saw Ron go striding into Dad's room and then come out with his arms up like that, as though someone pushed him back," recalled Diane years later. "He was gone." Walt's brother Roy was at the foot of the bed, massaging his feet. Diane remembered her uncle saying his goodbyes, "Well kid, this is the end I guess."[93]

The next day, the family held a private funeral for him at Forest Lawn Cemetery. Walt had wanted a simple ceremony. Instead of flowers, the Disney family asked people to support the California Institute of the Arts.[94] Walt hoped to create a new educational and cultural institution where artists could not only learn, but collaborate across media. This, along with EPCOT and Disney World, would be his legacy…and again, Walt was right. CalArts would go on to produce future leaders of the arts, specifically in the field of animation. "He said that if he could live for 15 more years," Ron remembered, "…he would surpass everything he had done in the forty years previous."[95] In his will, Walt left nearly half his estate to the development of CalArts.[96]

Ron said Walt's death "was the end of something that will never be seen again." It was now up to Ron and the others to carry on as best they could, without Walt.

"There was a tremendous void, an emptiness," said Ron.

Life after Disney.

Chapter 2

On the afternoon of October 18, 1967, hundreds of children from some of Los Angeles's historically marginalized communities were escorted down Hollywood Boulevard by the likes of Mickey Mouse, Snow White, and Captain Hook. The kids, ages seven to twelve, arrived in big yellow buses at Grauman's Chinese Theatre—home to handprints of Hollywood idols. The kids were treated like movie stars—a band welcomed their arrival and celebrity host Art Linkletter interviewed them for a TV show. This was the public premiere of Walt Disney's *The Jungle Book*, ahead of a more traditional red-carpet event that night. The kids that afternoon laughed loudly throughout the film, with one of the biggest reactions going to Baloo's line, "Man-village? They'll ruin him. They'll make a man out of him."[97]

The unadulterated enthusiasm felt by the audience that day would be repeated countless times as *The Jungle Book* rolled out in theaters over the next few weeks. *The New York Times* compared "this glowing little picture" to "an intelligent comic-strip fairy tale"[98] and *The Los Angeles Times* called it "very, very good Disney, indeed."[99] Walt Disney's last animated feature wound up being among his most popular. Made on a budget of approximately $4 million,[100] it earned six times that amount worldwide on its first release.[101] It was the smash hit Disney animation needed to stay alive, at least for the short term. With *The Jungle Book* successfully in theaters, production on *The Aristocats* ramped up. It was now an important test case: What exactly was a Disney animated movie without Walt?

Leading the production—with an eye on efficiency—was *Jungle Book* producer/director Wolfgang "Woolie" Reitherman. Woolie Reitherman was born in Munich, Germany, in 1909 and moved to the U.S. as an infant.

Part artist and part aviator, Woolie's coming of age coincided with the rise of aviation. He and his brother built a homemade biplane and would take it out joyriding over their Sierra Madre neighborhood, occasionally dropping water balloons out the back. Woolie also had great artistic ability. He enrolled in the Chouinard Art Institute in 1931, where his watercolor paintings won recognition,[102] leading to a fateful meeting with Walt Disney in 1934, when Walt was assembling a team for *Snow White*. Walt was impressed with Woolie's art, but Woolie wasn't initially keen on becoming an animator. "I didn't really like the idea of making drawings over and over. I told [Walt] so." Still, Woolie felt Walt's vision for *Snow White* was irresistible. "I had a feeling that this guy was going somewhere in terms of what he was trying to do with this animation. He was going to climb a damn mountain."[103] Caught in Walt's spell, Woolie overcame his hesitancy and signed up.

As an animator, Woolie seemed to have an innate gift for action scenes, whether it was Goofy learning sports in the *How To* cartoon series, Pinocchio's chase with Monstro the whale, or the dinosaur fight in *Fantasia*'s "The Rite of Spring." Just as Woolie was emerging as one of Disney's best animators, his career was interrupted by World War II. Given his background with planes, he enlisted in the United States Army Air Corp. By the end of the war, he had become a decorated transport pilot, navigating dangerous routes from India and Burma across the Himalayas to China. Wartime aviation required Woolie to become a careful planner—he knew even the slightest miscalculation could lead to disaster. After the war and a short stint as a commercial pilot in the Philippines, Woolie returned to Disney.

Over the next decade, Woolie kept pushing the limits of how dangerous animation could feel, and he became the go-to animator for climax sequences. His Headless Horseman chase in 1949's *The Adventures of Ichabod and Mr. Toad* runs a scant three minutes, but each second is filled with tension as Ichabod narrowly escapes one close call after another—until he doesn't. For *Lady and the Tramp* (1955), he helped create a kinetic showdown where Tramp confronts a rat in the baby's nursery. But Woolie's most memorable climax was *Sleeping Beauty* (1959). As sequence director, Woolie supervised the battle between Prince Phillip and the evil witch Maleficent in dragon form. Woolie's philosophy was to push the action as far as it would go, making the audience think the prince would indeed be killed. With the dragon's steel-like jaw and powerful streams of fire shooting from its mouth, the odds feel unfairly stacked against the Prince. The scene builds to the point of no return. Cornered on the edge of a cliff with a burning forest below him and the dragon closing in, Prince Phillip's only option for survival is to throw his sword at the dragon's heart and hope it hits its mark. Some animators questioned the sequence's logic, but Walt loved it "because it kept driving, driving, driving."[104] Like the Headless Horseman sequence, Woolie packed a lifetime of action into mere seconds of screentime. Maleficent is only a dragon for ninety seconds, but Woolie's sequence has become one of the most iconic scenes in Disney animation.

Around this same era, Woolie was installed as a member of Disney's animation board, established by Walt to handle key managerial duties: "hiring, firing, assignments, moves, promotions and training."[105] The composition of this group changed periodically but by 1950, the membership largely settled on nine supervising animators—a role that, at the time, was almost exclusively male. In addition to Woolie, the group consisted of Les Clark, Ward Kimball, John Lounsbery, Milt Kahl, Marc Davis, Frank Thomas, Ollie Johnston, and Eric Larson. Walt called this group "the Nine Old Men," based on the Supreme Court's nickname when Walt was younger. The animators weren't always sure if Walt's pet name was a compliment,[106] but they embraced it over time. Walt's Nine Old Men would go on to be among the most revered group of animators ever assembled.

After *Sleeping Beauty*, Woolie was promoted to director for Disney's next films: *One Hundred and One Dalmatians* (1961), *The Sword in the Stone* (1963), and *The Jungle Book* (1967). Walt's death occurred midway through the production of *The Jungle Book*, so it was up to Woolie to finish the movie without Walt's supervision. "[Woolie] knew he was going to get everybody there in one piece. He was going to finish the darn thing. He was going to make the journey and arrive successfully," said his son Bruce, who also voiced the man-cub Mowgli in *The Jungle Book*.

As Woolie now embarked on *The Aristocats*, he was aware of the turbulence threatening the entire Animation Department. "He appreciated that if they were to whiff on one of the shows, animation conceivably could have really been on the chopping block," said Bruce. As a result, Woolie's tolerance for risk was low. "It's an interesting combination. Pilots have it in spades. A willingness to do something really dangerous by making it as absolutely safe as they possibly can."

Bruce compared the uncertainty at Disney Animation to a black hole. "In the absence of somebody that has so much gravity.... It's like a huge sun around which everything else, all the other planets revolve. For that thing to blink out and go away, pretty surprisingly to everybody involved, it's a wonder that the whole damn thing didn't just scatter off into the cosmos."

The Aristocats benefited not only from Woolie's leadership, but from the other animation veterans as well. Each of the Nine Old Men had been working with Walt for three decades by this point. Though three of the nine (Marc Davis, Ward Kimball, and Les Clark) were now working on other Disney projects, the collective group had a shared history that allowed for an easy exchange of ideas.

"There was no fight for power," Woolie said. "[The other animators] respected me and I respected them. You could really say that four or five of us could've gotten producer credit because we talked all the time."[107]

The Nine Old Men were not the only veterans in the ranks of Disney Animation. Story Department veteran Otto Englander had recently been promoted to find new material for the Animation Department to follow *The Aristocats*, in case it was a *Jungle Book*-like success. Englander wrote a former colleague, "This is a great boost to the Animation Department here, because this move is a definite indication on the part of management that it is interested in going on indefinitely with this sort of picture, despite rumors to the contrary."[108] Englander knew those rumors, which had been circulating for months, were "depressing the spirits all around."[109] Despite getting a bigger office and more money, Englander had doubts about the new role. "What they didn't tell me to my face is that I'm probably the lone survivor of the old story team that goes way back to the infancy of feature cartoons—and that they didn't have anyone else to turn to," he wrote.[110] Englander had recently proposed one of the most ambitious new animated projects in the history of Walt Disney Productions, recognizing in it some of the same potential of the first animated features like *Snow White* and *Pinocchio*.

Englander had been working with Disney on and off since 1930—long before *The Jungle Book*, Disneyland, *Bambi*, or even Donald Duck. Englander was born in Bosnia in 1906, when it was still part of the Austro-Hungarian Empire.[111] His parents were Austrian Jews who later immigrated to America and he studied music and humanities in Vienna.[112] "He was an eternal student—his knowledge of literature, music, and all related arts was incredible," his wife Erna would later say. "He had a fantastic mind—photographic, in fact, and a total recall. His friends in and out of the Disney Studio called him 'The Encyclopedia Britannica.'"[113]

In the summer of 1924 at the age of nineteen, Englander left Europe to join his parents in New York where he enrolled at the Jewish Theological Seminary.[114] After he completed his studies, he found work as an art director for an advertising firm and wrote gags for magazines.[115] Situational humor came naturally for Englander.

Once, he submitted a story to a newspaper contest looking for one's most embarrassing moments. He wrote about his life as a young, single man in New York:

> I acted as a porter for the boss and escorted him to the railroad station. He instructed me to carefully watch his baggage while he purchased his ticket.

"Be very careful of them," he warned.

Two pretty girls came along and I forgot everything, including the precious baggage. Realizing they were gone I turned around frantically. The boss was standing behind me with his luggage and had been watching me flirt![116]

The setup could easily be a gag in an early Disney cartoon. Englander cast himself as the underdog; he often looked underweight at 5'8", 140 lb.[117] The story has a "heavy" in the form of the stern boss who issues the warning. Then, the payoff: the bags never disappeared. Now, imagine the story with Mickey Mouse, with Minnie Mouse subbing in for the two women and Pete as the boss. Based on his submission, it's easy to see why Englander's sensibilities fit in with the gag-centric 1930s Disney Studios. The submission earned Englander a dollar in the early days of the Depression.

Englander joined the Disney Studio shortly after arriving in California in 1930. His colleagues were among the vanguard of Disney Animation—directors Ben Sharpsteen and Wilfred Jackson, animators Les Clark and Norm Ferguson, and of course, Walt himself, who was as engaged with the medium as he would ever be.[118] It was around this time Englander met his wife Erna while traveling to Serbia.[119] They married in 1932, and she became a Hollywood correspondent for Serbia's largest newspaper, *Politika Belgrade*.[120] Although Englander bounced around to other cartoon studios, he rejoined Disney after a few years as part of the story team for *Snow White*. It was a career high-light. Years later, Englander looked back proudly at how revolutionary *Snow White* was:

Shortly after the picture started, everyone was caught up in the same excitement. They became alive to something very new and very entertaining. I was so impressed by the reaction that when my wife and I arrived home and discovered that our Scottish terrier had delivered seven puppies, we named them after the Seven Dwarfs.[121]

Englander then worked on the next three Disney features: *Pinocchio*, *Fantasia*, and *Dumbo*. These early films, along with *Bambi*, would become the standard against which all other animated films would be measured, even to this day.

Englander left Disney in April 1942 to join the United States Army Signal Corps, churning out war propaganda under renowned director Frank Capra. He was part of a team working on the animated *Private Snafu* films with colleagues like Ted "Dr. Seuss" Geisel and Warner Brothers animation producer Leon Schlesinger.[122] Englander was based in Hollywood for much of the war, but its horrors still hit close to home. Early in the war, Erna received a letter from her sister in Serbia. In response to a British-backed coup of the Axis-friendly government, the Nazis destroyed the city of Belgrade in April 1941. The devastating air attacks would become known as "Operation Punishment," as homes, cultural institutions, and synagogues were destroyed from above.[123] Erna's sister wrote them with news of the Nazi invasion. "Our beloved parents and sisters were killed, shortly after they were taken hostages in the invasion. How it happened, I cannot tell you yet…it is too horrible to bear."[124] Her sister added, "Their death is a blessing" compared to the fate of their other friends and relatives. At Adolf Eichmann's trial twenty years later, witnesses testified about the crimes against humanity committed by the Nazis in Yugoslavia at Eichmann's direction, including mass executions, starvation, and the use of mobile gas chambers.[125] The Nazi's brutality in Serbia rallied the Englanders into action: Erna became a volunteer for the Los Angeles war chest as they tried to warn Americans about the inhumanity of the Nazis.

During the war, Englander teamed up with screenwriter Carl Foreman (*High Noon*, *Bridge on the River Kwai*, and one of the most prominent figures caught up in the McCarthy-era blacklist) for a script called *Once Upon a Furlough*. Industry articles indicate the story was about a soldier returning from the Pacific front who undergoes evaluation by a female psychologist.[126] The intriguing premise suggests the film would grapple with how post-traumatic stress was affecting returning soldiers. Tackling a difficult subject in a format palatable to home-front audiences reveals Englander's grander writing ambitions; however, MGM ultimately shelved the film around the summer of 1944.[127]

After the war, Englander continued to branch out, working at MGM, RKO, and with the Marx Brothers. He found these experiences creatively liberating. Englander wrote, "Instead of feeling like Disney's little finger...I'm slowly beginning to feel there is a whole body—and maybe even a mind here somewhere."[128]

Eventually, Englander's old Disney colleague Ben Sharpsteen lured him back to work on the studio's expanding live-action output.[129] Back at Disney, Englander utilized his knowledge of music and culture to flesh out a biographical drama on Peter Tchaikovsky, which otherwise would serve as an infomercial for *Sleeping Beauty*. Even better was his script for *The Poet and the Nightingale*, focused on the platonic love story between Hans Christen Andersen and opera singer Jenny Lind. The project had been bouncing around Disney for years. Walt hoped to combine Andersen's biography with animated fairy tales like *The Ugly Duckling*. Englander's treatment is an affecting tale about a creative figure's frustration with his narrowly defined reputation as a successful children's author, something akin to what Walt was feeling.

Now in the wake of Walt's death, Englander's long and varied career gave him the trust and authority to select future animated projects. His mission was to bring animation storytelling back to those glory days of *Snow White*, *Pinocchio*, *Fantasia*, *Dumbo*, and *Bambi*. Those five films may have set a nearly impossible creative standard, but they could also serve as a guide for Englander. They featured life-and-death stakes, where sympathetic heroes were pitted against dangerous villains. They were often rooted in classic European fairy tales but flexible enough to include Disney's signature mix of comedy and pathos. One of the projects Englander selected was Lloyd Alexander's award-winning children's fantasy series, The Chronicles of Prydain.

The Prydain books were steeped in Welsh mythology and centered on a group of underdogs—an assistant pig keeper named Taran, a princess without a throne named Eilonwy, an unlikely bard named Fflewddur Fflam, and a creature of uncertain origin named Gurgi—up against the forces of evil. Englander thought it was perfect material for Disney and liked the series—especially the third book, *The Castle of Llyr*, where the princess is kidnapped. The Prydain books would likely be difficult to adapt but Englander had no way of knowing what he was proposing would ultimately be akin to opening Pandora's Box.

The Disney Story Department asked story analyst Inez Cocke to provide additional feedback on the books before acquisition.[130] Inez Cocke was a Louisiana-born journalist turned Hollywood literatus.[131] In the 1950s, Cocke branched out into screenwriting at Universal, specializing in adaptations of old films. Cocke's first major screenplay was a remake of a Wyatt Earp–inspired Western called *Law and Order* (1953), starring future president Ronald Reagan.[132] In 1955, she wrote a treatment for *Phantom of the Opera*, which eventually became a Hammer Films production.[133] She also collaborated with famed director Douglas Sirk—writing the script for *Interlude* (1957)[134] and the popular melodrama *Imitation of Life* (1959), though she did not receive screen credit for the latter.[135] By the time *Interlude* was released, she had already left Universal to join Disney.[136] Yet her best-known Hollywood work was a book—*Dear Mr. G*—about Clark Gable and Carole Lombard, coauthored by their personal secretary. The book was released in 1961, just months after Gable's death, and it garnered considerable attention. Cocke brought the writing to life. With a single line, she was able to capture what made Gable the "King of Hollywood": "He projected masculine sex, with a knowing, crooked smile."[137]

Now at Disney in 1968, Cocke read the third Prydain book, *The Castle of Llyr*, at Englander's request but didn't care for the material. She wrote, "The Prince does not win the Princess in the end (which is the way all good fairy tales end) but has the Princess vowing never to marry him and inclined to the pig keeper although she does not come right out and say so. Also the villains…escape punishment."[138]

Cocke finally concludes, "The story itself is over plotted with magic things happening at every turn so this does not seem over and above other fairy tales and legends for children. Certainly there is enough here for an animated feature but I do not think the story is outstanding."[139]

Englander's enthusiasm and Cocke's ambivalence about the Prydain series represent two opposing views that would continue to clash at Disney for the next seventeen years. Cocke's viewpoint won at first—keeping the lid on Pandora's Box closed for a little longer. It would take three more years before Disney acquired the property and the Prydain film was eventually titled *The Black Cauldron*, named after the second book in the series. Walt Disney's son-in-law Ron Miller would become the film's executive producer. Like Englander, he saw its potential as an important animated film. When Ron was ousted in a corporate coup led by his cousin-in-law Roy E. Disney, the film would be released to limited fanfare and ultimately earn a reputation as one of the biggest bombs in Disney history, which seemingly confirmed Cocke's initial instinct.

Sadly, Englander and Cocke's contributions to both Disney and Hollywood would be largely erased over time—overshadowed by their more famous collaborators. Neither lived long enough to see *The Black Cauldron*'s development. Records indicate Cocke died in 1972.[140] Englander had a fatal heart attack in 1969[141]; one of his last projects was writing a Disney educational film, *Understanding Stresses and Strains*, about how the accumulation of mental stress can lead to physical deterioration.[142]

Cocke's story analysis of the Prydain book is dated June 6, 1968. On that same day, just a short drive away from the Disney Studio, Robert F. Kennedy died after being shot by an assassin. It was not just Walt Disney Productions which was undergoing a radical transformation induced by trauma. So was America.

Chapter 3

Hints of societal revolution were omnipresent near the end of Walt's life, but the four years between his death and the release of *The Aristocats* were among the most turbulent and divisive in American history. It appeared Ron Miller and other executives at Walt Disney Productions tried to ignore the burgeoning counterculture and maintain the company's traditionalist values, but it was impossible to shut out the turmoil. Few sectors of American life were immune to the upheaval of the late 1960s, including Hollywood. Variety's top words for 1967 were "psychedelic" and "conglomerate," as both the counterculture and a new way of doing business invaded Hollywood.[143] The golden age of the studio system was ending; the moguls who had founded the major studios, including Walt, were now mostly dead or retiring. At the movies, *Easy Rider* and *The Graduate* were critical and commercial hits; they appealed to the notion of a generation gap between progressive Baby Boomers and their more conservative parents. These films were far edgier than anything being produced by Disney, whether on television or the big-screen, such as the musical *The Happiest Millionaire*.

The idea of going to a Disney movie seemed increasingly unhip to some film audiences. Still, Walt and his legacy continued to hold a special place inside Hollywood. The 1969 Oscars allowed the industry to pay their respects to two lost icons: Walt Disney and Robert F. Kennedy. Jane Fonda presented the Academy Award for Documentary Short

Subject to *Robert Kennedy Remembered*. She was immediately followed by Tony Curtis who announced Disney's *Winnie the Pooh and the Blustery Day* as the winner for Best Animated Short. Woolie Reitherman walked up on stage to accept the award on Walt's behalf, towering over presenter Tony Curtis. Woolie was grateful but solemn as he spoke. "To us who have worked with Walt, this is a very special Oscar," he said. He paused as he stoically tried to contain his sentiment. "And it's a memorable moment in all of the moments we all shared with Walt." He began to choke up before ending the speech with a simple "Thank you."[144]

Disney had one unlikely smash live-action hit in this era: *The Love Bug* (1969)—seemingly one of the rare Disney movies to acknowledge the changing times. The title itself is a nod to love as a state of harmony, like 1967's Summer of Love, and the "Bug" is the egalitarian Volkswagen Beetle, popular among Baby Boomers. In the film, the mechanic Tennessee (played by Buddy Hackett) implies Eastern philosophy—recently mainstreamed by The Beatles—may explain how the VW bug Herbie has come to life. Hippies are presented as benign comic caricatures.

The success of *The Love Bug* was a source of pride for Ron Miller. He had been the one to originally suggest the story material to Walt. The film proved Disney could still appeal to a large cross-demographic audience, even as cultural tastes evolved. "The sophisticates get so bugged because we can produce a picture about a thinking Volkswagen and make money with it," said Ron.[145] To promote *The Love Bug*, Disneyland even briefly called a truce in its ongoing efforts to prevent "longhairs" in the park. It held a contest for VWs drivers that included a special category for the most psychedelic Beetle.[146]

Disney had another unlikely counterculture hit: *Fantasia*. Three decades after its initial release, *Fantasia* found a receptive audience, including pot-smoking college kids. NYU's student newspaper called it "the most stoned out picture of 1970" extolling the film's psychedelic value. The review said, "the mind can run riot, sanity and reality becoming vestigial organs."[147] Disney made Day-Glo posters to promote the film, featuring the demon Chernabog sprouting pink wings surrounded by dancing mushrooms and sugar plum fairies. Malcolm Barbour,

Disney's East Coast production head, said, "Never before has the mass teenage and '20s generation looked upon a Disney film as being other than square."[148] He told a columnist the film was doing incredibly well in arthouse theaters, especially in college towns. The film, which notoriously lost money in 1940 and had a meager rerelease in 1957, was finally a success.

In this age of change, Walt Disney Productions attempted to convince observers of its own stability. In December 1967, Bob Thomas of the Associated Press was invited to the Disney lot to report on the company one year after Walt's passing. An AP photographer took a series of photos of Ron Miller (thirty-four) and Roy E. Disney (thirty-six). The implicit purpose of the photo shoot was showing the next generation of the Disney family carrying on in Walt's and Roy's footsteps. Ron Miller, now looking more like a hefty coach than a running back, seemed relaxed in a sweater, button-down shirt, and slacks. Roy E. Disney looked significantly smaller than his cousin-in-law and perhaps more earnest in his blazer and tie. In this series of photos, the men look like they are busy working together on a film, first exchanging script notes on a soundstage before heading to the cutting room to examine reels of footage. In the published photos, the two men never make eye contact, even when they are casually walking together at the intersection of Mickey Avenue and Dopey Drive.[149]

In truth, Ron and Roy Edward Disney never had a close professional relationship, according to Ron's son Walter. "I don't think Roy was ever part of my dad's group, which included [directors] Bill Walsh and Joe McEveety," he said. Almost everyone interviewed for this book liked both Ron and Roy individually and generally respected each man. Yet their professional rivalry and general dislike for each other would eventually threaten to destroy the company.

Roy Edward Disney was born in 1930, to his father Roy Oliver Disney and his mother Edna Francis. Roy Oliver Disney, born in 1893, was around eighteen years old when he met twenty-two-year-old Edna.[150] They had been introduced by Edna's brother Mitch, who worked with Roy Oliver at the First National Bank of Kansas City, a literal impenetrable fortress of commerce that had withstood a mysterious explosion just four years before Roy's arrival.[151] This is where Roy Oliver began his business career, which ultimately provided him the business acumen that allowed Walt Disney Productions to creatively thrive. Roy and Edna's courtship dragged on for more than a decade—interrupted by the First World War and then Roy's tuberculosis, which he contracted in the navy. Roy sought treatment for his tuberculosis at the Sawtelle Veterans Home in Los Angeles.[152] Contemporaneous reports from Sawtelle indicate many World War I veterans were languishing. "There are many disabled soldiers now at the Sawtelle hospital who would be pleased to receive…magazines in order to pass away many weary hours of just sitting around looking at nothing in particular," wrote an army captain.[153] Walt came to California in 1923 to persuade his brother to help him with his budding cartoon business and in that moment, the Disney empire was born.

After the Disney Brothers Studio was established, Roy Oliver finally wed Edna on a Sunday morning in April 1925. The simple affair was held at the house of Roy and Walt's uncle Robert; Walt and his soon-to-be wife Lillian were the best man and maid of honor. Roy and Edna had difficulty conceiving a child. According to Disney biographer Bob Thomas, they went to the unusual measure of having intercourse in front of their doctor so he could purportedly evaluate the success of the fertilization in real time.[154] Such was the state of fertility treatments a century ago. The difficulties didn't end there. Edna, about to turn forty, carried the baby to term but was in labor for three days before doctors finally agreed to deliver via a cesarean section.[155] Given the difficult circumstances they faced having a baby, it may explain why Roy and Edna only had one child.

Their son Roy Edward Disney was named after both of his parents—his middle name a nod to Edna.[156] Walt and Lillian were reportedly wild about their baby nephew. Roy Oliver wrote his mom that the infant "seemed somewhat afraid of Walt, but goes crazy over Lilly. Walt just doesn't know how to play with him yet."[157]

In Roy E. Disney's interview with the Television Academy Foundation, he said he was always aware of the family business, even at a young age. "When I was a kid in the '30s, it wasn't a huge, huge business the way it is now," he told the interviewer in 2007. "It was just this little cartoon studio with one little character."[158] As a child, he spent considerable time at the studio. When he wasn't in his dad's office, he would roam the halls to see the artists at work. His favorite location on the lot was the machine shop—and for a while, young Roy dreamed of designing airplanes. When the U.S. entered World War II, Burbank was suddenly one of the most exciting places inside the continental U.S. for a preteen interested in engineering. "There were B-17's and Lockheed Load Stars and P-38's, in the air around here, just constantly. And I wanted in the worst way to fly one of those things," Roy recalled.[159]

Roy Edward enrolled as an engineering major at Pomona College, with the hopes of pursuing a career in aeronautical engineering. However, Roy struggled with calculus, killing his aviation dreams. He needed to figure out a new direction for his future. "I'd always been fairly facile as a writer. And so I thought, well, I could major in English, cause I know I can pass that."[160] As an English major, Roy discovered Ray Bradbury who had just published *The Martian Chronicles*. "I remembered desperately trying to write like Ray Bradbury," but Roy couldn't quite pull it off. "Awful, but I tried."[161]

Roy's last name gave him a clear advantage in the entertainment industry—but his first job wasn't at the family's studio. "I think my dad kind of thought maybe Walt would be resentful of me and treat me...not as well as he might," explained Roy, though he added that was ultimately never the case. Instead, he became an NBC page.[162] In this role, Roy had a front-row seat to the golden era of television—including Groucho Marx's *You Bet Your Life* and Dinah Shore's show. The NBC building was down the street from the Brown Derby and RCA Victor, and the whole place had a neon buzz of energy, as large crowds lined the block to be in the audience of these radio and television shows.[163] Roy remembers being dressed up "in my little blue suit and suede shoes, trying to herd people in and out of the studio. It's a great lesson in the behavior of the public."[164]

After his time at NBC, Roy's father pulled some strings with the *Dragnet* crew—the cop show was filming on the Disney lot—and Roy was hired as an apprentice film editor. On *Dragnet*, Roy found stock footage of exterior Los Angeles locations to be spliced into the show. "It was really an amazing kind of a jigsaw puzzle of a show," said Roy.[165] Knowing how to piece together a story in the edit room would prove to be a valuable skill that helped Roy throughout his film career. By the time his stint on *Dragnet* ended, Roy was a member of the editors union. He parlayed the experience into work as an assistant editor on Disney's Oscar-winning nature documentary series, *True Life Adventures*. This series weaved a narrative out of assembled footage of animals in the wild; the theme was "nature away from the influence of man," according to Roy.[166] His first assignment was on *The Living Desert*, where the editors let him have a turn at putting sequences together. That film and its follow-up *The Vanishing Prairie* both earned Academy Awards for Best Documentary. Roy's next big project was a nature-based True-Life Fantasy, *Perri*, produced by Winston Hibler. On *Perri*, Roy traveled to Utah for the better part of a year and joined the crew as a camera operator. It had been Walt's idea. "He said, 'Why don't you take a movie camera along and try to shoot some of the behind-the-scenes footage," Roy remembered.[167]

In his twenties, Roy dated Patricia Ann Dailey, the New Orleans-born daughter of a *Look Magazine* editor. The couple was engaged in June 1955 and married three months later.[168] Their bridal party included Diane Miller and Patty's brother Peter Dailey, the future ad executive and ambassador to Ireland who three decades later would play a small role in the ousting of Ron Miller from Walt Disney Productions.[169] Roy and Patty had four children within six years of marriage.

Roy advanced at Walt Disney Productions, including writing the Oscar-nominated nature documentary, *Mysteries of the Deep* (1959). Winston Hibler and Bill Anderson also gave Roy the opportunity to write a couple of episodes of the popular tv show *Zorro*. "There wasn't much you could do to put your own spin on a *Zorro* show," Roy later remembered. "But it was fun to write."[170] As Roy grew as a writer/producer, it meant interacting more with his uncle Walt, the studio mogul. "When I did crappy stuff, he got mad at me just like he would with anybody else.… He never said 'great job'…you'd get a laugh or you'd get appreciation or you'd get it by him.… Cause just getting it by him was a compliment."[171] As the 1960s rolled along, Roy saw Walt age before his eyes. "You could see his health kind of beginning to decline those last couple of years," he remembered.[172] Yet like the rest of his family, he too was ultimately shocked when Walt died.

Walt's death put Roy O. Disney at the helm of the company, and he in turn installed Roy E. Disney on the board of directors. Yet the corporate ranks were not necessarily a place where Roy E. wanted to be. "I feel at home around creative people but I do not feel at home around business people who try to translate everything into formulas," recalled Roy. "So I really didn't participate in a way that maybe I might have, should have, could have."[173]

In that 1967 visit with Bob Thomas and his subsequent article, Walt Disney Productions seemed to be selling the Associated Press on the myth of a future Disney Studios creatively led by the team of Ron Miller and Roy E. Disney, but the truth was more complicated. Roy Oliver Disney was not interested in running the day-to-day operations of Walt Disney Productions but also didn't see a good alternative. He reportedly tried to give control to Disney board member and Bank of America president Clark Beise, but he declined.[174] Roy then decided on a split power structure, with one of Walt's loyalists Card Walker sharing control with one of Roy's advisers Donn Tatum. "I think [my dad] had envisioned a little bit as a partnership like he and Walt and it didn't work that way at all," said Roy. According to Roy E. Disney, there was an immediate personality conflict between Tatum and Walker after Roy O. Disney officially stepped down in November 1968. "Card Walker became the first among equals. And it was never really a partnership."[175]

As Roy O. Disney stepped away from managing Walt Disney Productions, he put all his energy into fulfilling his brother's final two dreams: CalArts and Walt Disney World. With Card Walker moving into power, Roy E. Disney found himself on shakier footing inside Disney. Outside, he was forming alliances more powerful than he could have imagined. His brother-in-law Pete Dailey was now running his own advertising agency. There, he installed Roy E. Disney on the board of directors, along with Dailey's lawyer Frank Wells, who (like Roy E.) had attended Pomona College. Wells, who was working for the law firm of Gang Tyre & Brown, had a young protégé named Stanley Gold, who had recently graduated from law school.[176] Roy wanted to untangle himself from the nepotistic tendencies of using Studio lawyers for any legal needs. So he asked Frank for a good lawyer and Frank recommended Stanley. "We just sort of hit it off. And have gradually become very close and business partners.... The rest is history."[177] Years later, Stanley Gold, Frank Wells, and Peter Dailey would all play pivotal roles in helping Roy E. Disney remove Ron from power and reshape the family's company to Roy's vision, forever changing the fortunes of Walt Disney Productions.

Chapter 4

When Walt Disney found out he had lung cancer, Ron saw something he had never seen in his father-in-law: fear.[178] Yet, a telegram from actor John Wayne seemed to cheer up Walt. It read, "WELCOME TO THE CLUB."[179] Wayne had survived lung cancer surgery just two years earlier[180]—which in turn, caused the Duke to re-evaluate his lifestyle. One of the serendipitous outcomes of Wayne's attempts at self-improvement was the sale of his Encino property to none other than Ron and Diane Miller in 1964.[181] The Wayne estate, nestled in the San Fernando Valley, was fit for a movie star but also comfortable enough to raise a family. Wayne's daughter Aissa fondly remembered the property in a 2008 *Architectural Digest* article:

> The main house was a sweeping Ranch home that sat at the top of the property, looking down over the expansive grounds that led to our poolhouse [sic], which was securely nestled into the lower side of the hill…. The land was located deep in the San Fernando Valley, far enough away from Hollywood to be a family home, yet close enough that my dad could drive to the studios. The grounds were surrounded by tall block walls with only one entrance leading through an electronic gate.

Those were the walls that kept us safe and apart from the world outside.[182]

Wayne purchased the 1939 ranch house and its five-and-a-half-acre lot about a decade after it was built.[183] Before the Millers acquired it, the home played host to dinners with director John Ford[184] and actor Dean Martin,[185] as well as fundraisers for Senator George Murphy.[186] In addition to the pool, there were tennis courts and a tiered garden.[187] Some years later, while on an overseas trip, Ron bumped into Wayne at a London hotel bar and introduced himself. It was Ron's last night in Europe, but the chance to have drinks with a childhood hero was too good to pass up. They got to talking about the Encino house. Ron mentioned how they had updated the pool house to look more like the rest of the property—removing the flat roof, which had decorative lava rock on top. As the conversation continued into the night, both men got drunker, until the point the Duke angrily told Ron he wasn't happy about the renovation—he liked the pool house and the lava rock the way it was. The two men clearly didn't see eye to eye on home décor. Still, for Ron, it was a dream come true to spend time with his idol, despite the "horrible hangover" the next morning.

By the fall of 1968, Ron was taking on increased responsibility at Walt Disney Productions. In addition to being named to the board of directors with his cousin-in-law Roy E. Disney, he was also promoted to executive producer of Walt Disney Productions.[188] With this new role, Ron was essentially the lead creative voice on television and motion picture projects. Bill Anderson stayed on to supervise production and studio operations, and the other producers on the creative committee continued to convene while heading up individual projects.

A typical day for Ron would see him leave the family's Encino house around 6 a.m. and drive about twelve miles in his Jensen Interceptor—a car he loved—before getting to the Disney lot. As soon as he'd arrive at the office, he would try to sneak in some reading before the first phone call of the morning—typically around 7 a.m.[189] The rest of his day was spent catching up on all the projects in development, which could mean giving a pep talk to a screenwriter, sitting through an executive meeting, or screening the latest episode of Disney's weekly show. He turned in twelve-hour days at the office before driving back home around 6 p.m.

Diane was an active mother, shuttling the kids between school and other activities in the family station wagon. She played host to members of the Encino Elementary PTA with a "Silver Coffee" meet-and-greet.[190] Diane insisted on cooking two dinners—one for the kids and one for herself and Ron. She thought the family dinner hour was an "overrated" notion—especially with seven children.[191] If Ron arrived home while the kids' dinner was still under way, he occasionally grabbed a snack off the lazy Susan in the middle of the table and head into the other room— probably to get a cocktail. On Sundays, the family would eat dinner out, often at the Mexican restaurant El Torito.

One of the ways Ron expressed his love for his children was in a way that came most natural to him—sports. He converted John Wayne's corral into a grass field where the family could play anything from football to baseball to volleyball. His son Walter remembers school friends coming over to play. "My friends were in awe of my dad," he said. "Probably because he was in the movie business. He made those funny movies they all went and saw.... But he was also just this giant of a man." Every Saturday, Ron would sneak in an early game of golf but would try to get home by the time the kids were up and ready. Occasionally on these weekends, he uttered seven magic words, "Hey, want to go to the studio?" The kids would enthusiastically take him up on the offer. On these special trips, the Miller children used the Disney lot as their personal race course driving little cars, similar to those at Disneyland's Autopia, which were built at the studio's machine shop. The kids loved driving through the Western-themed sets, because that's where they could kick up the most dirt. They spent hours in these go-carts while Ron ducked into his office to check on scripts or whatever business needed attending. They would then head to the top floor of the Animation Building to see Ron's office, which had also been their grandfather's office. Hanging on the wall was a portrait, drawn by Norman Rockwell, of their mom as a child. They would also peak into the Animation offices to see character sketches or funny caricatures of Ron and the other executives drawn by the artists.

When Ron took over as executive producer, *The Aristocats* was by far the most expensive production on Disney's ledger with a price tag just under $4 million. The 1969 budget for live-action pictures ranged from $1.75 million (*Rascal*) to under $900,000 (*The Computer Wore Tennis Shoes*, featuring Kurt Russell in his first starring role).[192] Ron believed an animated film would eventually earn back its money no matter its cost—both from rereleases but also the "enormous benefits" it provided to other parts of Disney.[193] When Bill Anderson later told Ron about Roy O. Disney's request to shut down animation, Ron felt it went against Walt's intentions. "Roy didn't have any right to do that," Ron told Anderson.

Anderson replied, "That's beside the point. I'm just telling you because you're going into it."[194]

At this point, Ron only had a general understanding of animation. He knew it was expensive but also the "bread and butter" of Disney. As he told the Associated Press, "The more cartoon features we have, the better off we are."[195]

In the weeks before Ron took over as executive producer, Woolie started to worry about *The Aristocats*'s budget. Twenty five percent of its allocated funds, or about one million dollars, had already been spent.[196] He had done his best to shield the Animation Department from internal and external turbulence up until now but going overbudget was not an option.

The financial constraints facing Disney Animation were a safeguard against runaway production costs that seemed to be dragging the rest of Hollywood into a recession, as the studios struggled to transition from old to new Hollywood. The big-screen epics of the 1950s and 1960s had once been a viable alternative to television, but now the habits and tastes of the audience were changing. MGM, once Hollywood's most glamorous studio, was quickly becoming a name associated with faded glory. Its biggest hits, *The Dirty Dozen* and *2001: A Space Odyssey*, couldn't earn enough to support a slate of underperforming and forgettable films;

MGM lost more than $35 million in 1969. Four other major studios—Fox, Universal, Paramount, and Warner Brothers—also lost money that year.[197] When Vegas financier Kirk Kerkorian eventually gained control of MGM, it became a brand more associated with casinos than movies. (Kerkorian would go on to become one of the corporate raiders threatening Disney's future in 1984.) At the 1971 Oscars, emcee Bob Hope joked, "The movie industry is in such a sad state the biggest grosser this year was the MGM auction."[198] Hope was referencing MGM's desperate attempt to raise capital by selling off its historic collection of props, costumes, and artifacts including the ruby slippers from *The Wizard of Oz*. What helped Disney avoid this fate was by keeping true to the same filmmaking strategy employed by Walt. Walt rarely chased after A-list stars or overly ambitious directors—major cost drivers at other studios.

In truth, Woolie could control only so much of *The Aristocats* cost since more than a quarter of the film's budget was devoted to the overhead cost of running the Animation Department, including employee benefits.[199] So Woolie had to look for efficiencies where he could. Animation had begun on *The Aristocats* in September of 1967, just before *The Jungle Book*'s premiere.[200] For that first year of production, the lion's share of animation was divided up among members of the Nine Old Men. Best friends Ollie Johnston and Frank Thomas were the most productive, with Ollie responsible for the most footage thus far. Not far behind was Milt Kahl, considered by some to be the Michelangelo of Disney Animation—who primarily focused on the film's human characters. Another of the Nine, John Lounsbery, had been working on a mouse character (voiced by comedian Arnold Stang) that had just been killed from the film—hence, most of his work was now on the cutting room floor.[201] It was an elite team, each at the height of their individual crafts, but Woolie needed to maximize productivity. He pushed the animators to try and produce ten feet of film a week, or about 160 drawings; Milt, Frank and Ollie were already churning out about nine feet a week at this point.[202] Character animation and touchups accounted for a quarter of *The Aristocats*'s budget. On October 28, 1968, Woolie issued a memo to assistant animators, warning of a "very serious budget problem" and said productivity was "considerably behind" where it had been on *The Jungle Book*. He asked them to pick up the pace by being more careful with rough drawings so only basic touchups would be required down the road. Woolie ended the memo, "I do not feel the goals are unreasonable and feel strongly that working in a more bold and productive manner will create a professional pride and help us put out a better picture."[203]

Even as he was worried about cost, Woolie was also trying to uphold the quality of animation that had long been associated with Walt. He held weekly screenings where the crew analyzed each shot—even individual frames—to make sure each moment was achieving its maximum impact. As production ramped up, more animators were brought on board, including Julius "Sven" Svendsen, a low-key and soft-spoken man who had once worked as an assistant for the comic genius of the Nine Old Men, Ward Kimball. Animator Floyd Norman credits Sven as an influence and calls him "a remarkable animator." "One of the things I learned from Sven was embellishing my animated art with what might be called supplemental animation," Norman said. "That is, secondary movement that may not be part of the main acting, but brings additional life to the character. Sven was remarkably good at this."

Sven's scenes in *The Aristocats* included some of the film's funniest slapstick, including when the villain Edgar the butler is thwarted by two country dogs, Napoleon and Lafayette. For months, Sven worked to heighten the comedy as the dogs confront Edgar on his motorcycle. Woolie encouraged Sven to let the scene play out. His transcribed notes read, "We need an anticipation on the dog, a bite and turn as Butler's fanny exits the scene showing his suspenders."[204] At Woolie's instruction, Sven kept refining the sequence. Even months later when the shot had been seemingly put to bed, Woolie continued to ask for tweaks, "Take the first 12 drawings and make the action twice as fast. The scene will be six frames shorter."[205] Such is the process in animation; every frame can be perfected. Sven would walk away from Woolie's screenings with dozens of notes. When a scene was considered done, he gladly crossed it off his sheet of notes and began working on several more shots assigned to him.

Ron credits *Aristocats* producer Winston Hibler with helping him learn the inner workings of the Animation Department. During internal screenings of *Aristocats* with Ron, Sven's sequence with the country dogs Napoleon and Lafayette attacking the butler in a zany motorcycle chase was getting some of the biggest reaction. After all, vehicular chases were a popular staple of Hollywood films in the 1970s. A new sequence was added for Napoleon and Lafayette, with another shorter chase involving the sidecar and a haystack.[206] Sven averaged eight feet of animation a week, only slightly less than what the Nine Old Men were producing.[207] He was becoming one of the top animators in the generation just below the Nine Old Men.

On the afternoon of Monday February 9, 1970, a rough cut of *The Aristocats* was screened by the public for the first time. The film was still unpolished, with some scenes presented in black-and-white animation and some sound effects and music missing. When the lights came on, the instant reaction was overwhelmingly enthusiastic. A sampling from the responses: "WOW!", "Precious!", "Very cute and enjoyable," "Great—terrific. Best yet!"[208]

As presented by the Disney team, the Paris of 1910 featured in *The Aristocats* is home to harmonious contradictions. Automobiles and motorbikes share the roads with horse-drawn carriages. Jazz and classical music are both in vogue. The working class and moneyed elites coexist with little conflict—except for one greedy butler. The Seine sparkles, though in truth, Paris had spent much of early 1910 coming back from the worst flooding it had seen in centuries.[209] Things are so good in this fictional world that cats even offer their food to mice. *The Aristocats* may have lacked the verisimilitude of 1910 Paris, but it couldn't ignore the realities of 1970 America. Concessions were made to try and appeal to the same audience that embraced the rerelease of *Fantasia*. As the film went to Ink & Paint, "psychedelic"[210] colors were added to two scenes— the dance sequence in the song "Ev'rybody Wants to Be a Cat" and again to the end titles.[211] Newspaper ads read "Meet the Swingin' Sophisticats" and highlighted a minor character, Hit Cat, who looks like a hippie in sunglasses.[212] Like *The Love Bug*, it was Walt Disney Productions' attempt to acknowledge a changing world. To the vast majority of that focus group assembled in February 1970, it all worked remarkably well.

The Aristocats is ultimately a love letter to two bygone eras—Europe's prewar Belle Époque and the age of Walt Disney; Walt's midcentury America now seemed as antediluvian as the France of 1910. The careful work of the Nine Old Men and other artists like Julius Svendsen allowed Walt's legacy to continue after his death. *The Aristocats* was the twentieth animated feature made by Walt Disney Productions, and as production wrapped, Woolie had lived up to his commitment to deliver the film on budget. After *The Aristocats* was finally released on Christmas Eve 1970, it earned more than twice its costs.[213] It also became Disney's highest-earning international release up until that point.[214] When author Christopher Finch assessed the Disney canon in his 1973 book *The Art of Walt Disney*, he wrote: "At least five of the postwar features—*Cinderella*, *Lady and the Tramp*, *One Hundred and One Dalmatians*, *The Jungle Book*, and *The Aristocats*—are excellent, each of them moving toward a more informal kind of entertainment. If we put these together with the first five features and the best shorts of the thirties and forties, we have an extraordinary body of work."[215] Over the years, *The Aristocats* has also acquired a surprising celebrity fanbase including Snoop Dogg,[216] Quentin Tarantino,[217] and Questlove, who was reportedly set to direct a remake of the cartoon.[218] Its real legacy, though, is that it secured the future of Disney Animation for at least another generation. The Animation Department was on much surer footing upon its release than when production began.

As *The Aristocats* wrapped production, some animators began work on sequences for the live-action musical *Bedknobs and Broomsticks* while the story team began fleshing out the next full-length feature, a comedic adaptation of *Robin Hood* populated by anthropomorphic animals. This animal kingdom take on Robin Hood was originally developed by Ken Anderson with some assistance from Otto Englander, making it one of Englander's final contributions to Disney before his death.[219] Woolie was again named director. With Ron Miller as executive producer, the department now had an inexperienced but supportive champion who wanted to see it thrive. For the first time since the 1950s, the department would be allowed to grow.

In the fall of 1970, Woolie presented leadership—Ron Miller, Card Walker and Bill Anderson—with a plan laying out "Ideas and Comments Concerning the Future of Animation in the Disney Tradition." He had worked on the plan in coordination with the other heads of the Animation Department—Ken Anderson, Frank Thomas, Ollie Johnston, John Lounsbery, and production manager Don Duckwall. The memo started off with a clear goal: "Obviously the main idea is to find and develop new talent to make up a new animation team for the future."[220] One way to do this was to let midcareer apprentices replace the Nine Old Men. However, this approach required years of patience and even then, "it is still questionable" whether these apprentices would rise to the occasion.

Woolie's memo offered a second, more holistic option, which was to instead train a new generation in the principles of Disney Animation, which would create a "new breed of animation." This new breed of animation would be centered around personality and characterization—stories that grow out of the character and vice versa. It would also embrace collaboration and feedback to improve the creative product. To accomplish this would require the creation of a new training program inside the studio, and Disney's "expensive and extremely well-analyzed animation will have to be de-emphasized somewhat." Still the rewards were greater than the risk. "…With a little luck, it might be possible that we create something new, fresh, and exciting. It might even be possible that we could create once again the excitement and discovery of the old days…"[221]

The response from the executives was enthusiastic. Card Walker wrote, "I am pleased that we have quit talking about this and finally are getting something done. Let's really get moving and get this off the ground."[222]

Chapter 5

Disney Animation was entering a new stage in its history. Instead of shutting down Animation, Walt Disney Productions was making the most significant investment in the department's future in decades. In addition to two big-screen projects—*Bedknobs and Broomsticks* and *Robin Hood*, it was launching a new animation training program. As envisioned by senior leadership like Ken Anderson and Woolie Reitherman, the program would identify artists who showed potential to play a greater role in Disney's future.[223] To prove themselves, these recruits were required to create two animation tests over the course of a two-month period. If successful, the trainees would be promoted and paired up with a mentor—and if they did not pass review, they would likely have to find work elsewhere. The first wave of trainees was largely internal candidates looking for a promotion—such as Dave Michener, Fred Hellmich, and Burny Mattinson, who were already assistants to supervising animators.[224]

Also among this first batch of recruits was a returning animator who would wind up being among the most polarizing figures in the history of Disney Animation—Don Bluth. More than a half century after he joined the animation training program in April 1971, the mention of his name can still elicit passionate responses from those who worked with him. For some, he was an inclusive and charismatic leader without whom the animation industry may have never regained prominence. For his detractors, Bluth was condescending, messianic, and responsible for an irreparable "artistic and personal and political rift" even before his highly-publicized departure from Disney nearly brought the Animation Department to its knees.

In the mid-1950s, eighteen-year-old Don Bluth worked under animator John Lounsbery on *Sleeping Beauty*.[225] Animator Floyd Norman, who was just a couple years older than Don, said he was "a very studious, methodical kind of guy. Extremely talented. He was a darn good artist, a good draftsman, good animator. And also I should say, very ambitious."

If Don was outwardly ambitious, his memoir *Somewhere Out There* reveals he was privately torn about his decision to leave Disney to serve a mission for the Mormon church. According to Bluth, when he told his mentor John Lounsbery he was leaving, Lounsbery was very quiet before saying "I respect what you're doing. It's very brave."[226] Bluth kept in touch with his contacts at Disney and returned as a temporary hire in the summer of 1961 to work on *The Sword in the Stone*. Years later, when Bluth decided to reenter the animation industry, he was hired by Filmation—a prominent animation studio focused on cheaper Saturday-morning cartoons and the occasional feature like *Journey Back to Oz*.[227] Don and his Filmation colleague Dale Baer would both be admitted into the initial class of Disney animation trainees before the *Oz* movie was released in 1972.[228]

When Bluth arrived back at Disney, he was given a few weeks to put together his first animation test as part of the training program. Don quickly graduated from the program and was placed with mentor Frank Thomas of the Nine Old Men.[229] Production manager Don Duckwall closely followed the progress of each trainee; he noted Bluth and Frank did not seem to work as well together as anticipated.[230] The biggest issue was that Bluth would make changes to his scene without first discussing the revisions with Frank. Duckwall addressed the issue with Bluth and the incident was seemingly not held against him.[231]

"I don't think that Don's personality really allowed him to pick up anything from Frank or Ollie or Milt," said Frank's son Ted. "Frank, I know, felt that Don was much more interested in production values like animating shadows than he was in character or personality, the things Frank could pass along and that made the earlier films so special."

Bluth was assigned scenes on *Robin Hood*—including where Robin Hood sneaks into Prince John's castle during the film's climax. When Woolie conducted screenings of the rough animation, Woolie was especially tough on Bluth's first scene. He said Bluth's Robin Hood lacked "attitude" and the animation was not "entertaining."[232] The feedback knocked Bluth for a loop, but he went back to his animation desk and spent the rest of that evening reworking the scene. Woolie's critique of Bluth that day seems harsher than the kind of notes he had given to Julius Svendsen on *The Aristocats*. One explanation could be that Woolie wanted to make sure the new crop of animators was held to the same high standards as the veterans who had just finished *The Aristocats*.

There were few women among the early recruits of the animation training program. Since the early days of Disney Animation, women were rarely given the opportunity to be supervising animators. Lorna Cook was an aspiring artist from Burbank who grew up under the shadow of the water tower on the Disney lot. She had intended to become an illustrator until financial issues changed her college trajectory. When a neighbor who worked at Disney recommended she apply to the studio's new training program, she submitted a portfolio of life drawings and was accepted. "It was a major accomplishment in my young life," she said. Lorna was excited to be accepted to this "really exalted place." As an animation fan, she had looked up to the Nine Old Men and was thrilled that one of them, Eric Larson, was now her mentor. "I loved every minute of it." Still, it was a challenge. Animation required a new approach to drawing—thinking in three dimensions. "Drawing is one thing, but animating is a whole other style of creating."

"I was very nervous. The first week, it was so overpowering to me. I was sick. I was just so like, oh my God, how am I gonna do this?" For her first test, she animated a dog chasing a ball and the initial feedback was positive. However, she later heard that a couple of the Nine Old Men thought her animation was not 'Disney enough' and she was cut from the program. "I was so devastated," she said. However,

Lorna did not give up on a career in animation. As soon as she was let go at Disney, she was hired by Filmation—and she walked away from Disney with meaningful connections, including Don Bluth. He would eventually help her return to Disney, where she later became a lead animator.

Another female recruit was Heidi Guedel, the daughter of television pioneer John Guedel (*The Adventures of Ozzie and Harriet, You Bet Your Life*). After high school, she enrolled in Chouinard Art Institute in the hopes of becoming an animator.[233] Frank Thomas's son Ted, who became friendly with Heidi at Disney, said she was "boisterous with a loud and easy laugh, outgoing, but self-conscious about being adopted. She liked to ride horses, had great energy and enthusiasm." The buzz among recruits was that some of the old guard would not let a woman become a full animator. She was determined not to meet the same fate as Lorna. Her Chouinard schoolmate Dale Baer took her to meet John Lounsbery, and suggested she could help with in-between drawings of Lounsbery's scenes on *Robin Hood*—specifically the Sheriff of Nottingham tying a noose. Her drawings were strong enough to win over Lounsbery and he backed her promotion out of the program and into a full-time job.[234]

Trainee John Pomeroy had been interested in filmmaking since he was a toddler, and recreated movie scenes using clay. When he was thirteen, he found one of the few books in existence about animation at his local library and from that point forward, he knew he found his calling. He decided he wanted to paint backgrounds for Walt Disney Productions. He began writing letters to the studio—about two a month—asking very specific questions like what kind of illustration board and brushes they used to create their backgrounds. In 1966, the teenager arrived at the Disney lot with his portfolio, but was turned away by the guard, who told him they weren't hiring. Undeterred, he continued his education at the Art Center College of Design in California. When Disney rejected him a second time in 1972, he took the feedback to heart and enrolled in an art course on perspective to get better. For John Pomeroy, the third time was the charm, and he was accepted into the trainee program in 1973.

"I had stars in my eyes," said Pomeroy. "I was on cloud nine for the first two or three years there of employment." It wasn't just because as a Disney employee he could visit the old *Zorro* set on the backlot or see the carousel horses used in *Mary Poppins* on any given day. It was also because he was able to work alongside great artists like Milt Kahl, Woolie Reitherman, Eric Larson, Frank Thomas, and Ollie Johnston. On his first day, a recent graduate of the trainee program, Gary Goldman, dropped by and asked if he wanted to grab lunch. "I can tell you all about the studio," Goldman offered.

Gary introduced John to his closest friend at the studio, Don Bluth. Gary had met Don after graduating from the training program a few months back. As Don would later tell the story, Gary was in the middle of a cigarette when they met, and Don instantly challenged him to quit smoking.[235] Gary accepted, and a lifelong friendship began. Likewise, John instantly clicked with Don and Gary. Don and John greatly admired each other's skill. "I was just ogling over the drawings on his desk," remembered John, "I thought he was a prodigy." In turn, Don was impressed that John's drawings were not just technically excellent but also seemed to come "from the heart."[236] Don, John, and Gary soon became a band of brothers.

John abandoned his pursuit of being a background painter and embraced the role of animator. He credits this to Eric Larson's nurturing instruction. His first major assignment, as it was for some others in the trainee program, was the short featurette *Winnie the Pooh and Tigger Too*, a follow-up to the Oscar-winning *Winnie the Pooh and the Blustery Day*. Before the featurette was in development, Ken Anderson had encouraged management to let "top young people" work on a lower-stakes project under the supervision of the veterans.[237] John was paired with Frank Thomas but looking back, John said he was never made to feel like this *Winnie the Pooh* film was "a training or audition vehicle." John was given a sequence near the end of the film where Rabbit tells Tigger he can't bounce anymore, after Tigger finally becomes unstuck from a treetop. He animated a dejected Tigger walking away from the camera and showed it to Frank Thomas. "He scrutinized the heck out of it," remembered John. It took John eighteen attempts until Frank felt the scene had been perfected.

Frank, whose extensive resume included the spaghetti kiss in *Lady and the Tramp*, was trying to teach John how to make the audience believe in a character. "Are they so captivated by the images that you created that they believe it's absolutely real? And are they rooting for that person or that character?" John said Frank was perhaps first among animators when it came to acting. "He passed on much animation knowledge that I use today. An amazing time."

The most intimidating presence at Disney for many of the young trainees was Milt Kahl, regarded by many as Disney's greatest animator. John approached Milt's office to ask for help with a close-up of Tigger's dejected expression. Other animators left their doors wide open, but Milt's was often closed during business hours. Before John could knock, two assistants popped up to warn him that the great and powerful Milt should not be disturbed. It was too late. Through the door, Milt yelled, "Come on in," but to John's amazement, it was said with a welcoming tone. John introduced himself and asked Milt for help getting the Tigger scene just right—after all, Tigger had been developed by Milt. Milt took out his pencil to find the best drawing of Tigger. Milt went to improve the drawing but wasn't happy with his own result, nor his second attempt, nor his third. "You know what," Milt said. "I actually like what you got better. Why don't you go with that."

"It was like the Heavens opened and I heard the Angels sing," said John.

As John got to know Gary and Don better, they told him about a project they had been moonlighting on in Don's garage, an animated story called *The Piper*. "The idea was that they needed to find out answers." said John. They were learning a lot about personality animation but, to their mind, not much else about filmmaking—like scoring sessions, story reels, budgets. For the next several years, Don, Gary, and John would become inseparable as they began to envision a project that would be their own. *The Piper* was soon replaced with a different idea, *Banjo the Woodpile Cat*. John said, "We thought if we were eventually going to fill [the Nine Old Men's] shoes, we gotta know something about the business so we know what we're doing."

Chapter 6

Disney's trainee program was beginning to yield viable recruits, but the ranks of the Animation Department were still surprisingly lean. "When I got there, there were only 55 people [in Animation], plus Ink & Paint," said Tad Stones, who joined as a trainee in 1974. "55 people were all that were keeping up the Disney heritage of animation features. It's crazy when you think of it now."

The program couldn't yet solve production challenges on *Bedknobs and Broomsticks* and *Robin Hood*. Disney continued to hire experienced animators from other studios on an as-needed basis. Among them was Floyd Norman, who returned to Disney after his attempt to launch an independent studio. His assignments were similar to trainee Don Bluth's, animating scenes of Robin Hood and the Sheriff of Nottingham, but he was let go as production was wrapping. "It was basically economics," Norman said with no hard feelings. "They knew they could hire an artist, a kid right out of school and pay him or her half of what they were paying me." Floyd Norman's dismissal was the kind of situation the Screen Cartoonists Guild worried about when they first heard about the training program in late 1970, warning the hiring of apprentices over experienced journeymen "seems contrary to the spirit if not the letter of the contract."[238]

The closest art school to recruit talent for Walt Disney Productions in Burbank—both geographically and spiritually—was the California

51

Institute of the Arts in Valencia. It had been Walt's final dream to create a fine arts institute for Los Angeles—a transdisciplinary arts school where one discipline could inform another. His approach for the school was ars gratia artis—art for art's sake.

CalArts had its roots in the existing Chouinard Art Institute, a Los Angeles-area school founded by artist Nelbert Murphy Chouinard. Nelbert, a gifted artist in her own right,[239] started the school after the death of her husband, army chaplain Horace Albert Chouinard. Horace died from cancer in September 1918,[240] less than three years into their marriage. Using her savings and her war widow's pension, Nelbert opened the Chouinard School of Art and Design in 1921. Many of her first students were returning veterans.[241] Still, she battled chauvinism from prospective students who called to enroll and asked to speak to her husband. Her terse reply was "I'm it!"[242]

In Chouinard's second year of operation, a Stanford Engineering student with a passion for drawing named Don Graham was walking by the school when he saw a sign and stopped inside to inquire about courses. After attending a life drawing class that day, he quit Stanford and enrolled at Chouinard.[243] Graham seemed to possess the unusual gift of strong artistic and analytical skills—the melding of the left and right brain. Nelbert wound up hiring him as an assistant teacher, and he became an important nexus between Chouinard and Disney. In late 1932, Don Graham began an after-hours program to train Disney's animation team, focused on life drawing.[244] Walt was impressed and began talking to Graham about designing a training program for the studio to help prepare his artists for the more sophisticated drawing that would be required for *Snow White*. In late 1935, Walt wrote Don Graham an eight-page memo stating his belief that to perfect the medium of animation, the artists needed a more uniform foundation in draftsmanship, caricature, acting, humor, story construction, dialogue, staging, music, and an understanding of the mechanics of animation. Walt believed there could be a "scientific approach" to teaching art. "We will thus stir up the men's minds more, and they will begin to think of a lot of these things that would never occur to them otherwise if the way weren't pointed out to them," Walt wrote.[245]

Graham's training program resulted in a major advancement in the art of animation. *Snow White* not only featured more realistic human figures than any previous Disney cartoon, but the focus on personality animation helped differentiate the miners, who otherwise were little more than adjectives: Grumpy, Happy, Sleepy, Bashful, Sneezy, Dopey (and Doc). Walt showed his gratitude to Graham and Chouinard by endorsing an animation prep program at the school in 1937, one of the first known animation courses in existence.[246] Graham's manual became the gold standard at Walt Disney Productions for decades to come and would be reused for the animation training program.

Throughout the 1940s and into the 1950s, Chouinard remained an important pipeline for artists at Disney, though Nelbert would later admit that Walt "had his eye on me more than I knew about him."[247] In 1953, Nelbert, who was now in her seventies, announced plans to retire. Her legacy seemed secure.[248] She had provided an education for tens of thousands of artists around the world, including Hollywood costume designers Edith Head and Bob Mackie, Disney color stylist Mary Blair, Warner Brothers animator Chuck Jones, and *The Endless Summer* graphic designer John Van Hamersveld.[249] Despite Chouinard's outward success, the school was on shaky financial ground reportedly due to alleged embezzlement from a Chouinard employee which threatened to shut down the school. Walt intervened, keeping the institution solvent.[250] Nelbert delayed her retirement.

In February 1961, students and alumni gathered to celebrate Nelbert's eighty-second birthday. "One thing I thank the Lord for is that I still have a good mind," she told *The Los Angeles Times* upon the occasion.[251] She also appeared on local television as her birthday coincided with the fortieth anniversary of the school. The show caught Walt's attention. He called her afterward and said, "Nelbert, tell me who's going to carry that school on?"

"I never thought of it," she replied. "It will die when I do, I guess."

"I will never let it die. You've done a wonderful job with that thing and I'll see to it that it's carried on," Walt said.[252]

Nelbert was grateful that Chouinard would be Walt's pet project. She told an interviewer a few years after this conversation that "I always feel that the school will go on no matter what happens to me. He will see to it that it will go on."[253]

To protect Chouinard's future, Walt joined forces with socialite Lulu May Von Hagen, who was helping another arts institution in decline, the Los Angeles Conservatory of Music. In late 1961, they hatched a plan to combine the two schools.[254] The merger excited Walt, who saw the potential to create something akin to what he had asked of Don Graham in 1935—a place where students could embrace a multidisciplinary approach to the arts. By 1966, Chouinard seemed ready to embrace its new identity as the California Institute of the Arts under the auspices of its board chair, Lulu May Von Hagen.

Nearly a year to the day after Walt's death, CalArts voted in H. R. Haldeman as its chairman[255]—the same H. R. Haldeman who would go onto become President Nixon's chief of staff and later convicted for his role in the Watergate coverup. In the 1960s, Haldeman managed the Disney account at the California-based J. Walter Thompson advertising agency[256] while also making a name for himself in the world of California higher education. Haldeman was president of the UCLA Alumni Association[257] and later appointed to governor Ronald Reagan's board of regents, where he supported Reagan's push to end free tuition and put the burden of rising college costs on students instead of the state.[258]

Before leaving for the Nixon campaign, Haldeman installed forty-year-old Robert Corrigan as CalArts's president—Corrigan's impressive credentials included being the first dean of NYU's Tisch School of the Arts.[259] Corrigan wanted experimental theater director Herbert Blau as the school's provost and lobbied Haldeman and the Disney family via Ron Miller to approve Blau's hiring.[260] Blau was well respected on the West Coast for cofounding the avant-garde San Francisco Actor's Workshop, but his recent tenure at New York's Lincoln Center ended after his shows were panned by New York critics.[261] According to school lore, the conversation between Blau and Haldeman went something like this:

> Blau: "You don't want to hire me. I'm pretty much a Marxist, and we don't believe the same things."
>
> Haldeman: "I'm told you're the most gifted theater artist in America."
>
> Blau: "I'm pretty good."
>
> Haldeman: "Then I don't care what your politics are."[262]

As Haldeman moved on to Nixon's presidential campaign and then the White House, he felt the school was in good hands but he continued to support CalArts from afar. In March 1969, within the first one hundred days of the Nixon administration, the Disney family was invited to the White House for a ceremony honoring Walt. There, President Nixon introduced a commemorative gold medal, copies of which would be used as a fundraising tool for CalArts.[263] It was a joyous day for all involved and a high-water mark for the relationship between Diane Miller's and Roy E. Disney's families. Ron and Diane's son Walter would fondly remember playing with his cousin Tim, which meant more to him than personally receiving one of the medals from President Nixon. At the North Portico of the White House, the entire family gathered to take a portrait—the patriarch Roy Oliver Disney stood off to the side while Roy Edward and Ron stood proudly together.[264] They were a family united in purpose—to celebrate Walt's legacy and in doing so, help his dream of CalArts come to fruition.

Haldeman wrote Corrigan a few weeks after the Disney family's trip to the White House to commend him on his "outstanding leadership."[265] Yet rising tensions were surfacing between CalArts leadership and the existing Chouinard staff. Those loyal to Nelbert Chouinard felt Corrigan and Blau were betraying her intentions. One of the new administration's most vocal critics was Edward Reep, head of Chouinard's freshman program. Reep, a respected watercolor painter selected by the Roosevelt administration to document World War II,[266] seemed to loathe everything about "Wrong Way" Corrigan. Reep compared the new president to a gigolo, writing "he had that naughty-boy charm wealthy woman find irresistible."[267] Don Graham, then chairman of the faculty, encouraged Reep to give the new administration a chance.[268]

In September 1969, Herbert Blau informed the vast majority of Chouinard instructors that they would be let go after that term. According to contemporaneous reports, only five of Chouinard's fifty-seven teachers would continue with CalArts.[269] The ousted design teacher Bill Moore, now chairman of the Save Chouinard Committee, began wearing pins that read "Pray for Nelbert's Baby."[270] Reep, Moore, and other faculty sued to get their jobs back. They also began a letter-writing campaign to plead their case to the Disney family and prominent Chouinard alumni. Yet Corrigan and Blau seemed to have the full support of the CalArts board of trustees, whose membership included Roy O. Disney, Ron Miller, Roy E. Disney, and Lulu Von Hagen.

Labor strikes delayed the construction of the Valencia campus of CalArts, so when the school was ready to accept students in the fall of 1970, it had to open a temporary home at Villa Cabrini, a former Catholic school in Burbank.[271] The setting couldn't have been more paradoxical for the anything-goes environment of the new CalArts. Nudity and drugs were not just commonplace but celebrated. Students were made to feel like artists in residence, so there were no grades and no fixed curriculum. Dogs roamed the campus. Shortly after CalArts opened, an Associated Press reporter interviewed students. "Please, could we just have some rules?" pled one student. Another complained, "I've always been a rebel, now I've nothing to rebel against, and I hate it."[272] When an earthquake struck in February 1971, it was as if God had personally brought down his wrath, leaving behind a scene out of the Old Testament. David Kirkpatrick, who was a teaching assistant in the Film Department, remembers, "The heads were off the statues. Oh, wow. It was just surreal. And then, the Valley had to be evacuated. We didn't know anything. It was like World War II and the sirens going off.

We went above the dam because there was concern it would've flooded the valley."

The following year, the permanent campus of CalArts opened in Valencia. Californian modernist architects Thornton Ladd and John Kelsey designed the main building to house all the departments under the same roof. Inside, the five hundred thousand square feet of classrooms and hallways created a spartan labyrinth of white concrete. To say the architects valued function over form would be to undersell the value of the walls as blank white canvases. One of the school's most impressive design features was a modular theater composed entirely of four-foot-by-four-foot platforms, any of which could be raised as high as ten feet off the ground by air pistons. Partially designed by Blau, the theater was promoted at the time as "the only playhouse in the world capable of breaking all precedent in the arrangement of stage and audience relationship."[273] Blau was beloved by his students, who saw him as the visionary genius who was never properly acknowledged by the New York theater scene. David Kirkpatrick remembers Blau's shows at CalArts, "were incredibly dynamic and actor-centric." Tony-winning actor Bill Irwin (CalArts class of 1972) said in 1982, "I learned as much from [Blau] as from anyone else."[274] However, the board increasingly blamed Blau for the extreme permissiveness at the school.

CalArts's lack of discipline—including reports of professors skinny-dipping with coeds—was the subject of increasing concern. In a public forum, one faculty member denounced the prudishness of the board and then reportedly proceeded to take off his clothes. Those in attendance largely viewed the incident as "theater," but when the Disney family heard about it, they were upset by the disrespectful display and what it said about the current management of the school.[275] It was the beginning of the end for Corrigan and Blau.

Equally problematic was CalArts's job offer to radical philosopher Herbert Marcuse. The aging German philosopher was a galvanizing figure blamed for student protesters in Paris, Berlin, and now the University of California San Diego.[276] His association with his former student Angela Davis of the Black Panthers made him a target of California conservatives,[277] who accused him of supporting violent protests[278]; his critics included governor Ronald Reagan, who said Marcuse promoted "a moral and sexual rebellion on the part of the young people."[279] After mounting pressure, the University of California San Diego forced Marcuse to retire due to his age.[280] The seventy-one-year-old professor would be a free agent, and CalArts offered him the job of running a new school of critical studies.[281] Although political philosophy may not seem to align with the original vision for CalArts, Marcuse believed art could be "a potential or actual weapon in bringing about revolution" through "a revolution of the aesthetic form itself."[282]

When Marcuse's hiring was put before the board for approval, the Disney family was reportedly so outraged they threatened to withdraw funding from CalArts.[283] The conservative Disney family would rather shut down Walt's dream than allow Marcuse to be part of it. In January 1970, CalArts informed Marcuse that they were withdrawing the job offer. When a newspaper asked if it was because of his political philosophy, he said "I would expect so."[284] The Marcuse affair soured Roy O. Disney on CalArts to the point where he began exploring merging it with another school.[285] When that failed, Roy instead asserted his influence over the administration[286] and Blau was dismissed as provost in the fall of 1971.[287]

"I think everybody knew the institute was built on a paradox," Blau said after his firing. "That you had a very innovative group of people with fairly searching ideas trying to find a correct premise of these ideas, being endowed by people who would be constitutionally suspicious of that. You put these two forces together and you're going to have conflicts."[288]

Blau's removal did not stop Edward Reep's pressure campaign against the administration of CalArts. He wrote Roy O. Disney on November 4, 1971, saying, "The removal of Herbert Blau will not solve the problem nor any one person for that matter. The school of art for one, must be reconstructed and restored to the sound program and principles it once enjoyed. This must be done quickly while there is still a chance to gather the heart and wisdom of the institution the Disneys believed in."[289] Roy Oliver Disney died before ever dealing with Reep's plea. On December 20, 1971—almost exactly five years after his younger brother Walt's death—Roy passed away from a stroke at the age of seventy-eight. Although Roy faced many stresses near the end of his life—including the launch of Walt Disney World in October 1971 and the hospitalization of his grandson after a serious accident—his wife would later say CalArts was "the place that killed my husband."[290]

Roy O. Disney's death was a major loss for Walt Disney Productions, but it was not quite as devastating as Walt's had been. "1971 wasn't nearly as dramatic as 1966," Ron Miller remembered. "Roy was a wonderful businessman. I think Roy had confidence in the staff Walt left the company with.… By '71, we were more or less in place and we were moving forward. And we were really comfortable with what we were doing."

Robert Corrigan stepped down as president of CalArts in May 1972, with Sharon Disney's husband, William Lund, named as a temporary replacement.[291] Ron Miller continued to help the school, including lending old Disney costumes and props for student films. He didn't care when the head of the Film Department, director Alexander Mackendrick (*Sweet Smell of Success*) dispatched his nineteen-year-old teaching assistant, David Kirkpatrick, to make the request. "Ron Miller was completely, completely open to us," said Kirkpatrick, who also called Ron "the nicest guy, salt of the earth."

From the beginning, CalArts had an Animation program, but it was run by experimental animator Jules Engel, who had briefly worked for Disney in the 1940s. Henry Selick (*Tim Burton's The Nightmare Before Christmas, Coraline*) was one of Engel's students. "The guy could draw like crazy and he could do the Disney stuff, but that's not what he chose to pursue." Engel was a Budapest-born, Chouinard-educated émigré who had an epiphanic moment when he first saw a Wassily Kandinsky exhibit in the 1930s.[292] *The Los Angeles Times* art critic Arthur Millier called that Kandinsky show "an event of first importance to all who keep abreast of contemporary art."[293]

"POW!," is the feeling Engel would remember from the Kandinsky show. "That opened the whole vista.... I, all of a sudden, felt that I wasn't alone."[294]

Engel arrived at Disney while production was underway on *Fantasia*. A ballet aficionado, Engel helped shape the film's two most memorable *Nutcracker Suite* sequences, the "Russian Dance" and "Chinese Dance," choreographing both numbers and placing them in abstract settings. On *Bambi*, his dramatic color styling accentuated the film's emotions.[295] When the war broke out, he joined the Air Force Motion Picture Unit, working with several artists who would later form a rival cartoon studio, United Productions of America (UPA).[296] With Engel, UPA would go on to revolutionize the look and feel of animation, embracing the abstract possibilities of the medium with flat, two-dimensional figures often set against a background divorced from naturalism. Today, UPA may be best known for the *Mr. Magoo* cartoons and the Oscar-winning short *Gerald McBoing-Boing*.

Engel's reputation as an abstract artist grew beyond Hollywood. His work *Red Poppies* hung in the White House during the Johnson administration.[297] As CalArts was looking for talent to run its film program, author Anais Nin brought Engel to the attention of Herbert Blau. Engel's first conversation with Blau felt more like an interrogation than a job interview. "Herb Blau had me over and had a kind of a rough cross-examination, lasted like three hours. I never talked three hours in my life before, and he just kept, you know, talk, pumping me and pumping me."[298] Blau, Corrigan and Alexander Mackendrick also screened Engel's experimental films. "What they were looking for at that time was a person who had a larger experience than just an animator.... I came to them as a painter who had been exhibiting, a sculptor, a printmaker, a designer, a graphic designer, and I had films both in live-action and animation, plus all the years of experience I had at the studios, and also a quality of taste that they saw in the work."[299]

Engel had no intention of teaching Disney-style animation. "That was not in my head to do that, nor in the head of Herb Blau or of Corrigan at that time," recalled Engel.[300] Still, the Nine Old Men tried to persuade him otherwise. "The questions came at me like arrows, and I had to answer them."[301]

Once Blau and Corrigan were gone, it's conceivable that Disney would ramp up the pressure on Engel to change his program. However, his students' films were beginning to get notice. Engel said, "We were sweeping every award that there was, student awards all over the world. In fact, I would say that by the end of the year we established the CalArts animation film graphics department as the most important new unit that was producing films of this caliber and of this consequence." The success of Engel's students "changed the whole situation." Still, Engel felt that the managers at Disney "were unhappy with me."[302]

Weeks before the release of Disney's 1971 musical *Bedknobs and Broomsticks*, animator Julius Svendsen rented a ship and took his two sons on a boating trip to the San Joaquin Delta. Sven had been working on the film's twenty-two-minute animated sequence that culminates in a soccer match between two teams of anthropomorphic animals, directed by his former supervisor Ward Kimball. Kimball and the animators stuffed 130 gags into the ten-minute soccer game,[303] giving the sequence an irreverent, go-for-broke spirit more typical of Looney Tunes than Disney. On that boat trip, Sven attempted to moor the houseboat after he put his sons to bed. As he was tying the boat to a tree, he slipped off the boat and hit his head. When the boys woke up, they discovered his lifeless body face down in the water.[304] Svendsen's death was a tragic reminder of the fragility of life, and in turn, why there was an urgent need to develop the next generation of Disney animators.

Chapter 7

With production on *Robin Hood* underway in 1971, the Animation Department began to look for new projects, and the most promising remained Lloyd Alexander's *The Chronicles of Prydain*. Before Disney's acquisition of the Prydain books, Lloyd Alexander was at the height of his literary career but still needed a day job to support his family. As part of the deal to secure the rights, Disney offered Lloyd "a mind-boggling amount of money to write a screen treatment"[305] which allowed him to forever say goodbye to the mundane grind of life that had plagued him since his days as a schoolboy.

Whether or not Philadelphia was experiencing a mild winter day on January 30, 1924, is entirely beside the point.[306] When author Lloyd Alexander would later recount the story of his birth, that January date was not just chilly but "bitter cold"; he'd occasionally throw in a nonexistent snowstorm for good measure. He'd blame the weather that day for "a certain bleak view of the world"[307]—a sardonic spirit that he carried with him the rest of his life. Yes, Lloyd was apparently born into a winter of his own discontent, and facts needn't get in the way of that story. Lloyd's childhood was full of wonderous moments like that. He claimed he "managed somehow to crack the code" of reading by staring at comics in the local newspaper.[308] These cartoons sparked a lifelong passion for storytelling.

Books were plentiful in the Alexander household. An overflowing shelf with eclectic titles seemed to be a status symbol for his parents— meant to be seen, though seldom read. "My parents, in fact, were invincible non-readers," Lloyd would say.[309] Easy access to books allowed Lloyd to devour whatever he wanted—from classics to "long-forgotten trashy novels. To me, it made no difference." He loved all genres, especially mythology and ancient history. "Nobody can read everything that's ever been written—but I tried."[310] He even convinced his mother to try and make foods mentioned in certain books. If Robin Hood consumed venison and beer, his mother's hamburger and ginger ale would be close enough to let Lloyd's active imagination bridge the gap. With hindsight, it may seem obvious that a young bibliophile with an overactive imagination would grow up to become an author, but young Lloyd had different pursuits in mind. He hoped to make his living as an artist—a painter, or, if he had to settle, a cartoonist. If that didn't work out, maybe a classical musician. "In time, sad to say, I realized I wasn't much good at either occupation" though he never fully abandoned these pursuits.[311]

Career was more of a verb than a noun in the Alexander household. His father Alan seemed to fail at every job he held: a stockbroker, a box-lunch vendor for factory workers, and a trader of Asian imports. When war broke out between Japan and China, the import market dried up, shuttering his father's business.[312] It forced Lloyd to reconsider his plans to attend college after high school, and he told his parents he intended to be a writer instead. They "nearly went into cardiac arrest," remembered Lloyd. His father urged him to find a steadier profession. "He was right, as I later found out."[313]

Lloyd had always preferred his own self-education to formal academics. "Tell the truth: much as I hated school, in fact I was a good student and won more than my share of honors," he wrote in an autobiography. "Does this seem curious and contradictory? No, not to me. School, after all, took up most of my life; and since it was the only life I had, I tried to make the most of it."[314] After graduating from high school at sixteen, he took a job as a bank messenger to save up for college but set aside time each day to write. Once he accumulated sufficient funds, he attended a teachers' college, but almost immediately chafed at being back in an institutional environment. "I, who had been a sophisticated man of the world for the past year, was obliged to shave my sideburns and wear a ludicrous freshman beanie. Worse, I found the courses so elementary as to be ridiculous."[315]

After the Japanese attacked Pearl Harbor on December 7, 1941, Lloyd decided to drop out of school. "The world was going up in flames and I was wearing a beanie." Lloyd had been concerned about the rise of Fascism in Europe since the Spanish Civil War, which he called "a defining moment, emotionally and politically (as Vietnam would be for a later generation)."[316] Now, like for so many Americans, the attack on Pearl Harbor made everything feel more urgent to him and he enrolled in the army. The gangly, bookish teen with a long, protruding nose felt like a misfit in the military until he was recruited for intelligence work, thanks to his French studies in school. He was quickly trained to help support the liberation of Europe after the Normandy Invasion. Lloyd was deployed to the United Kingdom. He was technically closer to the action but still not a part of it.

It was around this time Lloyd made a fateful trip to Wales. Decades later, this trip to "an enchanted world" would inform and provide the foundation for his most famous books, collectively known as the Chronicles of Prydain. "It seemed I recognized faces from all the hero tales of my childhood.… The Companions of Arthur might have galloped from the mountains with no surprise to me. Wales, to my eyes, appeared still a realm of bards and heroes; even the coal tips towered like dark fortresses."[317] *The Mabinogion*—a collection of Welsh myths dating back centuries to the age of oral storytelling—was one of the earliest versions of the Arthurian Legend. Lloyd would borrow characters and stories from *The Mabinogion* to form the basis of the Prydain books, but Wales represented more than a source of inspiration. For Lloyd, it was one of the last places he would visit while he still maintained a naive innocence about war, and by extension humanity. He wasn't yet dispelled from a fantastical belief in warfare informed by the tales he read as a child. "I saw myself performing great deeds of derring-do in a noble cause and quite possibly winning the war singlehanded."[318]

From Wales, he was deployed to the battle-scarred French country-side. As he moved closer to the front lines of the Lorraine campaign, he saw that his "delusion that a war was a technicolor movie spectacular had already started crumbling around the edges."[319] In its place, he witnessed the remnants of destruction. He encountered "an endless stream" of refugees fleeing destroyed villages, prisoners liberated from labor camps, and "everywhere, dead horses."[320] Lloyd knew his experiences were far less traumatic than what others experienced, and he also held firm to the belief that World War II was ultimately a justified war. "Yet, however righteous the cause, I think the process itself, the whole apparatus of killing, corrupts, to one degree or another, anyone involved in it."[321] From that point forward, he considered himself a pacificist. Years later, he wrote, "I grew up in the war and have no regrets about that. Even so, it stays in the mind."[322]

Lloyd spent the summer after V-E Day in Paris, where he met his future wife Janine and her child Madeleine.[323] He moved his new family back to the Philadelphia area, and supported them with a job at an advertising agency. Still, he clung to his dream of writing the great American novel. His early attempts yielded only rejection letters from publishers. When his first book was finally released nearly a decade later, it wasn't the overnight success he wished for despite personally lobbying local department stores to carry the book.[324] His follow-up works were also disappointments. At this point, he changed tactics and focused on becoming a children's author. To an outsider, it may have seemed like a compromise, but Lloyd found it to be "the most liberating and creative experience of my life."[325] He was able to express complicated themes in a more direct and satisfying way. *Time Cat*—about a boy and his time-traveling feline—was his first foray into children's literature. While researching different time periods for the book, Lloyd had a life-altering epiphany when he reencountered Welsh mythology. "Suddenly, it was as if all the hero tales, games, dreams, and imaginings of my childhood had come back to me, all in the setting of the land of Wales I had so briefly seen, and which had so enchanted me as a soldier 20 years before."[326] Lloyd constructed his own legends, set in a Wales of his creation which he called Prydain. The stories fused the ancient and the modern—time-tested mythology blended seamlessly with contemporary themes and characters. Lloyd didn't shy away from the Welsh origins, and created names for his characters which were uniquely unfamiliar to many readers: among them, Fflewddur Fflam, Princess Eilonwy, Gurgi, Gwythaints, Dallben. The first volume, *The Book of Three*, thrust readers into an adventure that unfolded at breakneck speeds, and yet the unusual setting and Lloyd's humanistic tendencies made for a compelling read. It also presented a protofeminist princess more than a decade before *Star Wars's* Princess Leia and two decades before Disney's *The Little Mermaid*. *The Book of Three* was a critical and commercial success and was followed in quick succession by the rest of the series: *The Black Cauldron, The Castle of Llyr, Taran Wanderer*, and *The High King*.

Never in the history of Disney Animation had a fantasy epic on the scale of the Prydain Chronicles been attempted, but it wasn't the first time it had been considered. After the completion of *One Hundred and One Dalmatians* in the early 1960s, animators Frank Thomas and Ollie Johnston began seriously exploring the possibility of adapting J.R.R. Tolkien's *Lord of the Rings* series. Frank's son Ted remembers the books lying around his house and how "excited" his dad was when talking about the prospect of turning Tolkien's books into a film. Yet according to Disney archivist Dave Smith, "As far as I know, we never purchased rights to *Lord of the Rings*. At least, there was never a production number set up for it, and over the years I have never found any proof that we had the rights. It is possible that Disney looked into buying the rights—and this very well could have happened—but it never progressed any farther than the talking stage." Some reporting has claimed Disney ceded the rights to United Artists (UA) in 1969[327]—though, if true, that didn't stop Frank Thomas from once again revisiting the idea with story artist Vance Gerry in 1972.[328] The film was ultimately made by Ralph Bakshi, who said Disney abandoned the project because it was too violent.[329]

In many ways, Bakshi was the anti-Disney alternative within the animation industry with edgy, contemporary adult cartoons, including the first major X-rated animated film *Fritz the Cat.* "The rest of the animation industry was all merchandising and misinformation," said Bakshi. He believed film was a director's/writer's medium, whereas Disney put the producer in charge. "Whatever Disney was doing was not interesting to me at the time," Bakshi said. His *Lord of the Rings* was released by UA on November 15, 1978.

With Tolkien's book out of contention, Frank and Ollie saw Lloyd Alexander's Prydain books as a promising alternative. Disney lore credits production manager Don Duckwall with helping acquire the books in 1971, but he wasn't alone in endorsing the stories. Frank and Ollie saw much of the potential that Otto Englander had first discovered three years earlier. Frank's son Ted was working at Disney in 1971 and carpooled with Frank and Ollie to the lot. On the way to work, these old friends would spend the car ride talking about the Prydain books—their Celtic mythology, the character relationships, and potential story points. "They were real champions of it," remembered Ted. "Both Frank and Ollie played a very strong role in convincing the studio to get the rights to it and then to think about seriously putting it into development."

Studio documents show the Story Department revisited its analysis of the Prydain books in early 1973. Otto Englander and Inez Cocke were no longer around to disagree about the stories' merits, and much had changed in the country. Nixon was now in his scandal-plagued second term, the draft had ended, and there was new hope for an end to the Vietnam War. In Hollywood, fantasy films were almost nonexistent. Disney had a new story analyst, Charles Embree, a jazz-loving beatnik hiding beneath the soft-spoken exterior of an aging suburban patriarch. Embree had moved to California after World War II and began writing for *Esquire* under his hepcat pseudonym "Riff Charles." Or, as he once put it, "Charles Embree is the actual name of a fictitious person whose reality exists in the imagination of others. Some imagine him this way; some imagine him that way, or some other way. He is most grateful to be imagined any way."[330] Embree's beat-era sensibilities stayed with him, even as he settled down and found employment at various Hollywood studios—including Paramount, where he worked under superstar producer Bob Evans.[331] His antiestablishment outlook was well suited to the new Hollywood of the late 1960s, but when he moved to Disney shortly thereafter, he had to retrain his thinking. "A Disney movie was a 'brand.' Like Campbell Soup. You knew what was in the can before you opened it," he later wrote. "It took me a while before I acquired what I suppose was the intuition to recognize a Disney script when I read it."[332] Embree was still relatively new at Disney when the Prydain books crossed his desk, but he may have been predisposed to like them; Embree and Lloyd Alexander were kindred souls. As children, both had wanted to grow up to be artists and musicians. Embree made a serious attempt at both. He studied painting under Thomas Hart Benton in Kansas City, and was a dedicated jazz musician. Like Lloyd, World War II changed Embree's path, and he emerged from it with hopes of being a great American writer.

The Prydain books now had a solid base of support within Disney from the likes of Embree, Frank Thomas, Ollie Johnston, and Don Duckwall. Likewise, Ron Miller liked what he saw. "It had a lot of elements that I felt were a little bit more mature than we had done in the past but yet still had all the elements that make for a good film," Ron said. "It had a good storyline and good characters." He ignored naysayer Bill Anderson, who thought there was nothing to the story. Lloyd Alexander's fantasy series shared some unlikely similarities with another Disney film of this era: 1971's *Bedknobs and Broomsticks*. Both stories fuse the folklore of medieval Britain with the idea of "total war." The Prydain books, set in the Middle Ages, present an all-out struggle between good and evil informed by World War II, while *Bedknobs and Broomsticks* is about a witch who calls up a deathless medieval army to stop the Nazi invasion of Britain.

After Disney acquired the rights, Lloyd Alexander was brought to the Burbank studio to collaborate on the story. From the beginning, he seemed slightly out of step with Disney. He enjoyed the first-class flight to California, paid by Disney, but he turned down their accommodations, which left them slightly perplexed. Instead, he decided to stay with his friends: author Myra Livingston, her husband Dick, and their family in Beverly Hills.[333] It was about thirty minutes away from the Disney lot, but it provided a homier environment. Lloyd had always enjoyed his visits with the Livingston family when he was in California. He was treated like a hero by Myra's young daughter Jennie, who was fond of Lloyd. When he visited the family for an unrelated trip in the summer of 1969, Myra wrote a friend how seven-year-old Jennie "wouldn't leave his side, and is now moaning that he is gone and asking me how many days until November when he returns!"[334]

Jennie Livingston grew up to be an independent film director—her most famous work is *Paris Is Burning*. She fondly remembers Lloyd's visits. "He was a great cartoonist," she said. He would draw birthday cards for the family, including one Jennie still keeps hanging in her house inspired by a "really really loud bird in our neighborhood." The illustration is called *The Giant Duck*. She also recalls Lloyd's bardlike tales of working with Disney. "He told really long hilarious stories about the studio," she recalls. "There was an incredulity in his expression, and an intricacy to how he mapped out the various things that were happening at the studio that he found fairly absurd. I'm sure it formed my views of film studios and may have kept me, as a filmmaker who works primarily independently, quite keen to avoid anything like what happens when a great tale like the Prydain series meets the Mouse Ears."

Whereas Lloyd had become accustomed to the lonely pursuit of writing, he was now collaborating—not only contending with others' ideas about his stories, but also trying to break into the Disney story team, which had well-established dynamics. Disney story artist Larry Clemmons wrote a comic retelling of a February 1974 story meetings, made to appear like "the minutes" of the session attended by Lloyd, Woolie Reitherman, Ken Anderson, Larry Clemons, Milt Kahl, Frank Thomas, and Ollie Johnston. Lloyd begins by announcing, "I have come up with a better outline" than the one from the day before. Before he can finish his thought, Woolie interrupts to tell everyone to stop interrupting. "My new story outline completely excludes the Black Cauldron…" He is interrupted again.

Ken Anderson jumps in, "Hold it!... You got no cauldron, you got nothin'!"

Woolie agrees. "Yeah, Lloyd, we gotta keep that big iron pot in there.... It's the gimmick—the BIG Weenie." Lloyd didn't seem to know what to make of this Disney term for a large, unifying icon to lure in audiences. As he tries to wrap his brain around it, Woolie jumps in and suggests a main character from the books, Gwydion, should be cut. As Lloyd tries to process that, Woolie suggests the villain should be the Horned King. "...a bad guy with horns on his head, we've really got something..."

Ken Anderson approves, "I can draw anything that breathes with horns on it."

Milt chimes in, "And NO dialogue. Who needs talk-talk, yam-mer-yammer, blab-blab-blab...we do the whole thing in pantomime." The others start to chime in and offer their takes on the number of characters, the relationship between the protagonist and antagonist as Woolie continually interrupts to remind everyone to let others finish their thoughts. As the meeting winds down, Lloyd has heard more suggestions than he's put forth.

Woolie ends, "Well, we've accomplished a lot—thanks to Lloyd's thinking on this.... Lloyd, do you have any further comments to make?"

"Just one," Lloyd says. "I'd rather be in Philadelphia."[335]

Again, Larry Clemmons' humorous take on the meeting is not meant to reflect what actually happened, but it does reflect Lloyd's discomfort working in a "writer's room" of a movie studio. Lloyd went home and spent the summer of 1974 working on the film's outline. He came back to Disney that October and spent days in marathon story sessions about the characters, their relationships, and the magical elements that would differentiate Prydain from traditional fairy tales. These story sessions showed the team coalescing around the primary characters who would later populate the film: Taran, the assistant pig keeper; Eilonwy, the princess; Fflewddur Fflam, the bard; Doli, a fairy; Gurgi, a man-beast; and the Horned King as the villain.[336] As evidenced by contemporaneous memos, the exchanges between Lloyd and the Disney staff show a deep commitment to properly develop the story, as challenging as it was to adapt a five-book series into a ninety-minute film.[337]

The Disney Animation Department which Walt had left behind was already evolving by the time Lloyd Alexander arrived at Disney. In an October 1974 story session with Lloyd, there were some new faces who had not been part of the core leadership team on *The Jungle Book* and *The Aristocats*—namely Don Bluth, whom Woolie was beginning to train to be a director, and the concept artist Mel Shaw.[338] Mel had only recently returned to Disney, having originally worked there three decades earlier, as part of the studio's glory days before World War II.

Mel Shaw had met Walt Disney playing polo as a nineteen-year-old in 1930s Los Angeles, and the young artist was hired in the Story Department working on *Fantasia* and *Bambi*.[339] During World War II, Mel was sent to Southeast Asia with the U.S. Signal Corps. As an official U.S. war photographer, he was responsible for documenting the leadership of Lord Louis Mountbatten (the grand-uncle of King Charles III), during the Burma Campaign.[340] During his time overseas, he witnessed the toll war takes on civilian populations, including the Bengal famine—believed to have killed 2.1 million people—and the brutal killings of communists by the Chinese army.

After the war, Mel opened an independent design firm with friend Bob Allen, out of which came the design for Howdy Doody—the iconic title character from one of the most-watched programs during the golden age of television. Mel Shaw's business partner retired in 1970, which left him at a crossroads, unsure if he would continue to run their business alone.[341] In a bit of fortuitous timing, Ron Miller found out that Mel would be at the same Beverly Hills holiday party he was attending with Diane. Ron had heard about Mel Shaw from longtime Disney veterans and he made it his business to seek out Mel, cornering him in conversation that night. Mel remembered Ron saying to him, "Animation is what made the studio in the first place and it should be rebuilt!"[342] Mel wasn't quite ready to say goodbye to his business, but Ron offered him the chance to work at Disney as a part-time consultant. Mel accepted and soon enough, he was devoting most of his energy to Disney.

When Mel joined the story meetings on *The Black Cauldron*, he noticed that Lloyd Alexander "seemed to be a very reserved man." Mel made a point of talking to Lloyd outside of the group setting, to learn more about the origins of the Prydain tales. Lloyd and Mel spoke at length about the historic underpinnings of the Prydain books—which were rooted in the ninth century Danish invasion of Northern England. "Lloyd Alexander let me get into his background of why he picked that particular part of the world to do a fantasy," Mel remembered. "The basics was a young man growing up and the coming of age where [he] could be part of the warrior group…the fantasy part and having a villain like the Horned King was something that had to do with a lot of the tribal problems they had in the northern part of England at that particular point in history."

Lloyd was having "a marvelous time"[343] with the animators—he would continue to correspond with some for years to come—but he was aware that Hollywood was not his calling. "I quickly realized that, for many technical reasons, the film version would be drastically different from the book. Even if I had been a competent screen writer, psychologically and emotionally, I wanted no part of the process.… What I came to understand was that a movie is a mass, public entertainment; a book, an individual, deeply private experience."[344] Lloyd flew home and withdrew from the film. His story would be adapted without further input from him, though his work with Mel Shaw would inform the film in its early development.

Two years passed, and—like a bad game of telephone—word began circulating within the children's literature industry that Lloyd had been mistreated by Disney. It prompted a Georgia schoolteacher, Kemie Nix, to write an angry letter to Ron Miller—claiming she heard false rumors Lloyd was fired over a clause in his contract and that he hadn't been paid for his work. She said she found it outrageous that "the greatest living writer of fantasy" would be treated in such manner. She warned that they would face a "whirlwind" of angry librarians, school teachers, and children if Lloyd wasn't treated right. Disney forwarded the letter to Lloyd, who wrote her back.

"There's no cause for alarm," he wrote. "It's amazing how rumors spread and it seems the more they spread, the less they have to do with facts…. Shabby treatment, not at all. Kindness, warmth and thoughtfulness would describe it better."[345] He also dispelled any myths around his contract or compensation. He told her that he was asked to give his thoughts on characters and storylines only and not to deliver a screenplay, a technical kind of writing for which he was not well-suited. As a happy byproduct of this angry letter, Lloyd Alexander and Kemie Nix became fast friends and maintained a correspondence until Lloyd's death in 2007. Whenever she taught literature to children, whether it was in Georgia or Kenya, Kemie Nix would forever start with the first Prydain novel, *The Book of Three*.

Chapter 8

In May 1972, veteran Disney animator Eric Larson traveled cross-country to help Disney establish relationships with major art schools outside California. The oldest of the Nine Old Men, Eric was a few months shy of his sixty-seventh birthday as he made his journey to schools like the Pratt Institute, the Philadelphia College of Art, and the Chicago Academy of Fine Arts.[346] Among his peers, Eric was admired for his wise and gentle spirit and his history of animating some of Disney's most iconic moments.[347]

Born on September 3, 1905, Eric Cleon Larson grew up in Cleveland, Utah—a small pioneer town where his father Lars Peter Larson ran a general store, which promised its customers "Come and Be Treated Right."[348] The Larsons left Cleveland for Salt Lake City around the time Eric was ten, in hopes of providing better opportunity for the family.[349] In high school, Eric blossomed. He earned praise as editor of the yearbook, ran for student office, and developed his artistic talent.[350] In 1921, *The Deseret News* published his Armistice Day drawing of Uncle Sam watching over a grieving soldier titled *Lord God of Hosts, Be with Us Yet, Lest We Forget, Lest We Forget.*[351] At the University of Utah, Eric's artistic talent helped him stand out as the art director of the yearbook and the satirical magazine *The Humbug*. When he joined *The Humbug* in 1924, the publication was adopting strict new humor guidelines—nothing risqué and no jokes about prohibition.[352] Even with these parameters, Eric's art and humor made the publication the talk of campus.

After college, Eric moved to Los Angeles, where he worked as an art director for Commercial Art and Engraving and married his wife, Gertrude. An attempt at becoming a radio playwright led to a chance encounter with Disney's publicity head, writer Dick Creedon. Instead of offering pointers on the script, Creedon convinced Eric to work for Disney.[353] Eric joined at a time when Walt was trying to inject his cartoons with more sophisticated animation—including the first attempt at a realistic human figure with Persephone in *The Goddess of Spring* (1934). As assistant animator to Ham Luske, Eric mimed the actions of Persephone to provide a sense of movement.[354]

Eric soon became one of the go-to animators for cute animal characters, including the woodland creatures of *Snow White*, the Silly Symphony's Ugly Duckling, and Figaro in *Pinocchio*. Figaro was a breakout for Larson, who gave the cat the personality of a willful toddler. It added vital humor to the early part of the film, sustaining audiences until Pinocchio comes to life fifteen minutes into the movie. Figaro embodied one of the most important qualities in Larson's animation: believability.

In the late 1940s, Eric codirected a documentary for the Church of Jesus Christ of Latter-Day Saints. *Church Welfare in Action* explored how the church helped its members through the Depression and World War II. It was Eric's first time in the role of director.[355] He followed it up with a second film, *The Lord's Way*, about a family struggling to support themselves after an accident. When Walt learned about the films, he offered his support and let Eric use a portion of the Silly Symphony short *The Grasshopper and the Ants*.[356] Eric's work on these Mormon films coincides with the period at Disney when he did some of his best animated work: Peter Pan's flight over London, Cinderella's dance with Prince Charming, *Alice in Wonderland*'s Caterpillar, and the character of Peg in *Lady and the Tramp*. Eric was promoted to director for Disney's *Sleeping Beauty*, the studio's attempt at a widescreen spectacle in the age of *Ben-Hur*, and *The Ten Commandments*.

Disney began developing *Sleeping Beauty* by 1951.[357] Walt's ambitions for the project kept expanding throughout the 1950s, even as he was getting more involved in Disneyland, television, and live-action films. Its visual style was a bold mix of midcentury modern graphic design and medieval tapestries, led by artist Eyvind Earle. Every frame was made to look like it could hang in a museum and the film was to be exhibited in a 70 mm widescreen format. Eric took the grandeur to heart as he set about directing what is arguably the most important sequence in the film—sequence eight, where Princess Aurora, hiding out as Briar Rose, encounters Prince Phillip while singing "Once Upon a Dream." Aurora has the least screen time of any Disney Princess, clocking in at just under eighteen minutes, and she doesn't have a single line of dialogue in the last third of the film. Sequence 8 is the only opportunity viewers have to get acquainted with Aurora, empathize with her loneliness, hear her sing about her desire to find love, and then see her rendezvous with the man she was betrothed to as a child who also happens to be the prince of her dreams. For Disney's *Sleeping Beauty* to work at all, sequence eight needed to excel.

Under Eric's direction, the sequence was indeed captivating but also exorbitantly expensive. Eyvind Earle's design style proved challenging for the human characters, slowing down the animators. In sweatbox meetings, Larson gave meticulous notes—further encumbering progress.[358] Walt grew increasingly concerned about the costs associated with sequence eight and demoted Larson, bringing in other directors, like Woolie Reitherman, to help finish the rest of the film.[359]

Floyd Norman, who worked on *Sleeping Beauty*, remembers, "Once the feature had been completed, Eric Larson returned to animation and his old office in D-Wing. I was working in the wing at the time, and Eric seemed content having returned to his old position as directing animator." *Sleeping Beauty* is now considered one of Disney's best animated films, but its box-office failure and the resulting layoffs haunted Disney Animation for years to come.

By 1972, as Larson embarked on his journey to recruit new talent, it seemed like his most significant work at Disney was long behind him. He had been at the studio for nearly four decades but recently had been relegated to side characters with limited screen time—like the Beatles-inspired vultures in *The Jungle Book* and the mouse Roquefort in *The Aristocats*. He couldn't have predicted that the next chapter in his life would go on to define his legacy—teaching and guiding the next generation of animators.

As he set out east, Larson planned to discuss why Disney needed candidates with good basic art training, and in return, how these artists could find "opportunities for self-expression in the animated art form" just as he had.[360] It seemed like an easy sell, but it turned out that few schools east of the Mississippi River were ready for the pitch. At the Art Students League in New York, the executive director left the meeting after a few minutes and stuck Eric with underlings: an assistant, a drawing instructor, and three students who were "well versed on Disney cartoons, yet never giving a thought to being part of them."[361] At Pratt, he couldn't get through to the head of the Film Department because the students were conducting a sit-in, trying to oust president Henry Saltzman.[362] The embattled Saltzman took the meeting with Larson but was gone by summer.[363] At the Pennsylvania Academy of Fine Arts, the administrator who met with Larson seemed "uninformed" about animation and "was quite surprised" Disney was seeking him out. Larson didn't feel discouraged even as administrators raised questions like, "Would the student be channeled into the Disney way of things, destroying his own individuality, or would there really be an opportunity for self-expression?"

Then there were practical considerations that Larson was not able to address, like how much would a trainee earn during this tryout period and who would pay for the travel and accommodations in California. "Is it worthwhile for a student to leave his environment and journey to the studio with no greater promise than a tryout?" These were all valid questions, and Eric raised them when he reported back from the trip. Still, he thought the schools were generally responsive to the idea, even if animation was "a whole new world to them. They haven't considered the creative possibilities it offers."[364] Ultimately though, relying on an

East Coast talent pool would be challenging. CalArts was still the most attractive option to create a feeder school.

Disney sent some of its new animators to talk to Jules Engel's class at CalArts—including John Pomeroy, Gary Goldman, and Don Bluth. The former trainees showed their rough animation from *Winnie the Pooh and Tigger Too*. For one of Engel's students, seeing these rough pencil animation made him feel connected to something larger than himself. Prior to this moment, that student, Glen Keane, felt out of place in Engel's class: "I didn't feel like I quite fit into animation.... I saw people flipping paper. It was like, what in the world is this? My drawings were very rough and loose. This style though, this rough animation, I knew I could do it." Future Oscar-winner Glen Keane would become one of the most prominent Disney animators of the post-Walt era.

Glen's father was *The Family Circus* cartoonist Bil Keane, who saw evidence of his son's talent at a young age. "I'm a cartoonist. You're an artist," Bil told Glen before the age of ten. That vote of confidence stayed with Glen for the rest of his life. "That was the most wonderful thing I think I'd ever heard," said Glen. "It was like being knighted." To further develop his son's gifts, Bil gave him the book *Dynamic Anatomy* by Burne Hogarth. Kids on the school bus made fun of Glen for his figure drawings, taunting him that he was drawing naked guys. "When you're a kid at that age and people are laughing at what you're doing, you stop. But not me, because I had my dad and I realized they didn't get it. And that made me feel really special. I just embraced this idea of being an artist."

As he was getting ready to graduate from high school, Glen was torn between playing football for Arizona State or going to art school. His school counselor tipped the scales by giving Glen a pamphlet for the newly opened CalArts. The Keanes drove to the new school on Easter break, but when they discovered the campus was closed, Bil asked the only person they could find—"a stoner"—if he could take his son's portfolio and turn it in for consideration at the art school. Glen got an acceptance letter from CalArts but was confused when he saw it was from the School of Film Graphics. Glen called the school. "There's been a mistake. I don't want to do film graphics. I want to paint. I want to sculpt. What is film graphics?"

The woman on the other end of the phone said, "Well…it's…um…film graphics, it's…you know, I have no idea, but this is the only way that you're going to come into the school."

Glen had been at CalArts for more than a year before Don, John, and Gary finally helped him find his path forward. He called Disney and found out that they were accepting applicants for the training program. When he mentioned he attended CalArts, the person on the other end of the line paused and then asked if Glen understood what material they were looking for in a portfolio. The Experimental Animation program was seemingly at odds with what Disney wanted. Glen realized, "[CalArts] was a negative check." Glen was undeterred, and he scheduled a portfolio review with Eric Larson.

Glen arrived at Disney for his appointment and earnestly greeted Eric that day as "Mr. Larson."

"Glen, it's Eric."

The young CalArts student was so eager for the portfolio review that he didn't listen. "Oh, okay. Yeah. So Mr. Larson…"

"Glen," Eric paused. "Everybody here is first name because we are all the same. We are all artists. It was that way with Walt. I'm Eric. You're Glen." Eric's welcoming approach finally sunk in. Glen was being welcomed as a peer by someone he respected. Calling people by their first name was a tradition at Disney, encouraged by Walt.

Eric continued to flip through Glen's portfolio but didn't spend much time on any one image. He finally paused on a very fluid unrefined figure drawing, which sparked a moment of self-doubt for Glen. He was surprised when Eric said, "Can you do more like that?"

Glen replied, "Yeah, I mean, that took me like 10 seconds."

"That's really natural. Yes. I can tell," said Eric. "If you can do more like this, with this rhythm and movement. There's an attitude that you're getting. This is animation right here. So go to the beach. Go somewhere with sketchbooks and draw."

Glen came back a week later with a stack of notebooks filled with seven hundred drawings. Eric went through them again, getting rid of anything but the best sketches leaving a "pretty good" average of ten drawings per hundred. Eric passed Glen's portfolio to the Animation review board and he was hired into the trainee program. Unlike others in the animation training program, Glen was relatively unacquainted with Disney Animation's storied legacy. "When I finally got to Disney, I just felt like I didn't fit in. Everybody knew about all of the Nine Old Men, they knew all the stories, they knew all the films. All I knew was I wanted to be an artist." Yet he was also in awe of what lay ahead. "The potential of [the medium of animation] was beyond anything that I could imagine."

What Glen now understood from Disney's initial hesitation upon hearing he attended CalArts was that those Experimental Animation students were considered too avant garde for Disney. "They weren't doing the kind of disciplined drawing and design that Disney needed." Whereas previous trainees Dale Baer and Heidi Guedel may have been seen as Chouinard alumni, Glen was the first exclusively CalArts student hired by Disney.

When Glen joined Disney, he considered himself to be a lapsed Catholic but still spiritual. "It had been years since I'd gone to Catholic church and I kind of pushed all of that back and then I got to Disney and I was busy working away. And then this incredible sense of spiritual bankruptcy—I guess, like I needed to know I was right with God— became even more powerful than learning animation for me." He walked down the halls of the Animation Building in those first days thinking, "Why does nobody else think about their soul and what's going on in a spiritual dimension?"

Within a few months, another trainee, Ron Husband, joined Disney. "He was a football player from the Las Vegas, Nevada, and he had his head shaved, [mustached], black guy, really strong," said Glen.

Ron Husband had grown up in Southern California but was an unlikely candidate for the training program since he hadn't watched a Disney cartoon since he was a kid. "I didn't know anything about animation," he said. Ron had been working as a technical illustrator for Honeywell but wanted to take on more creative projects, so he began taking classes at Art Center College of Design in Los Angeles. His instructor Sam McKim, one of the top designers for WED Enterprises, told him about the animation training program. He was accepted and upon completing the training program, he was paired in a room with Glen. Ron was doing in-betweens for Frank Thomas, and Glen for Ollie Johnston. Ron began to realize he was getting paid to do something he loved. "I never went to work a day in my life."

At lunch, Glen noticed that Ron wasn't joining the other animators. "Instead, he was sitting on the park bench reading his Bible," Glen said. "I'd never seen that before. I'd never seen anybody read a Bible." Back in their room, Glen asked Ron, "What does the Bible say about how I know I can be right with God?"

Ron replied, "Well, Glen, it's like I've been on that same search." Ron then quoted John 3:16 from the Bible.

From that day forward, Glen and Ron became close friends. They started a Bible study at Disney, composed of a group of about six or seven other employees. "That became such an important part of my life at that point, early, early on," said Glen. "People would make fun of me, us." At least one animator would later ask to be transferred out of Glen's unit because he was uncomfortable, coming from a secular background. Nevertheless, Glen's faith has been infused into the best of his animation—such as the Beast's transformation at the end of *Beauty and the Beast*, Ariel's longing to be part of a world she can't touch in *The Little Mermaid* or the spirit of the wind in *Pocahontas* guiding her path.

By the summer of 1974, the Animation Department heads were planning to create a Disney-sponsored department inside CalArts devoted exclusively to the the studio's animation methods. It would coexist with Jules Engel's experimental program, but the students would be handpicked by Disney and trained exclusively in the ways of Disney Animation.[365]

Artist Ken Anderson put much thought behind what type of student should be admitted to this new CalArts program. He took for granted that a candidate would have studied art in high school "and has good marks in work habits, cooperation, and attitude. In fact, I would not admit anyone who is deficient in those traits." However, Ken wanted more than those prerequisites. He wanted someone with an "insatiable curiosity," who could "accept guidance and discipline" but also had artistic ambition. After they graduated from the program, this ideal candidate "would have learned how to see and knows that the secret to seeing is understanding."[366]

That summer, Ken Anderson, Eric Larson, and Marc Davis held conversations with Alexander Mackendrick in the CalArts film program as well as Mel Powell, the head of the Music Department and Curriculum Committee chairman. The initial proposal was for an accelerated timeline that would see the character animation program launch in the 1974–1975 academic year.[367] For the small class of about a dozen students, they proposed generous scholarships from the Disney Family Foundation, a fund established after Walt's death.[368] They offered the job of running the department to famed animator Art Babbitt, who left Disney on acrimonious terms after the animators' strike of 1941.[369] Babbitt would later say the Disney family threatened to pull funding for the program when they heard he had been offered the job, according to his 1978 conversation with student Nancy Beiman. With Babbitt out of the picture, veteran Donald Duck animator Jack Hannah was recruited and the decision was made to begin the program in the fall of 1975.

The investment in training programs, both at the studio and soon at CalArts, showed the continued financial commitment to the Animation Department despite an overall decline in the economy. The OPEC oil embargo of 1973—spurred by U.S. support of Israel in the 1973 Arab-Israeli War—compounded problems for the already shaky U.S. economy. Gas lines were common. Inflation soared. Disney was not immune to these market forces. The company's 1974 annual report read, "Inflation, the crisis of confidence in government and the prolonged concern about the availability of gasoline had a profound effect upon business activity."[370] By March 1974, one analyst estimated that Disney stock had "lost $2.4 billion in market value" due to these external factors.[371] Walt

Disney World, originally an instant success, now threatened to be a liability as gas prices limited the number of visitors willing to make a long road trip. Still, Disney tried to project confidence in its stability. "We are a financially strong company with a young, aggressive management."[372]

At the 1974 shareholder meeting, chairman Donn Tatum and president Card Walker tried to reassure investors that Disney was in better shape than other media companies thanks to its diverse revenue streams: parks, merchandising, and of course, film and television. A summer blitz of reissued films helped the company break its all-time annual box-office record, topping $75 million (about $500 million in today's money).[373] It also released *Robin Hood* at Radio City Music Hall and had launched a "total Disney marketing" campaign—including radio and tv ads, merchandising and other promotion.[374] It was believed *Robin Hood* had eight billion total market "impressions" during its release.[375]

For one young aspiring animator in his late teens, *Robin Hood* indeed made an impression. Mike Gabriel was an artist and surfer in Huntington Beach, California, when he saw Frank Thomas and Ollie Johnston promoting the film on a television talk show. The two legendary animators showed a clip of Prince John and Sir Hiss in rough black-and-white animation. "I was mesmerized, and agape at the insanity of the animation that I saw. It was so well done I wanted to weep almost. It truly moved me. It shook my art brain. It confounded me," remembered Mike. "It instilled in me a greater furor than ever before to get into that studio. The simplicity in movement. The control. The clarity of every intention." When he finally went to see *Robin Hood* in theaters, he walked out on a "Disney high." It was more euphoric and illicit than any drug could be. "It made me feel almost lightheaded with joy and with all my artist senses on circuit-breaking overload."

As Mike Gabriel departed the theater, he was compelled to hold onto this special experience—even if it meant breaking the law. As he exited the theater, he spied large eight-inch-by-ten-inch lobby cards with scenes from the movie, joined together to make one giant poster. After making sure no one was watching, he attempted to rip down the cards in one masterful move, but the display was securely held together. He freed one of the cards but in so doing, it made a sound like rolling thunder. His heart started pulsing out of his chest, worried he would get arrested. Still, he was not deterred. He kept tearing down the lobby cards from the display, each time creating a louder sound than the last. As his pulse quickened, he was convinced he was going to have a heart attack. "I couldn't believe no theater personnel came, no matter how loud I was, and I got out of there when I had almost all of them." He raced home with the stolen goods and when he got to his bedroom, he taped up the lobby cards over the table where he drew. Like the outlaw Robin Hood, Mike Gabriel's theft would one day benefit others. "I stared and stared for years at those 8x10 lobby cards, drawing endlessly into the early mornings, trying to get as good as those guys who drew those images. They were my mountain I was going to somehow find a way to climb."

After that day, Mike applied to Disney multiple times and was rejected. Then in 1975, he received a letter from Disney Animation production manager Ed Hansen, who thought Mike would be a great candidate for the new character animation program being developed at CalArts. Hansen told Mike he would likely get a full scholarship if he applied, but Mike balked since he was already attending Golden West College. "I did not want to go to Valencia to a college for four years, I wanted to work for the studio in Burbank." Looking back, he regrets the decision. "I kick myself now over that stubborn, foolish block of a great potential doorway to the studio. I could have been a fellow student with the amazing Disney master instructors that all my Disney animator pals learned so much from. And I would have really bonded with the legendary first class of animation greats."

Chapter 9

The composition of the first CalArts Character Animation class invokes the Shakespearean adage: some are born great, some achieve greatness, and some have greatness thrust upon them.

Two of the first prospects identified by Disney to join the program seemingly fall into the first category. As high schoolers, Brad Bird and Jerry Rees were already spending their summers working and training with the Animation Department. Both young artists seemed gifted beyond their years.

From the age of three, Brad Bird was not just drawing, but storytelling with imagery; his rudimentary stick figures were designed in sequential order like a comic book or storyboard.[376] Brad liked movies—he saw *Pinocchio* and *The Sword in the Stone* multiple times in theaters, but it was *The Jungle Book* at age ten that sparked his interest in becoming an animator.[377] The following year, he began making his own short cartoon—a Road Runner inspired take on *The Tortoise and the Hare*. He had the good occasion to meet *Jungle Book* composer George Bruns through a family friend and at Bruns's invitation, Brad visited the Disney lot in Burbank, where he met some of the Nine Old Men.[378] It took Brad about three years to finish that *Tortoise and the Hare* film, but once he did, it opened doors for him. He won a local Young People's Film Competition; the short was then advanced to the national level.[379] He also sent the film to Disney, where the leadership team took notice and offered to train Brad. His mentor was none other than the legendary Milt Kahl. Milt's gruff demeanor had scared off people far older than Brad, but Brad wasn't intimidated, even if Milt could be "forthright in his criticism."[380] Brad was predisposed to Milt's candor and Milt was not shy in discussing what he saw as problems within the Animation Department—primarily the safe, easy approach to filmmaking since Walt had died.

In high school, Brad seemed to be a natural storyteller. He played Juror #3, the antagonist, in Corvallis High School's production of *Twelve Angry Men*. When others at the school worried the play would be too dull for students, Brad said, "The reaction will depend entirely on the maturity of the audience, and the enthusiasm, and the quality of the cast."[381] He also entered his school's photography contest with an entry titled *Sitting Dignity*, showing an elderly lady in a rocking chair staring directly into the camera.[382] It's as if Whistler's mother realized she was being observed. *Sitting Dignity* showed a progression in Brad's visual storytelling; Brad's prior entry was a simple portrait of his adorable schnauzer Max.[383]

Jerry Rees's love affair with animation began a little later than Brad's. Jerry grew up in the Seventh-day Adventist community in Loma Linda, where it was generally frowned upon to go to the movie theater; the church would occasionally rent family-friendly fare to project on 16 mm like *The Sound of Music*, though the picture quality was inferior, the sound muffled. Jerry found the whole experience annoying. One night, when Jerry was about twelve, his family was driving home on the freeway and passed a drive-in theater showing the climax of *Pinocchio*. Jerry couldn't believe what he was seeing. "The power and the reality of it," Jerry recalled. "The feeling that the character's in jeopardy and just the huge monstrous reality of [the] whale and the beautiful artistry of the sea in its monstrous power." He begged his dad to pull over and then when it ended, he asked if the family could stay to watch the next screening.

From that moment on, Jerry knew he wanted to be a Disney animator. He was not deterred that his family had no connections to that world. He took matters into his own hands. He purchased special pegged animation paper and rigged up his own Super 8 camera to create his own cartoons. Burning through real animation paper quickly became too expensive for Jerry's family, so he began replicating the pegged paper by using an industrial three-hole puncher at Loma Linda Medical University. When the supervisor of the school's audiovisual department found out what Jerry had been doing, he confronted the teenager. Jerry tried to explain why he had been using the three-hole punch—that he wanted to be an animator and this is how animators work. The supervisor chastised Jerry and explained that animators needed a specific kind of camera stand, consistent lighting, and on-and-on-and-on.... In short, Jerry's homemade animation wasn't good enough. Jerry's mom was in the doorway and witnessed this attempt to tear down her son's dream. As they got back in the car, she asked Jerry how he felt about what the man said. "He doesn't know what he's talking about," Jerry replied.

Jerry continued to use the industrial hole puncher, but it wasn't long before he got caught again. "Let me see what you're doing," the supervisor demanded. So the next time Jerry came, he projected his homemade animation of the penguins from *Mary Poppins*. Upon seeing Jerry's work, the man was taken aback.

"You did that?" asked the supervisor. "You didn't trace that? That's your work?"

The supervisor was sincerely impressed. He mentioned he had recently attended a lecture where someone from Disney spoke about how the veteran animators were about to retire, and they were looking for apprentices to pass down the craft. The AV supervisor wrote down a phone number for Jerry. It was the line for Ed Hansen, the production manager for Disney Animation.

Jerry looks back on this moment with bemusement. "[It was] the guy who said you can't do it.. It's like, because I didn't give up and I kept coming back and getting in his space, he finally saw my work. And then the guy who said no, handed me the most important phone number in my life."

Jerry called Ed Hansen and explained who he was and how he got Ed's number. Ed said, "Have your dad drive you down and bring your portfolio, show us something."

Jerry, now a high school junior, had his dad drive him the hour-plus distance to Burbank to have his portfolio reviewed. What Disney saw was impressive enough to offer Jerry an apprenticeship under Eric Larson. "They said, 'Anytime you can take a break from high school, visit us,'" according to Jerry.

One of the first things Eric taught Jerry was that it was okay for animators to draw rough figures in order to get the movement and action correct. It allowed the artist to see if the scene is communicating its intent. "Don't get yourself trapped in bad ideas because of pretty drawings," Eric warned him. Disney offered Jerry the role of a teaching assistant at CalArts, and they would pay any tuition not covered by scholarships.

Brad and Jerry were the ideal candidates for CalArts, but two kids do not complete a whole school.

"[Disney] had teachers, they had funding, they needed students," said Doug Lefler. "They were looking for people like me, who showed promise, who were about to graduate from high school and might fit into the Disney system." Doug Lefler didn't necessarily want to be a Disney animator, but he knew he wanted to work in the film industry. He attended an art teachers' convention at the Disneyland Hotel, where John Hench of Disney's theme park division, WED Enterprises, was speaking. Doug mentioned afterward that he and his friends made their own movies, and he convinced Hench to provide them with a tour of WED. They used that opportunity to show WED employees their homemade 8 mm movies, which were then brought to Ed Hansen's attention. Doug and his three other friends were all invited to submit portfolios. Of the four, Doug and his pal Bruce Morris both enrolled.

Before she enrolled in CalArts, Leslie Margolin had graduated from Wesleyan College, as a member of that school's first coed class. She had moved to New Mexico and studied art under Navajo code talker and artist Carl Nelson Gorman before appearing on Disney's radar.[384] She saw the potential of animation to do something far more profound than comic pratfalls. She would later write, "The animated film's ability to communicate beyond barriers of language and race, to instruct on the universal plane of visualization, imagination and movement, becomes more and more significant to me in promoting learning and worldwide understanding."[385]

Like Leslie, John Musker had also attended college before enrolling in CalArts. Musker had wanted to become an animator since he first encountered Bob Thomas's book *The Art of Animation*, a behind-the-scenes look at Disney during the making of *Sleeping Beauty*.[386] After graduating from Northwestern University, he applied to Disney, but his portfolio was rejected. Disney instead pointed him to CalArts.[387]

John Lasseter was an art major and water polo player at Whittier High School in California. He found Bob Thomas's *Art of Animation* book in his school's library, and reading it helped him realize adults could earn money making cartoons. "It changed my life," he said. "I knew that's what I wanted to do and I never shifted from it."[388]

Darrell Van Citters grew up liking Warner Brothers animation. He was attending the University of New Mexico and painting cels at a local low-budget studio when he heard about CalArts through a contact. In addition to submitting a portfolio, he shot some of his own animation on Super 8 and was accepted.

Mike Cedeno was still a year away from graduating from high school when unbeknownst to him, his dad submitted his portfolio to CalArts, and he was accepted.

One of the last people to emerge on Disney's radar for that first CalArts class was Nancy Beiman. As opposed to many of her future classmates, she was from the East Coast, and her interest in animation didn't come into focus until age sixteen. When she was a student in Cranford, New Jersey, her first 8 mm animated film was for a high school assignment—using paper cutouts to show a Model T blowing up after its tire overinflated. She had earned a spot at NYU's prestigious film program, but in her senior year, her film history teacher invited her to a presentation from the esteemed Croatian animator Zlatko Grgić. By coincidence, Disney's Educational Film Department had its office in the same town, so a representative also came to see the Grgić presentation. Afterward, the Disney representative asked the teacher if any of his students were interested in animation. He suggested they talk with Nancy, and she was invited to come to the office with her art.

Shortly after Nancy visited the Disney office in New Jersey, she received a letter from Don Duckwall in Burbank. He wrote to her, explaining that due to her age and her interest in furthering her education ("which we surely think wise"),[389] he thought she would be a good candidate for CalArts. He took the liberty of sending her work to Jack Hannah, who was heading the new "classical or character animation school" at CalArts. Duckwall explained, "It is being established at the urging of our studio animation people, and it will specialize in our kind of animation as opposed to the graphic animation CalArts has produced in the past." The letter was dated June 13, 1975.[390] She had never heard of CalArts and was already accepted at NYU; school was beginning in a few weeks. Jack Hannah called to follow up with Nancy and said CalArts could probably offer her a full scholarship; in fact, she would be awarded a "Disney Fellowship," personally sponsored by Edna and Roy E. Disney. Nancy and her dad took out a huge world atlas to find Valencia, California. All they could find was lots of brown space north of Los Angeles. Nevertheless, she packed her bags and headed to California.

Other people in that first year included future Warner Brothers animator Harry Sabin, future Disney Imagineer Joe Lanzisero, and producer Brett Thompson.[391]

"I think one of the reasons that it was such an extraordinary group is because all of us had come to the attention of Disney by dent of some creative ambition of our own," said Doug Lefler.

Jerry Rees didn't know anyone interested in animation before coming to CalArts. "For the most part, it was a very sort of lonely struggle," he said. That was true for most of the first-year students in the Character Animation class. Now, these artists were a collective with a shared passion, a shared goal. "Suddenly we were thrown together in one place," said Jerry. "There was jousting at first but then there was this dream of what can we do together."

For all the work that went into finding that first class, it became evident early on that the program wasn't for everyone. "We had a very high dropout rate," said Nancy Beiman, who estimated about a third of the enrolled students didn't make it through the first year. She said one of the only other women in the program decided to leave because the workload was too intensive while caring for her young daughter.

The Character Animation students also felt some resistance from others in the CalArts community, including from some in Jules Engel's Experimental Animation program. Jerry said, "The existing CalArts group that was already out there looked at us as corporate traitors. They really were not comfortable with us coming in, wanting to train for jobs. They felt like that was the betrayal of what the school was about. That the school was about experimentation and discovery and avoiding all previous molds that you were trying to fit into."

The teachers were an illustrious group, composed almost exclusively of former Disney veterans. Jack Hannah ran the program and taught animation. He had previously directed most of the Donald Duck shorts, as well as many of Walt's television appearances. Jack believed you needed ten years of experience to properly develop into a Disney animator, yet was concerned that studios no longer spent money developing young talent. Australian native Ken O'Connor focused his teachings on perspective, light, and shadow. Ken was one of the greatest layout artists to ever work at Disney—staging *Pinocchio*'s "Hi-Diddle-Dee-Dee" number with an overhead shot, designing Cinderella's coach, and developing the marching cards in *Alice in Wonderland*. He taught the students how to "plus" every scene and make it more visually interesting and dynamic. Elmer Plummer, who had once created vibrant pastels for *Fantasia*'s Nutcracker sequence, focused on life drawing. Former Chouinard instructor T. Hee—famous at Disney for his celebrity caricatures—handled character design. He guided the students through unusual exercises, like drawing with their nondominant hand or without ever lifting the pencil from the page. Disney also brought back Bill

Moore from Chouinard to teach design. The instructors that first year were largely inventing this program on the fly, yet they laid the groundwork for the animation renaissance to come. "The knowledge they gave us has always been unsung," said early CalArts student Tony Anselmo. He credits these instructors for developing the talent that emerged from CalArts, especially in the first five years of the Character Animation program. "They had the eye to see potential and they passed on their tribal knowledge to all these students who became figureheads in animation. They were pivotal in what would come later."

The summer before the CalArts Character Animation program began, teaching assistant Jerry Rees consulted with Jack Hannah about which classic Disney animated scenes to select from the studio's "morgue"—where all the old animation drawings were kept. Jerry was able to make high-quality copies using Ink & Paint's Xerox camera, so that when school started, the students could study these scenes frame by frame. Jerry was also tasked with carefully replicating the original animation exposure sheets, used to time out how a scene should play out against the soundtrack. Jerry had to replicate these forms by hand—every vocal modulation, every scribble changing from red to blue to black pencil. "I felt sort of like a monk doing illuminated text copies," said Jerry. "I would sit there and try to exactly match how the original exposure sheet looked." Jerry also took incoming calls from his future classmates. He remembers saying things like: "How do you spell Musker?" "Is that Berd, like e-r-d, or is it just like the regular Bird, B-i-r-d?"

The windowless classroom that would house the Character Animation program that first year was a nondescript space in the maze of CalArts corridors, numbered A113. Given the room's inauspicious early days, few could have predicted its fame. Brad and Jerry later started using the room number as a hidden gag in their early films. As the profile of the Character Animation alumni grew, this physical space became as legendary to animation fans as the people who once occupied it.

On the first day of Ken O'Connor's class, he came in to A113A, a smaller offshoot of A113, and asked the class to take out their supplies. Nancy Beiman held up a pitiful notebook, though she seemed slightly more prepared than others. In his Australian accent, which he still had from his childhood growing up in Perth, Ken scolded the class to get out of the room and go buy supplies at the school's tiny bookstore. He went home that night, discouraged by the lack of infrastructure for the Character Animation program, and told his wife how the room didn't even have desks. Ken's temper that day seemed out of character; future student Mark Henn said Ken was "a favorite of most of us" due to his dry wit and his endless patience.

"We all wanted to just animate," said Darrell Van Citters. "That was why we were there. That was the candy. That only happened on Fridays. We had to do our fundamentals the rest of the week."

In Jack Hannah's animation classes, he would review the students' work and make suggestions, but also allow the students to help each other. "He was a very, very good director in both senses of the word," said Nancy. "He knew how to time [the animation]. He knew how to tell you when something was not working properly."

Nancy Beiman looked at her art compared to her peers, including the other female students, and realized she was not at the same skill level. "I'm a token," she thought to herself. "I've got to work extremely hard to catch up. And that's what I did." She began sketching ten drawings each day, including a lot of anatomical studies, on top of her course work. Still, Elmer Plummer told her that she did not draw as well as the male students. "I was absolutely furious. But I can tell you, I was not furious at him. I knew he was right." She also adds, "The way some people talked back then, you couldn't do today."

Sue Mantle DiCicco joined CalArts two years after Nancy, but remembered being treated differently as a woman. Whereas her male peers got in-depth assessments of their annual reviews, hers just said "She's a pleasure to have in class." In interviews, another early Character Animation student Kathy Zielinski said only four of about thirty-five students in her class were female, but still recalled the time learning from Disney greats like T. Hee and Jack Hannah to be "inspirational."[392]

Looking back, Nancy Beiman said, "I worked incredibly hard, particularly on the stuff I didn't do well at, the life drawings and design classes in the first year, figuring I'd make up the animation later.... I got much better in the second year, and particularly in the design class."

On the first day of design, instructor Bill Moore entered "in a tizzy," as Nancy remembers. The former chairman of the Save Chouinard Committee had been brought back by Disney, not CalArts, and he was only working part-time—spending the rest of his time teaching at the Art Center College of Design. He wasn't about to let go of his campaign against CalArts, and he began sharing articles about what had happened to Chouinard. "Do you know what this place did to this beautiful school?" he asked the students who didn't seem to know or care about the school's backstory.

"I recall that the attitude of some people was, 'oh, we don't need a design class,'" said Nancy. "Well, we desperately needed a design class." In fact, Bill Moore's design class is often cited as the most memorable for the Character Animation students. He opened their minds to a new way of thinking about artistic principles—but his style of brutal honesty sometimes leaned a little too much into the brutal.

Tony Anselmo, who joined the program a couple years later, put it like this. "Have you seen the movie *Whiplash*?," referring to the Oscar-winning film about a demanding teacher. "That's what Bill Moore was like. We worked extra hard to please him because we respected him."

Darrell Van Citters said that Bill Moore "was probably the most influential instructor we had. He was a tough son of a bitch. He pushed you and you learned hard."

"He was amazing," said Mike Cedeno. When he worked at Art Center College of Design—between the stints at Chouinard and CalArts—Bill Moore once took his lit cigarette and proceeded to burn the students' art hanging on the wall. "Don't gimme this fucking shit anymore," Bill said. The following week, the students taped up matchbooks to their redone work, to make it easier for him if he wanted to torch their art. He laughed when he told the CalArts students about this encounter. Bill told the students to save their work, because someday they'd look back on it and "see how kind I was to you."

"Since I had no design training, I was terrible in his class," remembered Nancy. Bill would often use her work as example of what not to do. "Most weeks, he would say 'who did this piece of shit?' It was usually mine."

Some students felt it was better to be either the best or worst student of the week in Bill's class. If you were in the middle, he may not give you any feedback. Darrell Van Citters grew increasingly frustrated by Bill's approach and once blew up at him: "What the fuck do you want? I don't know."

A sample assignment could be to take a rectangle and break it into three different areas. He'd then challenge the class to come back tomorrow and blow him away. He began with the concept of black and white. Then he would focus on abstract shapes, eventually moving to more complex ideas, such as color design. Eventually the lessons would all start to come together to form more sophisticated ideas.

One time, when two of Nancy's pieces were picked apart, she felt the abuse was too great in the moment, and she left the room to compose herself. "I came back because you had to take it.... Today, the student would probably have gotten him kicked out. And I don't like that kind of teaching necessarily, but he was doing it to sort of knock it into our heads that we needed a design class and very badly. People were very cocky, and thought, oh we're just going to draw cartoons. Well you can't do it if you don't understand how to compose a shot, how to stage anything, how to block a scene or how to make it interesting visually." Looking back, she is shocked at how few modern animation programs have a design class. "I would require it in the first year," she said.

John Lasseter and Jerry Rees would often find themselves pulling all-nighters to finish the design assignments. They formed a pact that if they hadn't finished by 4 or 5 a.m., they would just stay awake until class by having an early breakfast at the restaurant Tiny Naylor's. These all-nighters "became kind of a social thing," said Doug Lefler, who recalled Brad Bird and John Musker among the group burning the midnight oil. "I tried it once and I found I didn't function well," said Doug.

In a school with no sports, extracurricular activities, or even many social outlets, work became a way to bond. "There were no activities. There was no transportation to go anywhere. There was nothing to do in Valencia," said Nancy. "I eventually got a car because I couldn't stand it anymore." For Nancy, CalArts was isolating at times, and a bit of a boy's club. "There was no socializing with the guys. They went out and did things. You'll hear a lot of funny stories. I was never invited. Neither was Leslie." She became friendly with kids in other CalArts schools, and eventually underclassmen in the Animation program. Still, she fondly remembers innocent teasing with her classmates, whom she liked and admired. When one of her peers claimed they thought maybe they saw her at the school's infamous nude swimming pool, she said, "If she had a gorgeous figure, it was me."

Walt Disney's dream of a transdisciplinary school wasn't what most of the Character Animation kids experienced. Only a few took part in classes outside the department. Nancy took kinesiology through the dance department. Mike Cedeno took a dance class, and a circus class. "I still know how to balance a spoon on the tip of my nose." Likewise, Jerry Rees remembers learning how to eat fire thanks to his circus class.

"It was a different world then," Doug Lefler reflects on the era and the cultural influences of the students. "*A Chorus Line* had just opened, *Jaws* had become the first blockbuster movie. I think at that time, Gerald Ford was about to leave the White House in a peaceful transfer of power to Jimmy Carter. All of us students there at CalArts, we used to listen to Elton John. Saturday nights, we would gather to watch this new TV show that had just aired that year called *Saturday Night Live*." These touchpoints would become a shared experience for many of the CalArtians.

Jerry compares that first-year group to a great comedic ensemble, like *Schitt's Creek*. "Every person is so different and yet the combination is so kind of perfect. And the CalArts first year, it was small enough, it was like a dozen of us. And it just had that feel to it where everybody got used to the quirks of the other people.... That CalArts group felt like that sort of a family of very eccentric individuals who are all eccentric in a good way."

The Character Animation students were treated to lectures from some of the all-time greats of animation, including the Nine Old Men. When Marc Davis came in to speak, Jerry Rees nudged Nancy to point out how much the out-of-shape older man still moved like one of his most famous characters, Cruella de Vil—right down to the cigarette holder. Warner Brothers animator and Chouinard alum Chuck Jones discussed pantomime with the class, mimicking the silent film star Oliver Hardy. The most intimidating figure to speak with the students was Milt Kahl, who came to show a preview of his work on the studio's latest film *The Rescuers*. His animation of that movie's villain, Madame Medusa, was a tour de force and ultimately, his swan song. It was clear from his talk at CalArts that although he was proud of his work on this new character, he found the surrounding film to not match his effort. He was candid in his assessment of the Animation Department's declining status. Nancy Beiman remembers being too intimidated at first to even ask Milt a question. However, Brad Bird, who had known Milt for a few years at this point, peppered him with questions. "Brad thought nothing of just chatting with him as if he could talk to one of us," said Nancy.

Brad pushed Milt further, asking him if he thought the films lost something with anachronistic moments—like the psychedelic lights in *The Aristocats*. Milt begged off the question at first but then added he was planning to leave the studio soon and cited *The Aristocats* example as a reason why. Brad then asked him about what would make him come back: "Would *Cauldron* do it?"

Kahl asked if the students had read the books. Several had. "I just think it's a wonderful piece of material," he said. "The possibilities there are just…I think it can be just wonderful." He got serious again though. "They deserve to be done really well or they shouldn't be done at all," he said. "I don't think this unit is capable of doing good work."[393] He mentioned his correspondence with Lloyd Alexander a few weeks prior, suggesting the author keep his fingers crossed that new people could be taking over the project soon. Still, despite his concerns around what he saw as creative malaise at the Animation Department, maybe someday he'd come back for *Cauldron*.

"I wouldn't shut the door. If I can be shown that there's a chance it can be as good a picture as I think it ought to be, and I thought people were capable of making it and I wouldn't be embarrassed by it, maybe I would. I don't know. I sure as hell would leave the door open."[394]

Nancy finally felt confident enough to ask her question, doubling back to the issues of the anachronisms in recent films, essentially asking who was to blame. Kahl looked her in the eye and pounded his fist on the table. "The trouble is Walt had to go and die on us," he said.

Kahl continued. "You see a lot of these people...if Walt were alive, they'd be alright, they'd be adequate in their jobs because he's there to be awfully goddamn critical all the time. Walt had the ability to get things out of people that they weren't capable of," Kahl said.[395]

"I respected [Kahl] as an artist, but my goodness, that was scary.... Brad was treating him as an old friend, whereas the rest of us were treating him as, you know, The Great Prince of the Forest," said Nancy, referring to the intimidating stag in *Bambi*. "[I was] sort of curled up on a chair in [a] fetal position."

As was the custom at CalArts, the Character Animation students were not given grades. Instead, they would work toward an annual capstone assignment, in which each student was required to submit an animated scene. Many took the challenge seriously and aimed to create what was essentially a student film. That first year, Brad and Jerry had decided to team up and were pretty far along in their collaboration before the faculty shot down their plan. They had to scramble to complete last-minute individual showcases.

According to Nancy, that first year screening was held in A113, with Frank and Ollie in attendance. She was excited because she had animated an albatross thinking no one had ever attempted it before. Brad burst her bubble before the event saying, "I hate to disillusion you but they're making a film called *The Rescuers* and there's an albatross in it. And Ollie Johnston is animating it and he's coming to see our show." She began dreading the screening, thinking Ollie would hate her work compared to his. When her animation played, there was little reaction. As Frank and Ollie were leaving the room, Ollie said to Nancy in a fake stage whisper, "Stick with this. We need more women in the business." Nancy would always remember this kind gesture at the end of a very difficult year, and it began a lifelong correspondence with Frank and Ollie.

The Disney team was brought back to review the students' work at the end of the second year. After seeing their films, they hired four students—Brad Bird, Jerry Rees, John Musker, and Doug Lefler—to join the Animation Department after only two years at CalArts. The CalArts experiment was beginning to pay off. Over the next few years, the Character Animation program became a reliable feeder school for Disney. Students at CalArts would include a flood of future directors—Chris Buck (*Frozen*), Tim Burton (*Beetlejuice Beetlejuice*), Rob Minkoff (*The Lion King*), Bruce W. Smith (*The Proud Family*), Kelly Asbury (*Shrek 2*), Gary Trousdale and Kirk Wise (codirectors of *Beauty and the Beast, The Hunchback of Notre Dame*)—as well as other artists and animators who would play significant roles at Disney in the years to come, including Mark Henn, Joe Ranft, Mike Giaimo, and Kathy Zielinski, to mention just a few. The arrival of these new animators would shake up the company—bringing with them a flood of new energy and ambition, and an eagerness to challenge the status quo and bring Disney Animation into the modern age.

Chapter 10

The Black Cauldron continued to cast a spell at Disney for the vast majority of the 1970s, with seemingly everyone in the Animation Department hoping to crack the story. "The guys who had been there with Walt wanted to go out on [*Cauldron*] as their swan song, to really do a fantastic piece that would rival *Snow White* or *Pinocchio*," said Tad Stones, who joined as a trainee in 1974. "It was also at the same time being used as the carrot for the young people."

Several members of the Nine Old Men spent considerable time and energy trying to get the story in shape so it could move into production. Under them, the story kept coalescing around the same group of characters—the hero Taran and his pig Hen Wen, the princess Eilonwy, the creature Gurgi, the bard Fflewddur, the fairy Doli, the witches who hide the cauldron and the Horned King who seeks it for his power. Frank Thomas and Ollie Johnston kept refining their own versions, discussing how to best develop the relationships that would drive the narrative. Milt Kahl joined in as well. "Frank—I tried a 'straight ahead' approach on this thing just to see where it would lead." In longhand, Milt dashed off a multipage outline but didn't get to the end. "This is as far as I got with it—I had to leave," the note concludes. The occasionally cantankerous animator signed off with hearts around his initials.[396]

Woolie, Frank, Ollie and Milt met regularly about *Cauldron*, along with Mel Shaw, Ron Miller and a revolving door of story people and animators. At one meeting, Mel Shaw gave a story presentation for *Cauldron*, when one person asked the group, "What do you think about doing this [version]?"

As Mel Shaw remembered it, "Milt Kahl stood up and said, 'Hell, man, this studio can't do this thing. I'm the only one in the studio that can do this type of picture.' Of course, [Milt's outburst was] kind of a shock to a lot of the guys."

Ron Miller shot back, "Okay. Make me some sketches of what you think Taran would look like and some of the characters."

As newer artists came into the Animation Department, they too were drawn to the project. Ron Clements—codirector of *The Little Mermaid*, *Aladdin*, and *Moana*—submitted a treatment for *Cauldron* in 1976,[397] and again in 1978. He wrote it has "enormous potential" citing its themes, characters, and the "great opportunity to do something very special in areas such as animation, effects, layout, background, color and music."[398]

Even those in the greater orbit of Disney could not resist the lure of *Cauldron*. On December 5, 1975—on what would have been Walt's seventy-fourth birthday—the ultimate Disney Animation fanboy/historian/journalist John Culhane signed a release with Frank Paris to have his treatment of *The Black Cauldron* considered. Culhane held a sincere belief that *Cauldron* was destined to be the most important film ever produced at Disney, and he wanted in on it. He wrote to animator and friend Frank Thomas, enthusiastically describing his hopes and dreams for the project:

> FRANK: YOU AND OLLIE MUST NOT RETIRE UNTIL YOU HAVE TOPPED SNOW WHITE.... Now you have accumulated the experience and now at last you have found the story with the "single piercing emotion", the "single theme and idea." You can top Snow White with the story of THE BLACK CAULDRON because it has the right vibes....

Like your greatest fantasies, SNOW WHITE, BAMBI and PINOCCHIO, THE BLACK CAULDRON is about the victory of life over death, but it has the unity that PINOCCHIO lacked, and unlike BAMBI, in which Thumper and Flower aren't even involved in the crucial forest fire, its characters motivate the action.

THE BLACK CAULDRON can be as entertaining as 101 DALMATIANS, as full of rich characters as JUNGLE BOOK, as paced with sparkling situations as ARISTOCATS, can have a great relationship between funny personalities like ROBIN HOOD, and yet top those good films, because its plot and images strike archetypal chords as they do not. I predict that when the Black Cauldron is rent asunder, audiences will applaud as they do today when the witch in SNOW WHITE plunges to her death....

As writers who have wept with the dwarfs at the death of Snow White, and rejoiced at her resurrection—and felt a chill along our spines when we first surmised the horse's head was toward eternity, we should be inspired to win another victory over the Destroyer of Delights and the Sunderers of Societies.[399]

Frank was blown away by the letter's enthusiasm, but less so by Culhane's story treatment, which he thought relied too much on the human characters. Culhane's submission had another problem. It had arrived on the heels of another treatment, from British playwright Rosemary Anne Sisson.[400] Sisson had become a favorite screenwriter of Ron Miller.

Rosemary Anne Sisson was a decade older than Ron Miller, born in North London in 1923. Growing up, she had been a solid student with a passion for writing, drama, and horse riding but her education was cut short by World War II. For the first year, the war provided an illicit thrill. She and her sister would wake up and run outside to see if they could see Nazi planes fly overhead. Yet as the war grew more serious, Rosemary felt its dehumanizing effects.[401] She wrote in her journal: "The war is so weary and slow. There is no joy in it, and no wonder. It is a great engine moving steadily forwards, churning everything it comes to.... I sometimes wonder if we shall ever again know gladness."[402]

She had once believed war was hardest on the elderly, who didn't want their final years defined by conflict, but as World War II dragged on, she realized it was youth who suffered most. "I was wrong. We can't spare this time. We sacrifice more than anyone...our careers, the filling of our brains, the training of our bodies and minds, but we sacrifice also much more, we lose the undoubted right of youth to be careless, ignorant and foolish, to be irresponsible and improvident."[403] She joined the Royal Observatory Corps and on D-Day, she helped keep track of the positions of Allied aircraft, never leaving her post on "the longest day." When she arrived home and her family told her the invasion was underway, she was surprised to learn the importance of her work.[404]

After the war, Rosemary turned her focus to writing. Her dream was to be a successful playwright, but her historical dramas about the royal courts of the past were considered old-fashioned in the age of the "angry young man" plays of 1950s Britain. She found work writing for the BBC—where historical dramas were still popular—and built a career working there on a variety of projects throughout the '50s and '60s. It wasn't until she was nearing fifty that she finally hit it big as one of the writers on the 1970s hit *Upstairs, Downstairs*.[405]

Walt Disney Productions first contacted Sisson in 1968, hoping to use her for a live-action remake of *Black Beauty*, but the project never got off the ground. Five years and one successful television show later, Disney contacted her again to write an adaptation of James Aldridge's novel *The Sporting Proposition* (later known as *Ride the Wild Pony*), an Australian story about a working class boy and a paralyzed rich girl who separately claim ownership of the same horse, leading to a court case to determine ownership. When Story Department head Frank Paris asked Rosemary to work on the film, she wanted to know if she needed to write for any specific actor.

"No," Frank replied. "Disney is the star and the most important thing is the script."

She quickly dashed off a one-and-a-half-page outline and sent it back in. Frank asked to meet with her, and he wasn't entirely pleased. He said, "Listen, you know what you're going to do, and I know what you're going to do, but Disney are going to say 'Did we bring this woman all the way here from England just for this [page and a half]?'"

"Ah, I see what you mean," she replied. Grateful for the second chance, she went back and expanded the outline.[406] She worked on a treatment throughout the early fall of 1973, collaborating with actor turned Disney producer Jerry Courtland while staying at the Hollywood hotel Chateau Marmont. At first, she found Disney to be a bit "soulless," writing the people are "outwardly, immensely cordial and 'we're all one big, happy family' but when you get down to it, you eat alone!!" She also noticed there was no liquor on the campus, but she seemed to soften her position on Disney's social life and its employees after she was invited to the *Robin Hood* wrap party in October 1973.[407]

Ron read Rosemary's treatment in early November 1973 and liked her work. The following summer, he brought her back to Hollywood for script meetings. "I told Ron, 'This is a very gritty story. Both children are such little brutes. I don't want to lose that.' He said, 'We don't want it to be saccharine,' and after that, everything was all right."[408]

"Can I ask a silly question?" he said in one of their sessions. He began questioning Rosemary over what she would later concede was a weak point in the film. "Didn't [the characters] know that already?"

"Ron, I don't like your silly questions" she joked. "They always mean fifteen pages of rewrites."[409]

Rosemary thought Ron was "very intelligent and very helpful" and she trusted his instincts. She also cherished these give-and-takes with him. She was finally beginning to feel a part of the Disney family. While meeting with Ron, she would have presumably recognized that The Animation Building was its own version of *Upstairs, Downstairs*—with Ron Miller and other executives on the third floor, producers and directors on the second floor, and the animators on the ground level.

Before *Ride a Wild Pony* went into production in Australia in the fall of 1974, Rosemary was hired to work on her second Disney film—another sensitive live-action film about children trying to protect mining ponies in Yorkshire, England. It would be titled *The Littlest Horse Thieves*. On February 12, 1975, Rosemary went to see a rough cut of *Ride a Wild Pony* at Pinewood Studios in the UK. Afterward she wrote, "I was thrilled with it—it's beautifully photographed by [acclaimed cinematographer] Jack Cardiff, beautifully directed by Don Chaffey, marvelously cast, and made me cry. I don't think there are nearly enough films or plays today which make you cry, so I'm hoping some other people feel the same. The Disney people have been kindness itself throughout, and I really enjoy working with them."[410] She spent the rest of the day catching up with Ron on *The Littlest Horse Thieves*. "All his suggestions excellent, as always, and we got on so well together."[411]

Ron believed *Ride a Wild Pony* was a great movie, in a different league than Disney's average live-action slapstick releases, but he wasn't sure it would be a hit. He told a reporter he thought it could make money, "If we can get people into the theaters..."[412] Disney wrestled with how to release the movie—considering more than 130 alternate titles, before deciding *Ride a Wild Pony* was indeed the best option.[413] They also thought it may stand a better chance in the marketplace as a prestige film, starting its rollout with a limited release for awards consideration before expanding widely.[414] It was ultimately a naive play. Released in Los Angeles in December 1975, *Ride a Wild Pony* failed to receive a single Oscar nomination during one of the most competitive Academy Awards seasons ever—which saw major contenders like *Jaws*, *Dog Day Afternoon*, *Nashville*, and *Barry Lyndon* lose Best Picture to *One Flew Over the Cuckoo's Nest*. Only a few critics noticed that *Ride a Wild Pony* was a special film when it was eventually given a wide release in spring 1976, playing as the second part of a double feature with the rerelease of *101 Dalmatians*. *Ride a Wild Pony* may not have lived up to Ron and Rosemary's expectations, but their partnership continued to flourish, and he soon asked her to work on *The Black Cauldron*.

Ron brought Rosemary to a *Black Cauldron* story session led by Mel Shaw. It was also attended by Woolie and other head animators. In the months since Lloyd Alexander visited the lot, Mel had developed dozens of beautiful pastel sketches for *Cauldron*, each a work of art. To present them to a group, he would prepare slideshows, using two projectors and music. According to Rosemary, he "gave a sort of magic lantern show, telling the story according to his outline, illustrated with slides of his excellent pictures. He never acknowledged my presence or hinted in any way that I had written an outline, and been brought 3,000 miles to do it!"

Rosemary sat quietly through the presentation until Mel had run out of things to say. Woolie piped in. "Rosemary, you haven't said anything. What do you think?"

Ron jumped in. "She's wondering when the next 747 goes back to London."

"You're right," she laughed. "Well, I see it quite differently." She went on to explain that *Cauldron* wasn't a fairy tale, "but myth and legend, which is a sort of memory of the days when there was magic, and when men and animals lived together."

Woolie chimed in that he had been impressed by her outline. The room went back and forth about how to simplify the story and make it stronger, often going back to suggestions made by Rosemary in her outline. "So poor old Mel was routed—for the moment," she reflected on the day. "I really don't like power struggles, and I was mad to be put in such a stupid position—but rather pleased with myself to have come out of it so well. Mel's storyline was very muddled and shapeless!... If I hadn't been a lot tougher than I look, it might have destroyed me...."[415]

Despite her frustration with being pitted against Mel Shaw, Rosemary would later look back on this period with nostalgia. "I think some of the happiest weeks of my life were spent laughing, arguing and striking sparks off each other in the Animation Department," she wrote.[416] She realized there is no fire without friction. It was also true that Mel Shaw's visual concepts for *Cauldron* had captured the imagination of many people at Disney Animation and would be used to both drum up publicity for *Cauldron* and as a recruiting tool for new animators.

In August 1976, *The New York Times Magazine* ran an article called "The Old Disney Magic: Can a New Generation of Artists Make Audiences Cry the Way They Did for Snow White?" The author was John Culhane, who did not disclose that he had submitted his own treatment for *Cauldron*. The article was accompanied by Mel Shaw's striking concept art for *Cauldron*—showing the Horned King bringing his undead army to life. The inclusion of the *Cauldron* art is notable because at this point, the Animation Department was primarily focused on the 1977 film *The Rescuers*, which features a caricature of Culhane named Mr. Snoops. Yet this article was clearly an attempt to reinvigorate public interest in Disney animation and of course, Culhane saw *Cauldron* as the way to do that. Ron Miller told Culhane, "I think the young guys feel like they're sort of breaking out of jail.... It's time for us to let them get out on their own or else we're going to find ourselves with our pants down."[417]

Culhane also interviewed Don Bluth, who said, "Right now, enthusiasm for a story called *The Black Cauldron* is boiling through the studio, and we hope that the new generation can touch people with that story in ways that Walt never dreamed of." The article talks about how this new generation has it in them to make *Cauldron* even better than *Snow White*. Bluth is introduced as a member of the "nine young men"—a group of up-and-coming male animators, though Culhane acknowledged the growing ranks of female assistant animators.[418]

By the time Culhane's article was published, the Nine Old Men were already a vanishing breed. Ward Kimball was the first to officially retire in 1973, around the time his syndicated television show *The Mouse Factory* was canceled.[419] Ward was just shy of sixty years old when he left Disney, but he came back a few years later to work on EPCOT Center.[420] Les Clark retired a couple of years later, ending his career as Disney's then longest-serving employee; his time with Disney predated the creation of Mickey Mouse.[421] Although Marc Davis was still working on Disney theme parks, he had left the Animation Department more than a decade earlier.

At the start of 1976, the majority of the Nine Old Men—Woolie, John Lounsbery, Frank, Ollie, Milt, and Eric—were leading the Animation Department through its latest production, *The Rescuers*. The film is about two mice who work for the United Nations-inspired "Rescue Aid Society" and their efforts to save an orphan girl from her kidnappers who are using her to collect a hard-to-reach diamond. *The Rescuers* was serving as a transitional film, allowing the remaining Nine Old Men to work alongside the people they had personally mentored to take over. In 1976, Disney announced that the next film after *The Rescuers* would be *The Fox and the Hound*, followed by *The Black Cauldron*, budgeted between $5 to $6 million.[422]

The trainees had brought an influx of youthful energy, which hadn't been experienced at the Animation Department in some time. The old pranks and hijinks that were once a defining part of the early days were returning. One day, trainee Randy Cartwright looked out the window from his office on the second floor and saw a dead rat lying under a tree. He and another trainee went outside and scooped up the rat with animation paper. They then proceeded to create a small coffin out of art supplies, and then using pencils as forceps, they dressed the rodent up in a yellow raincoat and umbrella to look like the main character Bernard of *The Rescuers*. Randy carried Dead Bernard around the studio, whistling a funeral dirge and freaking people out when they went to see what was in the coffin. People egged Randy on to leave the corpse outside Milt's door, but he chickened out. Instead, he brought it to Woolie for his reaction. Woolie didn't flinch when he saw Dead Bernard. "That's a rat," said Woolie. "Bernard is a mouse."

The Nine Old Men treated even the youngest artists as peers. Brad Bird and Jerry Rees were visiting the studio while on break from CalArts, when Frank and Ollie asked them to come look at footage from *The Rescuers*. On a Moviola machine, they played a rough scene where the orphan Penny is in a cave struggling to not be swallowed by a tidal whirlpool. Dramatic moments pass before suddenly, Penny is pushed back into the cave by the force of the water. "It was so visceral because you can imagine yourself trying to hold your breath for that long. They were really pushing it to the edge. We felt so exhilarated," said Jerry.

Frank and Ollie said to their young colleagues, "Well, you're probably the last two people to see it because Woolie wants us to cut it shorter." They explained that Woolie was concerned the scene was too intense. The four launched into a conversation about how scary Disney films had always been, like the transformation of the Evil Queen in *Snow White* or the drowning of Pinocchio. Brad and Jerry got so worked up they said they were going to go speak to Woolie. Jerry acknowledges he and Brad probably seemed like "a couple of college punks" when they went into Woolie's office, but they made an impassioned plea to preserve the intensity of the scene. Woolie patronized them for a bit before explaining that he didn't want to get letters from concerned parents in the Bible Belt that the film was too scary. "They were getting really sensitive to trying be really G-rated, so overly kid-friendly," said Jerry. Jerry was forever disappointed by Woolie's attitude that day, which he viewed as a betrayal of the spirit of Disney Animation.

Among the younger animators, it wasn't just Brad and Jerry who were concerned about the direction of the department under Woolie. Don Bluth, Gary Goldman, and John Pomeroy were also not satisfied. "It looked like they were always trying to play it safe and cheap," said John Pomeroy. "It just felt like we were in a creative rut and there was no way out of it."

A generation gap was emerging between the veterans and the new generation; the young animators deeply revered their mentors but sometimes wished the veterans shared the same ambitions. "I don't want to say it a nasty way, but it just felt like a retirement villa," said Andy Gaskill, who joined Disney in the animation training program around the time of *Winnie the Pooh and Tigger Too*. "It just felt very slow and, and for us kids, we were looking for a little more excitement."

Winnie the Pooh and Tigger Too had created unexpected friction on *The Rescuers*. Since the trainees on that short received screen credits as animators, it would seem like a demotion if they went back to being assistant animators. Tad Stones was once told it would take a trainee ten years to become a directing animator; *Winnie the Pooh and Tigger Too* seemed to speed up that timeline for some trainees. Tad said some of his peers insisted on staying animators and "made noise like they would walk or find something else. It changed the dynamic in that suddenly these very young guys moved into animation."

In turn, that meant other artists in the generation between the Nine Old Men and the trainees were overlooked for opportunity. "There was a lot of bitterness because then they would get the animation that we did as young artists coming in, and then they would have to clean up our drawings and put it onto model," said Glen Keane. "They were complaining, they were angry, they were bitter. There's a lot of tension between that middle generation and the young generation."

Still, the reverence for the Nine Old Men by the younger generation was strong. Randy Cartwright recalled bumping into John Lounsbery in the hallway. The veteran said, "Hey, you're new around here, aren't you?" He welcomed Randy to watch progress on *The Rescuers* with Woolie, Milt, Frank, and Ollie. "The old animators and me sitting there watching the movie. It was, yeah, it was quite amazing," said Randy.

Glen Keane recalled the day he asked one of his animation heroes, *The Rescuers* codirector John Lounsbery, to review his drawings. "I just fell in love with [Lounsbery's] drawing of the wolf in *Sword in the Stone*," said Glen, reflecting on Lounsbery's body of work. "And also *Peter Pan*. *Peter Pan* was my favorite movie." Glen noticed that Lounsbery used Blaisdell pencils, the "self-sharpening" pencil popular at the turn of the last century. "I thought if I could just get one of those pencils, maybe I can draw like John Lounsbery with these really bold, fun shapes. I ended up buying all there were left on the market." For the rest of his storied career, Glen adopted the Blaisdell as his pencil of choice. He said he showed Lounsbery his drawings that day in February 1976—shortly before Lounsbery had a scheduled heart test at St. Joseph's Hospital. According to animation historian John Canemaker, Lounsbery lost consciousness during the angiogram and died on Friday, February 13,

1976.[423] "I always felt like, 'oh man, my terrible animation killed John Lounsbery'" said Glen Keane, only half joking.

Lounsbery was the first of the Nine Old Men to die. His sudden demise threw off the balance and stability of the Animation Department. Ron Miller had reportedly been developing Lounsbery to replace Woolie as lead director, but longtime animator Art Stevens was now thrown into the job on *The Rescuers*.[424] Days after Lounsbery's death, Ron Miller called Rosemary Sisson to discuss how the changes in the Animation Department would be impacting progress on *The Black Cauldron*. He explained the project was "being given to the young men—especially Don [Bluth]." Rosemary, who had continued to revise her *Cauldron* treatment, was glad that the slow progress wasn't "that they'd lost enthusiasm for it. Very good news and exciting to be working on something new, with the young men," she wrote.[425]

Lounsbery's passing was soon followed by increased strife among the Nine Old Men. Milt Kahl had long been known for speaking his mind in the office, often in outbursts which bordered on abusiveness; even Walt faced these eruptions from time to time.[426] However, on *The Rescuers*, Milt's anger was beginning to wear on his colleagues. Frank Thomas's son Ted was working at Disney during this time and remembered the tension. "Milt, particularly at the urging of his then wife, had been lobbying for more recognition of his work and even asked for single screen credit on *The Rescuers*." At a time when the rules around screen credits were so strict that most assistants and in-betweeners were never acknowledged, this request was unprecedented. "Frank and Ollie felt that it went against the way they had always worked, whereupon Milt announced that he wasn't going to work that way anymore. He wanted his scenes, he'd do them on his own, and turn the finished work in. Done. Basically, he didn't want to have anything to do with his former colleagues."

After Milt launched a particularly nasty verbal attack against Frank and Ollie, the pair brought it to the attention of Ron Miller. "My dad recalled how shaken they both were by Milt's outburst," said Walter

Miller. He remembered the incident in part because it was unusual for Ron to discuss personnel matters at home.

"[Frank and Ollie] were hoping that Ron, as the overall head of the studio, could be the peacemaker and keep them all together," said Ted. "Ron then met with Milt, but he wouldn't budge. He'd had his fill."

Milt would later say, "Ron Miller and I didn't get along to start with and so I just decided the hell with these guys. And I made a lot of demands…and Ron wouldn't go for any of it. He didn't give me a goddamn thing."[427]

Milt also erupted over the work of the young animators, though rarely directly. "Don Bluth related to me that [Frank, Ollie and Milt] did have an argument over a scene I did featuring 'Penny,' 'Snoops' & 'The Alligators'," said John Pomeroy, about his work on *The Rescuers*. "Not sure if it was about me being cast in that scene, or the acting direction or how it was drawn." Pomeroy added that despite hearing about this incident secondhand, "it didn't hurt my relationship with Milt. He and I got along great." Glen Keane discussed a similar incident where he heard Milt blew up at the review board over one of Glen's scenes, but Milt chose not to engage directly with Glen.

Milt left the studio at the end of April 1976. "My memory is not so much a retirement as a departure," said Ted Thomas. "Milt was there one day, and then he packed up and left." With Milt's abrupt exit and Lounsbery's death, only four of the Nine Old Men were still left at Disney Animation: Frank, Ollie, Woolie, and Eric. The balance of power in the unit was beginning to shift away from the veterans and toward the future—specifically Don Bluth. When *The Rescuers* was released in the summer of 1977, it would be the final credited film for John Lounsbery and Milt Kahl, and the final directed by Woolie Reitherman. Years later, *The Los Angeles Times* credited Woolie as "one of the highest-grossing directors of all time," thanks to his run of hits from *One Hundred and One Dalmatians* through *The Rescuers*.[428] More importantly, he had safely guided Disney Animation through the first decade after Walt's death, proving that there could be Disney Animation without its creator.

The next project for the Animation Department was *Pete's Dragon*—another musical that combined live-action and animation. *Pete's Dragon* had been an original story Walt himself purchased in 1957, with the hopes of turning it into a television vehicle for child actor Kevin Corcoran, who became a breakout star with *Old Yeller*.[429] By the time the film went into production twenty years later, Corcoran was now an adult working behind the scenes on the film he was once supposed to star in.[430] Don Bluth was promoted to animation director—his first directorial assignment, where he would lead several of the former trainees, including his good friends Gary Goldman and John Pomeroy, as well as Ron Clements, Glen Keane, Randy Cartwright, and others.

Pete's Dragon featured an eclectic cast: "I Am Woman" singer Helen Reddy, in her first starring role; 1930s box-office star Mickey Rooney; method actress Shelley Winters; Oscar-winning comedian Red Buttons; child actor Sean Marshall; and British actor Jim Dale. The live-action portion of the film went into production shortly after the nation's bicentennial celebration in July 1976 and took about four months to complete.[431] The animated dragon Elliott was originally slated for about ten minutes of screentime but when the first scenes came back, the filmmakers loved what Bluth and team accomplished.[432] "We got to have more dragon!" Gary Goldman remembered the executives saying. "Suddenly, our footage was doubled but our budget remained the same."

Pete's Dragon had been booked at Disney's favorite New York venue, Radio City Music Hall, for early November 1977. Yet Elliott's increased screentime created a production crunch for the animators. To meet the deadline, Bluth and team had to work around the clock—sometimes seven days a week and late into the night. The Bluth group's experience moonlighting on their own short *Banjo the Woodpile Cat* had given them the confidence and skills to tackle the project. "All the little tricks that we had explored for the last four and a half years, were suddenly there," said Don Bluth.[433]

Even as the animators were facing the production crunch on *Pete's Dragon*, Don was also working on *Cauldron*'s story. In January 1977, Ron invited Rosemary Sisson back to Burbank to see Don's work with

Mel Shaw and Tad Stones. "I *love* what they've done," she wrote effusively. "A young, very talented boy, [Tad] Stones, has rewritten my Treatment most sensitively, simply improving it and Mel Shaw's drawings are splendid. There's a young director, Don Bluth, the one who liked my ideas when no one else did except Ron, and it will be lovely to work on it with them. I'm to pass my comments on to Ron and then we meet and see what the next stage is. It will still take about seven years!"[434]

Rosemary was so busy with other Disney projects during this time that the seven-year timeline didn't faze her. She had been on set for the filming of *The Littlest Horse Thieves*, and then again for the live-action comedy *Candleshoe*, whose cast included future Oscar-winner Jodie Foster alongside previous winners David Niven and Helen Hayes. Rosemary was simultaneously developing *The Little Broomstick*, an animated film that never went into production.[435]

The Littlest Horse Thieves opened in the U.S. in March 1977. It was Disney's Easter release, and most venues showed it as a double feature with *The Many Adventures of Winnie the Pooh*, an anthology film combining the existing Pooh featurettes. Ron had told Rosemary the previous year, as *Horse Thieves* was being released in the U.K., that he loved the movie so much that "he didn't mind whether or not it made money."[436] The reviews were generally positive with critics praising Rosemary's script, but it was not a massive hit. It was also the last Disney film to be released before Hollywood was taken by storm by a movie so massively popular it would change the entertainment business forever: *Star Wars*.

Chapter 11

*S*tar Wars's impact on popular culture has been well documented
in the half century since its release. It ignited Hollywood's obsession with summer blockbusters, science fiction, trilogies, $100
million dollar box-office grosses, fantasy, high-quality special effects,
John Williams, toys, merchandising, "world building," IP (intellectual
property), creatures, franchises, robots, and Harrison Ford. It also was
the beginning of the end for the adult-centric cinema that had domi-
nated Hollywood for the last decade. George Lucas himself was quoted
in a 1977 article, "I wanted to make a children's movie, to go the Disney
route;" his target audience was fourteen and under.[437] Lucas created
a modern fairy tale for kids that could also be enjoyed by the kid in
every adult. It was a universal success and by the end of 1977, it had
outgrossed every other film ever made. What is less well-known about
Star Wars's impact is the deep impression it made on many of the young
animators who would go on to reshape Disney.

Tad Stones left work early to go see *Star Wars* on opening day at
Mann's Chinese Theatre in Hollywood with a group of fellow animators including Ron Clements and Ed Gombert. As they were waiting
in line to go in, Andy Gaskill and other animators were coming out of
the theater. "It's great. It's great," Andy told the group. Tad said that *Star
Wars* was not just a major influence on his generation, but from that

point forward, the animators bonded by seeing the latest George Lucas or Steven Spielberg film together.

Many of the CalArts animation students were equally enthused about *Star Wars*. Doug Lefler didn't know much about the film before he went to see it. He received a call from John Musker asking if he wanted to come see a new movie that was supposed to be good, and if so, come to the Chinese Theatre in the next thirty minutes. Doug got there right as the movie was starting, so he rushed inside with no context for what he was about to see. "The lights were already going down as soon as my butt hit the cushion. The opening scroll went up and the movie began. We were all just blown away," he said. "Spielberg, Lucas and Coppola were really reinventing the industry at that time."

Jerry Rees was also left in awe of this Holy Trinity of new cinema—Lucas, Spielberg and Coppola. "It was such a key moment [seeing *Star Wars*]. I remember walking out of the theater at night in Hollywood and just going, 'Oh my God, I, I want to do that.' And then I was thinking to myself, I am part of a movie studio and we can make whatever films we want. So we can do that," said Jerry. "We were thinking animation belongs there, it should feel at home in the company of their films."

As popular as *Star Wars* was, not everyone was as enthusiastic. "I wasn't one of the *Star Wars* people," said Henry Selick. "I thought it was fun and like, a great B movie." However, he generally preferred edgier films like *Easy Rider* and *Five Easy Pieces*.

Ron Miller was similarly ambivalent about *Star Wars*. Tad Stones, still coming off his *Star Wars* high, bumped into Ron Miller in the halls. "I don't get it," Ron told Tad. "It's like Saturday morning serials. I don't see the big deal of it."

The Rescuers was released on June 22, 1977, a month after *Star Wars*. It proved to be a solid hit for Disney, earning more than $45 million worldwide. It even outperformed *Star Wars* in West Germany.[438] Still, *Star Wars* was too big a phenomenon to ignore. Later that year, Ron greenlit a science fiction film titled *Space Probe*—later renamed *The Black Hole*. "Maybe Walt would have made *Star Wars*," Ron told a reporter, after announcing the $10 million production of *Space Probe*.

"I went in to see it with that in mind.... It's an intriguing question. But academic. Nobody offered it to us."[439]

The Black Hole went into production in late 1978,[440] with a cast of notable actors including two Oscar winners Maximilian Schell (*Judgment at Nuremberg*) and Ernest Borgnine (*Marty*), *Psycho*'s Anthony Perkins, Yvette Mimieux, and Robert Forster. It was a prestige ensemble with actors not typically associated with Disney. Every soundstage on the Disney lot was used for the film, and in a rare move, the sets were closed to visitors to "insure [sic] the secrecy of story and design."[441]

Disney had a fundamental problem it couldn't control. Its natural audience base was shrinking. At that point in time, Disney largely saw itself as a company catering to U.S. families with young children. Yet the trailing years of Generation X saw a decrease in key population metrics like the U.S. birth rate and total fertility rate.[442] The causes of the decline are multifaceted, but larger economic trends like inflation are widely considered to have played a role.

Walt Disney Productions had been able to skirt through the 1970s releasing largely undemanding fare—notably six live-action comedies starring Don Knotts in the span of four years. Disney had been pleased enough with the box office results from two of its 1975 films—*The Apple Dumpling Gang* (with Don Knotts) and *Escape to Witch Mountain* (without)—that both received sequels. However, audiences were largely abandoning Disney live-action films. To change that for *The Black Hole*, Ron Miller wanted to make Disney's first PG-rated film. The Motion Picture Association of America (MPAA) rating system was introduced in 1968, more than a year after Walt's death. Walt never had to grapple with the audience implications of the ratings system, and the studio's library titles were G-rated when rereleased, regardless of their content.

"It became more and more obvious that a G-rated film, for whatever reasons, young people out there just wouldn't be caught dead walking into a G-rated film," said Ron. "You know, that sounds like an exaggeration when I think about it. I remember sitting there. I remember all of us this sitting around saying, 'God, you know—if it's almost typical of what we did before, and it's not provocative—it doesn't have stuff for the young people.'" In addition to *Star Wars*, non-Disney hits like *Grease*, *Superman*, and *The Bad News Bears* all proved family audiences were getting more comfortable with innuendo, violence, and profanity. Following the model of those films, *The Black Hole* would include mild profanities and intense action—the first movie made by Disney to be rated PG.

Ron wanted to tap *Freaky Friday* director Gary Nelson to helm *The Black Hole*, but Nelson needed convincing. Ron suggested he meet with Peter Ellenshaw to see his concept art for the film. Nelson would later tell *The Hollywood Reporter* "[Peter] showed me these *incredible* paintings that he had done for the movie, and I fell in love with them. And I said, 'Well shit, if this is what it's going to be like, count me in.'"[443]

Matte artist David Mattingly said *The Black Hole* was a leap forward for Disney effects. "It had the most technical breakthroughs, with the computer-controlled matte camera that allowed moves on matte shots. Before that, most matte shots were stationary, or if there was a move it was very difficult and expensive to do. With computer control, the camera was freed up so you couldn't immediately spot a matte shot." The film would go on to be nominated for an Oscar for Best Visual Effects, losing to *Alien*.

"I met and shook hands with Ronald Reagan after the premiere [of *The Black Hole*]—this was before he was President. I asked him what he thought of the movie, and he replied 'Very interesting.' A very political answer," recalled Dave Mattingly. "I felt after having worked so long and hard on the show, it should have been a masterpiece."

Looking back forty years later, director Nelson was happy with the final result. "I think *The Black Hole* holds up well…. A lot of time and lot of effort to make a pretty good movie. Not a great movie. Not some outstanding movie. But a pretty good movie that will, no matter what, probably stick around for a long time."[444] *The Black Hole* was not a financial success like *Star Wars* or even Paramount's *Star Trek: The Motion Picture*, which was released two weeks before *The Black Hole*. Critics at the time were not particularly kind to *The Black Hole*, many using it as an opportunity to say what they had been thinking for several years—that Disney was no longer making good movies and seemed to have lost its way. Instead of critics seeing the film as a turning point for the company, it was lumped with the Don Knotts movies as a subpar live-action film. After *The Los Angeles Times* wrote negatively about the film, Diane Disney Miller wrote a letter to the editor: "*The Black Hole* is the most expensive film made to date by Walt Disney Productions. It is also the largest grossing film for the studio for a first-time release. It will continue to make money as part of the Disney film library."[445] She wasn't just defending her father's legacy, or her husband's career. Her son, Christopher, was an assistant director on the film.

Disney had been facing this kind of criticism, internally and externally, for the last few years. Roy E. Disney had voiced such concerns before he left the company as an employee in 1977. Roy was increasingly alienated at Disney after the death of his father. In the 1970s, he became vice president of 16 mm production—a precursor to the home video market that allowed Disney films to be rented to nonprofit organizations like schools and churches. His direct manager was Ron Miller,[446] and that chain of command did little to improve the relationship. Ron would tell an interviewer that Roy "tried to get involved in motion pictures, and he submitted a couple of scripts, or at least one script to me, which I didn't care for. That was the extent of it."[447]

According to Roy, Card Walker still looked at the company as having a "Walt side" represented by Ron and a "Roy side."[448] The competing loyalties were an increasingly false dichotomy with neither Walt nor Roy O. Disney around. "Ron was a much easier guy for Card to bring under his wing," said Roy. "I think I was all prickles and thorns. And I would rather argue about something I don't believe in." Over time, those tensions led Roy to question if he wanted to continue at the company. "It wasn't any fun to work there anymore. And I just simply didn't feel at home there," he said. "I finally just said, hey, you know, I don't need this in my life."[449]

When Roy decided to leave his family's company, he and his lawyer-partner Stanley Gold asked for a meeting with Card Walker and Donn Tatum. Roy wanted to leave with a contract that would allow him to make independent films which would be distributed by Disney. Such deals were common in Hollywood, like Bob Evans's contract with Paramount, which allowed him to make *Chinatown*, but it was unheard of at Disney. Card Walker flat out refused. Worse, he insulted Roy by asking, "What do you want to do, Roy, make *Deep Throat*?" While Roy was interested in less-sanitized fare, he was insulted by the suggestion that he wanted to make a pornographic film.

Gold quickly jumped to his client's defense. "We're just trying not to do *Herbie the Love Bug* for the fifteenth time. It was cute the first time."[450]

Roy decided his best path forward was to step down from his day-to-day role at Walt Disney Productions, even without a distribution deal. In his resignation letter, he cited "deep and irreconcilable philosophical differences with present management" as his reason for leaving. He expressed concern that Disney was making and remaking the same films with diminishing results, and he complained that new releases were being paired with classic animated films to help their box office—likely referring to the double feature of Ron's beloved *The Littlest Horse Thieves* with *The Many Adventures of Winnie the Pooh*. Roy finished the letter saying he planned to "express myself" with other projects while remaining on Disney's board. "As the largest individual shareholder and a director, I naturally expect to be consulted in advance of any proposed changes in management or corporate financial policy which may affect the future of the Company and the interest of the shareholders. —Regretfully yours, Roy E. Disney"[451] He resigned on March 4, 1977.

It would be several years before Roy would reenter the picture at Disney in any significant way. His reemergence would threaten everything Ron had built. But for now, Ron was focused on the creative future of the Animation Department and the man who Ron thought could lead the unit into a new era—Don Bluth.

Chapter 12

The unofficial wrap party for the *Pete's Dragon* animation crew was a Halloween party at animator Heidi Guedel's house. Among the attendees were Frank Thomas's son Ted, who showed up with animator Andy Gaskill—they dressed as Chicken Boy, the Paul Bunyan-like chicken mascot of an LA restaurant. Animator Glen Keane went in an upside-down costume, with a head between his legs to make it appear like he was doing a perpetual headstand, and his wife Linda was dressed as a ladybug. Assistant animator Jane Baer went as "Mama Jane," (Guedel later described the costume as a "flamboyant hooker") while her husband Dale dressed as a shirtless biker.[452]

"It was a pretty fun night as I recall, although as the evening wore on there were sort of two parties," recalled Ted Thomas. "Don Bluth and his little group played their own party games in a corner, and then everybody else partying. That part was a little weird, and sort of pointed out the direction of what eventually became the split in the department."

Don Bluth, Gary Goldman, and John Pomeroy thought they would be rewarded for the nearly impossible task of completing the animation for *Pete's Dragon* on time. After all, they had worked around the clock and been given no additional resources to produce double the amount of work that was originally envisioned for the film. Instead, production manager Don Duckwall asked to meet with Bluth alone. When Bluth came out of the meeting, he explained to Gary that Duckwall had chewed him out for going $95,000 over budget. "Don felt like, 'God, I did everything I could to try and make sure this worked and do a good job,' only to have his ass chewed when it was all over," said Gary.

Members of the animation crew were compensated with extra days off, instead of paid overtime. "Inwardly, I seethed," Bluth would later say about the unfair lack of recognition for the team.[453]

Pete's Dragon was a modest success for Disney. Within the first few months of release, *Pete's Dragon* had earned more than $16 million in film rentals,[454] against a budget advertised as $11 million.[455] *The New York Times* critic Janet Maslin called the film "the most energetic and enjoyable Disney movie in a long while."[456] Not every critic was as effusive, and like *Bedknobs and Broomsticks*, it had to contend with the legacy of *Mary Poppins*. It was also the last Disney film to premiere at Radio City while the venue was still functioning as a movie house. Disney would continue its relationship with the venue when it reopened the following year, using it for Disney's first major foray into New York theater with a 1979 musical adaptation of *Snow White*.

Don Bluth seemed poised to take over the Animation Department. He generally had the support of the rank-and-file animators and he been brought into story development of *The Black Cauldron*. However, as Bluth's time on *Cauldron* progressed, Tad Stones saw increasing tension between Don and Ron. "[Don] hated the idea that one day Ron Miller came in and gave notes and said no to something, and yes to something else. Don didn't want [to be in] that position."

After *Pete's Dragon*, the next project up was a Christmas featurette *The Small One*—about a boy and his donkey who would play a pivotal role in the birth of Jesus. Development had been started by story artist Pete Young, before being greenlit by Ron Miller.[457] *The Small One* seemed poised to be Eric Larson's return to directing after his *Sleeping Beauty* demotion. Eric had earned enormous goodwill among the new trainees with his patient guidance and gentle demeanor. "We were totally looking forward to having our mentor direct us in a featurette. It wasn't going to take forever to do and we were gonna get some real hands-on training from our teacher," said Jerry Rees, who said Eric was like "everybody's papa."

"We were excited about it," said David Block, who entered as a trainee in April 1977. "Not so much for the property itself but because Eric [Larson] was going to direct it." Most trainees graduated from Eric's area on the second floor down to a production desk on the first floor of the Animation Building, but David was holding out so he could stay near Eric for as long as they'd let him. "I witnessed some things that really pissed me off. There was this conflict, political conflict between John Pomeroy wanting to be the lead on *Small One*, and Glen Keane." Two of the best animators of their generation were both auditioning for Eric with pencil tests of the little boy. David could see Glen and John's competing designs play on Eric's Moviola machine from his desk across the hall. "There was no question that Eric was leaning towards going with Glen."

Glen said, "I had the greatest admiration for Don Bluth and John Pomeroy." After all, their presentation at CalArts inspired his career. "They were very gracious helping me as well," Glen added, referring to his first years at Disney. He was among the many young animators who went to Don's house to work on *Banjo*, even chipping in to help buy mirrors for Don's house so the artists could better study movement. Still, there seemed to be undeniable tension growing. "*Small One* became the flashpoint really," Glen said. "I was working with Eric Larson a lot. I had designed the character of the Small One and done some experimental animation on it. Jerry Rees did some cleanup on it. Around that time, Don talked to Ron Miller about the importance of the young people taking charge and he would lead the group. So Ron Miller told Eric Larson that he was not going to direct that movie, that it would be Don Bluth."

"All the feedback I heard was that Eric was pushed out of the job because Don went and told them, 'I am the leader of a number of the young people. I am a younger man. Eric is old. He's about to retire. He's old news. I can take things into the future. I am the future. Ron, use me,'" said Jerry Rees.

Burny Mattinson, who had once been Eric's assistant animator, would tell the story that all the developmental artwork for *Small One* was stripped from Eric's second-floor office one weekend and brought downstairs to Don's area, without warning. Eric arrived at work that next Monday and didn't know what to think.[458] When he found out Bluth would be taking over, he was crushed.

"That whole group of CalArts folks, we were so angry and frustrated, offended by that. Eric was very hurt by it," said Glen. "But Eric was always very gracious. He would never talk down about anybody. He was just a wonderful example of just how positive a spirit you needed to be at Disney."

As one of the last members of the Nine Old Men still at Disney, it's conceivable such a betrayal could have led Eric to retire. Instead, he dedicated himself to continuing the training program. Tony Anselmo joined Disney from CalArts a couple years later and trained with Eric. "He had been in a really happy marriage and his wife passed away," Tony said. "He told me he would've retired, but when he didn't have Gertrude anymore, his other love was this work. He knew that they needed somebody like him and he loved doing it."

To be fair, Don Bluth's version of events differs. He told historian John Canemaker that Eric was never set to direct *Small One* and had just been working on storyboards.[459] In his autobiography, he expanded on this by saying Ron assigned him to *Small One* because Eric was too busy running the training program.[460]

John Pomeroy offered additional perspective. After *Pete's Dragon*, he and Gary went to Ron's office to ask for raises because their recent pay bump didn't seem like fair compensation for the work they were churning out. It seemed to particularly bother Gary, who was supporting a young family at the time. However, their approach backfired. "Ron got very upset," recalled John, who tried to defuse the situation by getting Gary out of the office as quickly as possible. Rather than more pay, they got more responsibility. "Their way of compensating was awarding us *The Small One* production," said John.

Regardless of what exactly transpired, certain things seem to be true. First, Eric's supporters say he was visibly upset by the project going to Don Bluth. Second, the CalArtians would perceive these events to be Don's fault, and they would hold that against him for years to come.

"You had three factions in the studio. Walt's people, Don Bluth and his bunch, and the CalArts group," said animator Dan Haskett, who was sympathetic to the views of Walt's people but would become associated with the CalArtians. "Each group had its own thing they wanted to get out of the studio. Walt's people were concerned [that] everything they loved would be going down the toilet. They were perhaps most aware of what was happening in the executive suite at the time. It looked like the studio may be on its last legs. For Walt's guys, it was how can we maintain what kept us popular. How can we keep making money so that we keep the department alive. On Bluth's side, he felt the studio had lost its way and wanted to bring production values back to the standards of the 1930s," referring to Bluth's obsession with shadows, reflections and other effects animation. "Meanwhile the CalArts group wanted to do something different. George Lucas and Steven Spielberg were becoming the new Disneys."

"I personally loved Don Bluth," said *Beauty and the Beast* producer Don Hahn, who worked under Bluth at Disney and would later direct the documentary *Waking Sleeping Beauty*. "I think he was both the Messiah and a Walt wannabe. He was both," said Don, referring to the seeming cultlike devotion of Bluth's followers. "For whatever reason that was my take on him, but I probably wouldn't be doing what I am doing [without him] because he gave me tremendous opportunity."

Don Bluth had initially hoped to win over the CalArtians by mentoring the group. One day while Don was attempting to hold court, he asked why people chose to get into animation. According to Jerry Rees, Brad Bird gave the following summation of his personal philosophy: "There's something miraculous about taking a stack of blank paper and when you're done, if you do it well and you show all your drawing in sequence, you'd swear that that character has thoughts and feelings and you care about it. And it's almost like a god-like act of creation." What

Brad was describing was "the illusion of life"—which is why the medium derives its name from the Latin word animare, which means "to give life to." Don Bluth seemed dismissive of what Brad said and proceeded to launch into his own motivations, involving childhood memories of the movement of his mother's dress. To Jerry, it seemed Don's speech was fine if you're a visual effects supervisor but not for a character animator.

"I think [Don] got challenged too many times—and rightfully so—by people like Brad Bird, Dan Haskett, John Musker and I did too," said Henry Selick. Selick said some of the dissension came from Bluth's version of cutting corners—asking the animators to rotoscope (or trace) live-action footage on *The Small One*. "It's something you have to learn how to use it well so it doesn't just look like a tracing."

"Some of his films turned out pretty good. His approach though, as a teacher and a leader, it was the antithesis of the group of people that I was with," added Selick. "We wanted to have more input. We wanted to be able to question things. And Don just wouldn't stand for that.... From his generation, when he'd actually started working at Disney, the idea of questioning your superior, you would never do it."

Selick added, "I remember he lost his temper and was basically saying, 'You haven't paid your dues. You've never done this before. Stop bellyaching.'"

According to Selick, Bluth's outburst led Dan Haskett to jump in saying, "Well, you've never directed a feature before." Selick said this was the final straw for Bluth. This remark reportedly prompted Bluth to lash out and call them all "The Rat's Nest" – a label that was meant to imply treachery but instead became a badge of honor.

For his part, Dan Haskett did not remember exactly what was said but added, "[Don] saw us as interlopers. He saw us as people who were plotting and planning to take Disney some place it should never go." "The Rat's Nest" grew united in their dislike of Bluth.

When a newspaper came to do a feature on the growing ranks of animators, the warring sides were brought together to present a united front. The photographer wanted them to talk among themselves in order to take a candid shot. According to Glen Keane, "We're sitting there like, 'Gosh, this is weird.' Then Don said, 'So what do we talk about?' 'How about Glen's receding hairline?' Then everybody laughs and they're looking at me and I'm kind of laughing."

"[That photo] looks like we're all casual and having fun but it was a really awkward moment," said Glen. "It was a good year where no one spoke to each other."

Randy Cartwright said he was one of the people who fell out with Don. "It became a very big split at the time where like, when you walk down the hallway, if it's one of Don's people, you wouldn't even smile or say hello. You'd just ignore. They'd ignore you, you'd ignored them. Very strange split."

After departing *The Small One*, Glen Keane moved on to *The Fox and the Hound*; his animation of the movie's bear fight was a highlight not just of the film, but of the entire Disney canon. "I was really trying to push boundaries for me. To [John Pomeroy], I was really ruining—I don't know—the heritage of Disney. Then he came in and said that very clearly. Those were the last words that we had together." It would be years before the pair would speak again, eventually repairing their friendship and collaborating again on *Pocahontas* (1995).

For all the behind-the-scenes tension, *The Small One* wound up being an important film in terms of providing opportunity to new talent. Six people were promoted to the title of animator during its production, including three female animators: Lorna Cook Pomeroy, Emily Jiuliano, and Heidi Guedel.[461] In her book *Animatrix*, Heidi writes, "several male trainees had achieved their promotions in less than two years while Lorna and I had to make it there through circuitous routes, sheer determination, and stubborn refusal to give up."[462]

That refusal to give up was also part of Ron Husband's journey. When he first arrived at Disney, a production executive told him that he would never rise to the ranks of animator at the studio. He ignored that and dedicated himself to learning. Soon, his quick sketching abilities were noticed by management. On *The Small One*, he earned the distinction of being the first Black animator to receive screen credit at Disney. As Ron explained it, "At Disney feature Animation you had to animate a hundred (100) feet of animation on a production to get a screen credit and only the 'head' of a department (story etc.) got a screen credit." (Floyd Norman's work as an inbetweener or story artist on earlier Disney films was never acknowledged with screen credits due to the hierarchical rules around opening credits, which finally changed when Disney switched to end credits with *The Black Cauldron*.)

"Particularly in those days, they weren't looking for a quota," said Ron Husband. "They weren't looking to be politically correct. It was just, 'can you do the job.'"

Other talented Black artists of the era were also breaking barriers at the Animation Department—among them Mike McKinney, Dan Haskett, Louis Tate, Louis Scarborough, Donald Towns, Pixote Hunt, and Lenord Robinson. "They were just at the very, very beginning of any kind of diversity," said Dan Haskett. "I don't think they were thinking in terms of diversity. That came later." When the NAACP publicly challenged Disney in 1982 to do better to meet its "moral commitment" of employing a more equitable workforce, the Animation Department was held up as an example of progress. Fifteen Black animators joined Disney's training program in its first decade, though only eight remained by 1982. At the time, 10 percent of Disney's workforce was Black. The NAACP pressure campaign led Disney to agree to a fair share deal that would, among other agreements, see "increased participation of blacks in the creation, production and performance in films and television" as well as Black representation on the board of directors, a first for Disney. [463]

During production on *The Small One* in May 1978, Ron Husband was experiencing serious health issues. His symptoms were dizziness and a loss of equilibrium. His doctor refused to write him a note to excuse his absence from work, so he figured if his doctor wasn't that concerned, he shouldn't be either. "I didn't realize how sick I was." He couldn't keep food down, his speech began to slur, he began losing weight, and his eyes began to turn yellow. "It happened over a long period of time, so it wasn't like [it was] really noticeable." When he made the thirty-mile trek from home to Burbank, he tried to avoid changing lanes so he wouldn't have to look right or left.

It finally caught Ron Miller's attention when he saw Husband walking down the hall, using his hand to balance against the wall so he could keep his equilibrium. Miller inquired about Husband's health and when he learned that doctors were unable to diagnose the problem, Miller intervened and had his secretary book an appointment with a neurosurgeon. It was discovered that Husband had a cyst on his brain, near his neck that needed to be drained. His wife was told that he would probably die on the operating table, or if the eight-hour surgery was successful, he would be paralyzed from the waist down.

"My recovery was pretty dramatic," said Husband, whose athletic background as a football player helped him regain physical function. It would be three months before he could return to work part-time. Husband credited Disney's close-knit community ethos with getting him the essential surgery he needed. "People cared about one another. That was just part of the family. 'We have a sick guy in the family, let's see what we can do about it'. Ron [Miller] intervened. I'm sure he would have done that for any number of people." Ron Miller viewed the employees of Walt Disney Productions as not just *a* family, but *his* family.

"When *The Small One* was over, [Ron] felt like the crew, the young guys, didn't want to be led by Don Bluth," said Gary Goldman. Don reportedly spoke to management in November 1978 and asked to no longer be a director—between the budgets and ego management, he was done. Don's account is that when he informed Ron Miller of his decision to step back, he was told several of the younger animators had already been up to Ron's office to say Don was "arrogant, self-serving and an elitist."[464] The criticism stung and reinforced Don's decision to not continue as a director on *The Fox and the Hound*, which had already begun production.

"A lot of young guys coming in from CalArts in those days were actually going up to Ron Miller saying things like, 'Why are you choosing him? He's not much older than us,'" said Gary. "Basically trying to undermine Woolie and Ron Miller's acceptance as Don being the next guy to run the show for animation."

"It just got to a point where we said 'Gee, is it worth it to work this hard and to have nobody say thank you," said Gary. "And at the same time, have no one on the crew that wants you to be there either." They were still hopeful they could convince Ron to purchase their short film, *Banjo the Woodpile Cat*. Disney management had been following *Banjo*'s progress—production manager Ed Hansen even visited Don's Culver City garage to see the *Banjo* bootcamp and acknowledged it was its own animation school. However, Ron was not interested in buying the cartoon. It was a blow to Don, who was using a home loan to cover *Banjo*'s production costs.[465]

Don, Gary, and John acknowledge that once Ron rejected *Banjo*, they began viewing the film as a calling card for outside opportunities. It was at this point that the trio got serious about leaving, although Tad Stones, who worked on *Banjo*, claimed such discussions began years earlier. "They were openly talking about leaving. This was years before they left and they kept up a story, oh no, they were just teaching themselves. That wasn't true at all."

Regardless of when the decision was made, it was clear their departure would be a bold move that would shake up the industry. "It was like, 'Oh my God, I just got back here and you guys are talking about leaving,'" remembered Lorna Cook, who had recently married John Pomeroy, making her a coconspirator. "It was a gamble. To leave the studio in the way we did, it was not a conventional thing."

Ron Miller began to hear rumors that Don Bluth might be planning to leave. "That didn't bother me. I liked Don. Don was creative in his own right," said Ron. "I found him to be financially irresponsible, but that's beside the point. So many people are." What concerned Ron were reports from Production management that Bluth was going to take several artists with him. Ron confronted Don in his office. "I said, 'Don there's a rumor going around that upsets me. The rumor is that you're leaving.' Don denied it. I said, 'Well, the other thing that really bothers me more than anything else Don is that you are going to take some of my staff and that really bothers the hell out of me.'"

According to Ron, Don Bluth looked him in the eyes and said, "Ron, I would never do that to you."

"I said, 'Okay. Fair enough.' And then he did one other thing. He said, 'Ron if I ever choose to leave, you will be the first person that I tell.' That's the last that I ever talked to the guy, the last I ever saw him. He was a coward."

September 13, 1979, was Don Bluth's forty-second birthday—and also the date of his departure from Disney. "It reminded me of a scene out of a Western. I felt like Doc Holliday with the Earp brothers walking to O.K. Corral," said John Pomeroy. "All three of us were walking down Dopey Drive and turning onto Mickey Avenue, coming up to the Animation Building." From the second floor, director Art Stevens saw them through his office window and made a beeline downstairs to production manager Ed Hansen's office.

"The temperature was one of regret and sadness and sorrow, but well wishes," said John Pomeroy of the moment when he, Don, and Gary resigned together.

Gary had packed up his office and was leaving the Disney lot for the last time. He was only a few paces away from the Animation Building when he heard someone shouting after him: "Hey Goldman!"

Gary turned around and saw Ron Miller on the steps of the Animation Building.

"Good luck!" Ron shouted.

"Thank you!" answered Gary.

"You're going to need it." Ron seethed, turning around and walking back into the building.

Years later, Ron didn't deny confronting Gary, saying "Wouldn't you?" and then adding, "I'm glad they recognized the fact [that] I didn't like what they did."

If Ron thought the departure of Don, Gary, and John was a betrayal, it was the next day when the resignation became a mutiny. The following morning, nine more animators resigned. "It was a very difficult day," said Lorna, who was part of the team leaving Disney.

"The second day, when people started coming in one at a time and tendering their resignations, it went from well wishes to anger. They felt we had betrayed them, misled them, lied to them," said John Pomeroy. He compared the group's departure to young children leaving the nest, but he also learned to understand the anger that accompanied their departure. "When I train somebody and they go work at somewhere else, there is a certain amount of hostility that brews in me, because I have just given all of my knowledge and time and attention to someone who I was grooming to help me, or help this production that I'm working on, and they take that knowledge and go off on their own or go somewhere else."

Gary said some of the Nine Old Men were just as angry as Ron. "They thought [we] were disloyal, arrogant sons of bitches."

The Bluth group's departure made headlines in newspapers and television stations around the country. When asked for comment, Ron Miller was not shy about his contempt for Don. He told *The New York Times*, "The atmosphere and the climate here in the last few days have been wonderful. It's like getting rid of a thorn. They complain of our training program, but, if it hadn't been for our training program, Mr. Bluth wouldn't have had all those trained people to go with him."[466] *The New York Times* pointed out the glaring fact that several of the artists leaving with Bluth were female which Bluth attributed to the "sometimes oppressive" atmosphere for women.

Lorna Cook, Linda Miller, Diann Landau, Emily Jiuliano, Vera Lanpher Pacheco, Sally Voorheis, and Heidi Guedel all joined Bluth, as did Carmen Oliver from the Ink & Paint Department. Lorna said Don Bluth fostered a more inclusive environment for female animators. "He was extremely open and helpful. My feeling is if you could do the job, if you have the talent, gender does not matter. And he never saw it as a guy's world exclusively in animation ever. Women were a big part, in a world that essentially was at the time a guy's world. I still feel we have a long way to go in that regard too, with women directors in animation and live action," said Lorna, who years later would go on to direct the Oscar-nominated *Spirit: Stallion of the Cimarron*.

CalArts student Nancy Beiman was working at Disney that summer leading up to Bluth's departure. She can understand why so many of the female artists chose Bluth over Disney. "Every woman who's ever worked in animation has been told at one point she's difficult to work with. And that's because the sexism is so ingrained, they literally cannot even see it," said Nancy Beiman.

Nancy was once introduced to a female assistant animator by some-one who said she was the wife of one of the male animators. "Why would they tell me she's married to somebody?" Nancy remembered thinking. "To introduce somebody as the wife of somebody was, to me, irregular. It has nothing to do with her merits. She is being judged by someone else's merits." Nancy's concerns over incidents like that led her to ultimately seek employment elsewhere after graduating CalArts, though she's quick to point out that she still holds Disney in high regard. "I never lost respect for the company...in a cutthroat, miserable, high-ly-dodgy industry, Disney was a class act...highly, highly ethical stan-dards." She would go on to work for Disney consumer products in New York and animated remotely on *Winnie the Pooh and a Day for Eeyore.* "In New York City, without any of the politics...they loved my work when they couldn't see me." As times and attitudes changed, she came back to Disney in the 1990s and had wonderful experiences working on *The Goofy Movie* (1995) and on the Fates in *Hercules* (1997), codirected by her former CalArts classmate John Musker.

Bluth's departure left a gaping hole in the animation staff. More than a dozen animators, fully trained in the Disney way, were suddenly gone. The time and investment in their training also went with them. For the management of Disney Animation, this was a tragedy—the generational torch being passed on from the Nine Old Men was nearly extinguished. When the experiment to save Disney Animation began, the Nine Old Men were all active at Disney. Now, John Lounsbery and Les Clark were dead, and the others essentially "retired" to make room for this promised infusion of new blood that wasn't to be.

"Let's face it, we were wiped out when Don Bluth encouraged all those people to leave with him," said Ron. "It left us with a tremendous void," which is the same phrase he used to describe the loss of Walt. "We had a number of people who refused to leave with them and they were talented people but for the most part, we had to basically start over."

It would also be a setback for Disney's *The Fox and the Hound*. More than a third of the film still needed to be animated and it was no longer possible to ready the film for a Christmas 1980 release—it would be pushed to the following summer.[467] In turn, production on *The Black Cauldron* would also be delayed.

Don, meanwhile, had secured funding from Aurora Productions—founded by former Disney executives—for both *Banjo* and a feature-length film, based on the Newbery Award–winning book *Mrs. Frisby and the Rats of NIMH*. Ken Anderson had recommended the book to Don before his retirement in 1978, though Disney wasn't keen on yet another mouse movie after *The Rescuers*. Don asked Gary to look into it. "I read it. I loved it. Don read it. He gave it to John Pomeroy. He read it and said, 'This is great,'" remembered Gary. Bluth's film *The Secret of NIMH* would be the first major animated movie to challenge Disney's dominance in decades. The Bluth team now had to deliver on its promise.

"It wasn't a publicity stunt," said Lorna. "We had to be good on our word. We took some big chances and it happened to turn out well. We shook up the industry and got people to think about things. I look back and we were pretty gutsy to do it."

"We equated it to us being in our own little dinghy, rowing from the Queen Mary out to the open sea," said John Pomeroy. "Very exhilarating but very scary."

"When [Bluth] left and took a big chunk of the department with him, there was worries that the whole department would go down," said David Block. Longtime production manager Don Duckwall retired in the wake of Bluth's departure. Several members of the Rat's Nest were also gone within a matter of months. Nevertheless, morale was restored. "It was like a breath of fresh air to those who were left," Block said.

Without the Nine Old Men or the Bluth group, Disney Animation's survival once again hinged on the ability to assemble a new team. This time, they weren't starting from scratch, although it may have felt like it in real time. Their investment in the CalArts Character Animation program was providing a steady flow of recruits. The CalArtians and other like-minded young artists would soon flood Disney Animation with raw talent and grand ambitions.

Chapter 13

Timothy Walter Burton grew up in a modest home in Burbank, a short drive but seemingly a world away from the Disney lot.[468] Tim's father William had been a baseball player in the minor leagues. "Burbank Bill," as he was known by the press, was considered among the most popular members of the Fresno Cardinals at the time of his engagement to Tim's mother Jean Rae Erickson.[469] The Cardinals threw a wedding shower for Bill and Jean at Fresno State College Park just before a game in August 1953—presenting twenty-three-year-old Bill and twenty-year-old Jean with a heaping pile of finely wrapped gifts. During that same game, Bill was hit in the face by a wild ball, leaving him unconscious and requiring emergency dental surgery on his two front teeth, which had been knocked out of his mouth.[470] Tim said his father would entertain people by taking out his false teeth: "When the full moon would come out, he could pull it back and his side teeth would seem to stick out and he'd pretend to turn into a werewolf."[471] (The perils of dentistry would loom large in Tim Burton's early animation career.)

Bill Burton continued to play ball for a few more years after the accident but retired from the minor leagues after another injury. Tim would later say, "Obviously, you're an athlete and then you have an injury, and you're not able to do it—it's kind of something a bit sad."[472] Bill Burton was twenty-seven years old when his dreams of a baseball career ended and he began working for Burbank's Parks and Recreation Department; Tim Burton was born the following year, on August 25, 1958.[473]

As a kid growing up in the 1960s, Tim fell in love with movies and animation when he saw *Jason and the Argonauts*. "That one stays," Tim said, specifically referencing Ray Harryhausen's stop-motion special effects. "[Ray Harryhausen] was a name I knew before other actors and directors." Tim also loved watching sci-fi monster movies. "That's why I wanted to do movies or draw or do anything. I don't know if it was coming from a very low middle-class suburb…it was kind of a hermetically-sealed world. You were always looking for ways to escape mentally, emotionally and through these kinds of movies, it was very easy."

Tim has credited his high school art teacher Doris Adams with encouraging his artistic talent. To her, Tim was quiet, introverted—a modestly dressed student with a wildly creative imagination.[474] Though just a short drive up the freeway from Tim's home, CalArts was seemingly cost prohibitive for Tim and his family. However, Disney was still offering generous scholarships to attract prospective students to the Character Animation program, which is how he was able to enroll. "It was a new thing, it kind of attracted a different group of people that wouldn't ordinarily have that kind of outlet for things," Tim told a reporter, adding that he happened to be there "at the right time."[475]

CalArts proved to be a liberating experience for Tim—not just because he could walk around in his birthday suit. He found other "geeks and freaks" interested in animation—a band of misfits who shared "camaraderie, rivalry, friendship, espionage and intrigue."[476] Tim's creativity was not contained to the classrooms at CalArts. He renovated the door of his standard-issue dorm room to resemble something out of the German expressionist movie *The Cabinet of Dr. Caligari*.

"Tim knew he was special," remembered Ralph Bakshi, who hired Tim for his *The Lord of the Rings* adaptation. "At that young age, painting cels, he had all the confidence in the world telling me where I was wrong and why. It made me laugh. I called him 'kid.' God, he loved that."

Tim's third-year CalArts film *Stalk of the Celery Monster*, about an evil scientist who is revealed to be a family dentist, was funny and stylistic enough to help him get hired by Disney. Tim was placed in Glen Keane's unit. "I don't think people really at that point sensed the weight of the future of Disney on our shoulders," Glen said. "I was having him animate Vixey, which was totally wrong casting for Tim. But it's the work that I had. Just doing that was killing him to draw this cute little fox. Female fox. Sandy Duncan's voice. And he'd come into my room like 'Aaaaaaarrrrrgggghhhh! I just can't do this.'"

"When I was back in animation, it was like the dark days," said Tim, referencing not just his frustrations but also his feeling about Disney's films of this era. "I was a bad animator in a way. Animators are very special people because I always felt that you have to be: A) an artist, but B) you have to be very disciplined. You have to have a lot of different disciplines. I could never get those two sides of my brain connected, so I was quite frustrated as an animator. Good animators are a real rarity and a real special people because they have to straddle both sides of the brain, big time, at the same time."

Glen remembers arriving at work in the winter of 1980 and taking off his coat. Tim was hiding in the narrow wardrobe near Glen's desk. "I'd take my coat, put it on his head, shut the door and then I'd go in and animate. I come back out open it, Tim is still there with the coat on his head. I mean he'd be there for hours like that."

Tim started around the same time as other young artists who would become his close friends. CalArts student Sue Mantle DiCicco was visiting her former CalArts classmate John Lasseter for lunch on the Disney lot when he told her, "We could really use you here. You should see if you can get on staff because we need more people.'" He introduced her to Ed Hansen, who asked her to come back with her portfolio. Shortly after lunch, she returned with a portfolio and was hired.

Mike Gabriel, the surfer who had once stolen lobby cards from *Robin Hood* to imitate the Nine Old Men, had applied multiple times to Disney. "I was still a failure-to-launch 24-year-old kid with a dream to work at Disney Studios," still living at home with seven of his siblings and driving a Ford Pinto. He thought *The Small One*, that Bluth Christmas short that had caused so much internal consternation, was such a downgrade in animation quality that he worried Disney's heyday was over. "I wondered if h'oh, did I miss it? Is it over? Is Disney dead? But almost as quickly I realized something. If that is where the studio sits now, talent wise, I think I am probably good enough to get in." He applied again and showed his portfolio to Don Duckwall, who thought it needed more loose action sketches. Mike submitted a revised portfolio the following Monday, but the entire week passed and he didn't hear anything. Fearing another rejection, he called Disney to see if they received his updated portfolio. "HEY MIKE!," exclaimed Production manager Ed Hansen. "We got your sketches, you forgot to leave us your phone number!!! We have been trying to reach you for days!!!" Mike Gabriel began his decades-long career at Disney Animation on October 11, 1979—four weeks after the Bluth group's resignation. Tim, Sue, and Mike became inseparable friends.

"[Tim and I] got along great right away. Immediately. We clicked, like I did with all the CalArts people for whatever reason," said Mike. "I loved Tim. He was a great friend. He was always FUN! One of the funniest guys I had ever met. Hilarious and hilariously original in every way."

Tim's irreverent sense of humor was at least partially forged by the kitsch of the era. Mike Gabriel remembers "his appreciation of the weird in the entertainment world like show biz banter and Vegas lounge acts. He loved the absurd and the quirky.... Every day, we had our ten o'clock break, [with Tim] rehashing the cheesy but wonderful low budget horror film he might have seen the night before, by Ed Wood, like *Plan 9 From Outer Space*, or a John Waters film, *Pink Flamingos* with Divine. He would have us all laughing 'til tears were streaming down our cheeks. He would be so animated and excited talking about the cheap effects and bad acting—but you could tell he loved it."

Jerry Rees, who first met Tim at CalArts, felt protective of him. When Tim needed money for much-needed dental surgery and had nowhere else to turn, Jerry gave him money to help out. Tim's dental surgery became a community event at Disney, when he stopped at the office to show everyone his tooth. The red trail on the office's linoleum floors led to Tim, blood dripping from his mouth and down his shirt, posing for photos with his friend Joe Ranft.

Jerry was at a party where Tim thought he would get a reaction if he donned a straitjacket. As the night wore on, Jerry realized Tim was outside alone on the diving board, tied up. He began to worry Tim could accidentally fall in the pool and drown. Partygoers looked on from inside, mildly amused at the gag, but dismissing it as just another quirky Tim moment. "This is somebody who's undoubtedly going through some stress and therapeutic explorations right now in a lot of danger" Jerry thought, as others laughed at the antics. "It's not a goof right now." Jerry kept watch over his friend to make sure he made it through the night safely. Jerry witnessed other outlandish behavior by Tim, who was eager to make his friends laugh. "I didn't feel like that was the essence of Tim. He would do these things because he saw crowd reaction but I just saw a really sweet, creative person that just wanted to sort things out."

Tim's idiosyncratic sensibilities were being shaped and sharpened by his peers. During breaks, conversations would center around bands like Oingo Boingo or Madness, also CalArts alum Paul Reuben's *Pee Wee Herman Show* on Sunset Boulevard. "It was a creative powder keg for me to be thrown in with people so explosively talented and clever and hip in a very artsy way, not forced, all natural and true to themselves," recalled Mike Gabriel. "It was no wonder Tim got to direct Paul in his first feature *Pee Wee's Big Adventure* within a few short years, and use Danny Elfman as his film composer almost exclusively."

As *The Fox and the Hound* tried to recover from Bluth's departure, the younger artists on the film felt they had been handed a chore rather than a chance to exercise their talent. It was a sentiment that had been hanging over the department for a good chunk of 1979. Earlier that summer, Glen Keane met with director Art Stevens, Don Duckwall, and Ed Hansen to tell them that the "majority of us feel that *Fox and Hound* is not our picture." He urged the production team to look for new leaders among the ranks—pointing out that Jerry Rees and John Musker were natural leaders and that many of the animators—including Rees, Musker and Lorna Cook Pomeroy—could all be good directors if given the chance. He urged management to find the best utilization for the artists' talents—including suggesting Tim Burton would be an excellent fit in character design. Glen's most important message: "WE HAVE TO TAKE SOME RISKS!"[477]

Glen was already taking big swings, supervising the climax of *The Fox and the Hound*—a thrilling fight between the title characters and an enormous bear. With the help of John Lasseter, Glen Keane created an action sequence that transcends the rest of the movie. "John [Lasseter] and I really felt the climax of the film wasn't what it needed to be," said Glen. "Mel Shaw had done a pastel of a huge waterfall with a bear fight going on, but the bear fight wasn't that interesting. But the waterfall, with the sound of it, we both just said, there's nothing as powerful as that waterfall in the whole movie. What if the bear fight took place on that waterfall?" Glen began to storyboard the sequence and draw thumbnail sketches, but it lacked power. He began to read about real-life bear attacks to add to the scene's believability. "I just kept drawing the bear bigger and bigger and bigger. I had to cover mass. A large mass of dark bear shape. I started doing that with charcoal."

A new CalArts graduate named Mark Henn was put in Glen's unit to assist on the bear sequence. "Sometimes the bear was so big, it just filled the entire sheet of paper," said Mark. "It was a great opportunity and yeah, it was a fun sequence.... I got along great with Glen both artistically and personally."

Frank and Ollie had retired from animation but were still on the studio lot writing the definitive history of Disney Animation, *The Illusion of Life*. They began to hear about this new guy working on this amazing bear fight sequence. They seemed surprised when they finally learned the buzz was about Glen, whom they had now known for several years. Still, they were so impressed with his work they included it in their book, alongside the best work ever created by Disney.[478]

Jerry Rees led a team of CalArtians—including Darrell Van Citters, Brad Bird, and John Musker—who were hoping to create a similarly thrilling opening, where a mother fox is running for her life. As Jerry envisioned the scene, the mother fox ran through a series of small hills, dipping in and out of view. "She's a little closer on the next horizon, a little closer, so it's like you're going to get there, you're going to get there. Then finally there was a gunshot. Birds came up from between the hills. The camera kept moving back and she did not appear at the next horizon. Then the camera slowly gets it and slows [down] and stops and just looks at the meadow and there's nothing. And it just told you she didn't make it."

When he showed it to codirectors Art Stevens and Ted Berman, they both looked at him and said, "She's dead!"

"Yeah, that's the story. It's about an orphan," he replied.

"No, no, no. We have to think maybe she got away," they insisted.

"Really? Is this a story about not an orphan but a delinquent mother who leaves the cub?"

Jerry was equally frustrated by their reaction to his animation of Dinky the sparrow. He decided he wanted his animation to capture the way birds flit around in real life. If the bird was about to fly, he'd take one drawing and keep it still, then move the next drawing ever so slightly—and then, the next drawing would be a streak of a blur indicating the bird took off. When the directors saw the test in a Moviola, they loved his animation. But when they reviewed it drawing by drawing, they thought his approach was too cartoony. He conspired with his cleanup artists, including another young artist named Rebecca Lodolo, to show the directors the drawings they thought they wanted to see but then once approved, put it back the way Jerry intended before it went to Ink & Paint.

Around the same time, Jerry Rees and Tim Burton teamed up to codirect *Luau*—a homemade 16 mm comedy that starred Mike Gabriel along with many other animators. It was mostly an excuse to get the gang together on weekends, but *Luau* is an important anthropological document of the underground humor coursing through Disney Animation. "It was a *Beach Blanket Bingo* American International send up surf movie," said Mike. "The Tim oddball outsider twist was his character. He starred as the villain, an outer space alien, who is nothing but a head…looking for a body." The film is as irreverent and politically incorrect as many 1980s comedies, with the production value of an Ed Wood Z movie. Most of the comic dialogue was adlib. "I had never been around people this glib, inventive, creative and so damn funny!" said Mike. Among them was a new CalArts arrival whom Mike called "the great one we all adored"—Joe Ranft.

"Joe Ranft arrived and ignited all our creative gunpowder into a constant explosion of hilarity and comic genius. He became an epicenter of good times, big laughs, and brilliant social insights. He was the hippest of us all even though you would never know it right off looking at him, but his total commitment when improvising a character bit, and fearlessness in his adlib social commentary were truly stellar in a Lenny Bruce way but with a sweet laugh not a sneer. He was so comfortable in his own skin. He had the confident cool factor," said Mike Gabriel.

For the younger artists, the Disney lot felt like college, and not just because its carefully manicured aesthetics were used as a school campus in the film *Midnight Madness* (1980). Hijinks—from pranks to rubber-band fights—were regular occurrences. The comic sensibilities of modern Disney films were developed in this environment. Yet for management, it felt like a regression. "[Bluth's leaving] really panicked Ron because he really took our best people and that was one of the reason that the kids were coming in from CalArts. [Management was] determined that they were going to keep them pretty happy so they could do no wrong," said veteran Joe Hale. A director or producer may encounter an animator practicing his guitar in one room or a group in the middle of a headstand contest in another. "I would go to Ed Hansen who was head of animation and say, 'God, can't we do anything about that?' He said, 'No, you can't fire anybody.'"

The generation gap was felt in both directions. Gary Trousdale (*Beauty and the Beast*) remembered when Joe Ranft visited CalArts after joining Disney. "We were all thrilled. Like, 'Yeah, Joe! Go show them! Go take that place by storm!'" Joe had been out of school six months but he was no longer enthusiastic about Disney. "'All the old guys at Disney might be dying off, but they're training a bunch of new old guys,'" Joe told Gary.

Ron Miller extended peace offerings to the young animators working on *The Fox and the Hound*—inviting them to a party on his boat. He also unexpectedly accepted a challenge from animator Darrell Van Citters, sent via interoffice mail, to play a winner-take-all volleyball match—live-action producers versus animators. The stakes were high: whoever won the game got control of Walt Disney Productions. Ron and the live-action producers came in long-sleeved red uniforms. On the opposing team: Mike Gabriel, Darrell Van Citters, Tim Burton, Chris Buck, Jerry Rees, and Jay Jackson. John Musker played the role of Howard Cosell, delivering play-by-play commentary to Randy Cartwright's camera. Despite a valiant effort by the producers, the animators—who were about twenty years younger—won handily. "We totally skunked the producers. It was almost sad," said Mike Gabriel. "[Ron] showed great sportsmanship and class, and invited our team to have burgers." Given the talent involved, it's fun to imagine what would have happened if Ron made good on the contract and handed over control of the studio to these future industry leaders, even for a day.

Chapter 14

"Why Disney? I'll tell you," Bette Davis, the aging Hollywood icon, put down her cigarette long enough to answer the reporter's question during production on Disney's *The Watcher in the Woods*. "They are about the only company around who treat their workers with respect, and who make movies with the style that Hollywood used to have. I've enjoyed every moment I've been associated with them." As the interview was winding down, she circled back to the earlier question about why Disney. "Oh, and the other thing is that Disney have never had a flop—it is rather nice to be associated with success."[479]

The Watcher in the Woods was to be a showcase not only for Bette Davis but for a small team from the Animation Department that was helping with the film's special effects. Davis reportedly asked Disney to have the film finished by April 1980 to coincide with the fiftieth anniversary of her film career and her seventy-second birthday.[480] The film would premiere at the plush Ziegfeld Theatre in New York, followed by a celebrity party at Tavern on the Green in Central Park, with a guest list that included Andy Warhol, Bianca Jagger, Roy Scheider, and Tammy Grimes.[481] When the lights went down at the Ziegfeld, hopes were high for *The Watcher in the Woods*. Davis had reinvented herself as a horror queen with the film *Whatever Happened to Baby Jane?* (1962); *The Watcher in the Woods* was Disney's first foray into the genre. The credits offered the promise of thrills, as eerie music played over voyeuristic footage. As the story unfolded, viewers learned that Davis's character's daughter had gone missing many years ago and now seemed to be haunting the new teenage neighbor, who is her doppelgänger. In the final minutes of the movie, just as the story is climaxing in a frightening séance, a B-movie monster alien is summoned out of nowhere and takes the neighbor into a '70s era futuristic–looking "other world," where she rescues Davis's daughter, who has been trapped inside a prism. The audience was alleged to have burst out laughing when the monster appeared on the screen—likely reacting to how little this "other world" sequence resembles the rest of the movie.[482] *The New York Times* critic Vincent Canby mocked the special effects[483] and columnist Rex Reed called the film "a horror movie in more ways than one."[484] Ron Miller showed the film to distributors in other parts of the country, and they said they would only run it if the ending was changed.[485] Ron and Card Walker made the unusual decision to pull the movie from circulation after two weeks to rework the ending.[486] The film's coproducer Tom Leetch would later blame the special effects on the rush to release the movie in time for the gala honoring Bette Davis's fifty years in Hollywood.[487] Ron knew that wasn't the full story though. "*Watcher in the Woods* was a big mistake," Ron said. "We should have developed [the monster/ending] long before we did. We waited much too long to find out that we had a problem with what we developed there."

The small crew working on the *other world* sequence was largely composed of members of the Animation Department: Henry Selick, Andy Gaskill, Rick Heinrichs, and Joe Hale. Henry Selick put the blame on director John Hough, who never bothered coming to Burbank to see their progress. "I have no respect for the guy.... Your whole movie hinges on what is the Watcher in the Woods.... A smart director would have been there and seen this isn't working out and would've worked with a writer to say, 'okay, here's what we can do.'"

"They wanted me to design the monster and the director [had] just seen the new *Alien* film. He said, 'Oh yeah, make it look like that. Make it look just like that.'" Selick was also critical of Disney's visual effects department at that time. "They couldn't make something amazing and spectacular. It wasn't about the idea, it was the execution. They didn't realize how far their abilities had fallen from what the rest of the world had done and how much physical effects had advanced.... They should have made it more like a shadow thing that's glimpsed or just eyes and never given it away."

Rosemary Sisson had written the original draft for *Watcher in the Woods*. However, she chose not to go on location because she found director John Hough to be "unpleasant." According to her recollection, he then "hired another writer, and between them they hatched a different ending." When she heard about the audience reaction, she reached out to Disney and offered to help with reshoots. "We managed a new ending which, though not as good as my original one, or the one I had later thought of, did at least work pretty well," she later wrote.[488]

David Mattingly, the film's matte artist, said, "I remember they had no ending on the movie, and called in everyone they could think of to give suggestions after the rest of the movie was shot." Ultimately Disney asked visual effects artist Harrison Ellenshaw, who had just completed work on *The Empire Strikes Back*, to help revise the ending. The new version of *Watcher in the Woods* was released in 1981, after an additional $1 million was spent fixing the film. Reviews of the later cut were generally positive, but the film was not the success Bette Davis once assumed it would be. Disney would lose nearly $7 million on the film.[489]

During the whole mess of *Watcher in the Woods*, Ron got better acquainted with Animation Department veteran Joe Hale. "He had the unfortunate job of coming up with the creature," remembered Ron. "We had thrown a couple of things to him.... I got to know him and I started talking to people about Joe. People felt that he had the ability [to take on a big project], that he was conscientious." Ron was looking for veterans of the Animation Department who could help lead it back to where it was before Bluth left. Joe had a good rapport with the small group of younger artists working on *Watcher in the Woods*. Henry Selick said Joe was a "funny, likable guy." David Mattingly, though not in animation, worked with Joe on both *Watcher in the Woods* and *The Black*

Hole and remembered him being very serious and diligent. For all the problems on *Watcher in the Woods*, internal politics did not seem to be one of them.

Tad Stones had heard good things about Joe's management style on *Watcher in the Woods*. "I saw how well Joe was working with people and I was in Ron Miller's office every once in a while. I would go in and just shoot the breeze—again the company was so small.... [people] don't realize how tiny the company was. I remember saying Joe Hale works great with the young guys. Lo and behold, Joe was put in charge of *The Black Cauldron* to work with the young guys." Ron hoped Joe could take charge of the young CalArtians without alienating them like Don Bluth had. It was also clear that despite Woolie's track record, it was time to move past his approach to filmmaking. Woolie's films had become formulaic, safe, and featured a repertory company of sitcom stars like Eva Gabor, Pat Buttram, and George Lindsey. Steve Hulett, who worked on story for *The Fox and the Hound*, has said Woolie's failed attempt to add a song to that film—sung by Phil Harris of *The Jungle Book*, *Aristocats*, and *Robin Hood* fame, as well as the Spanish entertainer Charo—seemed to be the end of the road for Woolie.[490]

In May 1980, Ron offered Joe the position of producer on *The Black Cauldron*. More than $500,000 had already gone into *Cauldron*'s development under Woolie.[491] Hale wasn't sure he wanted to take on the responsibility of running the film—and by extension, the whole department. Yet the story spoke to him. Like the main hero Taran, Joe had once been a young kid on the farm with dreams of glory on the battlefield.

Joe Hale's life changed forever in April 1943, the month he entered the Marines. The scrawny teenager had listened to stories of the Great War, like *All Quiet on the Western Front*, for as long as he could remember. When the Japanese had attacked Pearl Harbor, Joe was still too young to enlist but he wanted his chance to be a tough marine defending his country. When a WWI veteran told Joe that the U.S. was going to defeat Japan in six months, Joe feared his chance to fight for his country would disappear.

Of course, the veteran's prediction was wrong. So as soon as Joe was eligible to enlist, he hitchhiked his way to Detroit, which was about an hour from his hometown in Chelsea, Michigan. At his physical, Joe weighed all of 112 lb. A disappointed Sergeant said, "You're not exactly what we are looking for. But, we can't find anything wrong with you so I guess you're in."

He was shipped off to the Pacific and less than two years later, Private First Class Joe Hale was directing artillery fire for an infantry battalion of the 26th Marines. War was now a dangerous reality for this small-town Michigan boy. He faced the fiercest fighting of his war experience at Iwo Jima. About two weeks into the Iwo Jima campaign, Joe was dispatched to the frontlines to rescue one of his superiors, who had been shot and was now bleeding out. Although Joe reached the lieutenant and helped get him on a stretcher, he had to hunker down for the night before he could return to the command post. The first foxhole he encountered was overcrowded; two rifleman were already using it. He scurried to another spot to ride out the night. At four in the morning, intense, heavy shelling fell down around him. "The ground was shaking and clouds of dust and choking cordite drifted over us. I curled up in the foxhole with my knees pulled up against my chest and my hands pressed over my eyes trying to make myself as small as possible.... Our foxhole that had seemed so cramped earlier now felt huge and exposed. For the first time since setting foot on the island, I was sure that I was going to die."

"I experienced a terror that I cannot possibly express in words," Joe would later write. "I can remember praying and eventually everything seemed to retreat into my head.... Finally, after what seemed an eternity, but in fact was only a few minutes, it was all over." When dawn broke, Joe left the foxhole and saw several marines gathered nearby looking down at the remains of a marine and two Japanese soldiers who had died overnight. As he looked more closely, he realized he was looking down at the first overcrowded spot he had tried to climb into. Joe knew he was lucky to be alive.[492]

The military now says Iwo Jima was "one of the bloodiest battles in Marines Corps history."[493] Although estimates range, around twenty thousand marines were wounded and another seven thousand were killed.[494] As harrowing and unforgettable as Joe's war experiences were, it was an entirely different event in April 1943 which changed his life. Just before he left for boot camp, Walt Disney's *Bambi* debuted at Joe's local movie theater in Chelsea, Michigan. It was unlike anything Joe had ever seen—to him, it provided that rare euphoria one encounters when they connect with art. Joe had always loved going to the movies, since he was a small boy in the Depression and his mother would give him a dime to go the movies after weeding crops at a local onion field. "I grew up in the movie theater," he said. Most of the time, he didn't care what was playing, but he typically liked the short cartoons and musicals. But *Bambi* was different. Joe would later say that if he was in a burning building, and he had to choose between saving the Mona Lisa or the last remaining negative of *Bambi*, he'd choose *Bambi*. Since the film was only showing for three days, Joe squeezed in as many screenings as he could. By the time it left town, he had seen it five times. When he finished boot camp in California in June 1943, he found a San Diego movie theater playing *Bambi* and saw the film two more times. From these screenings, Joe knew that he wanted to be an animator.

After the war, Joe went home to Michigan and enrolled in an art school, courtesy of the G.I. Bill. "It was a wonderful, wonderful thing that they did for us GIs, not that it was done out of the goodness of their heart…they didn't want 20 million unemployed veterans running around." Michigan hadn't changed very much but Joe had. He had outgrown the quiet life of his childhood. Even the art school seemed limited compared to his ambitions. The final straw came in 1947, when a big blizzard hit. "Everything was snowed in for days and I had been in the tropics for the last few years and I thought I couldn't handle this."

As soon as he was able to dig out, Joe said goodbye to subzero winters and hitchhiked his way to California.

A trucker gave him a lift and asked Joe, "Where you going, son?"

Although Joe hadn't thought out his plan exactly, he blurted out, "I'm going to California. I'm going to work for Walt Disney."

When he arrived in Los Angeles, he enrolled at the Academy of Fine Arts to learn how to sketch human anatomy. By 1951, he felt he was ready to work at Disney. He brought his portfolio to the gates of the Disney Studios in Burbank, ready to be hired until the guard stopped him in his track. "Do you have an appointment?"

Joe replied no.

"Do you know anybody in the industry?"

Joe again replied no.

The guard told Joe to hold on while he made a call. Within minutes, Joe was in front of the head of publicity for Disney animation. After reviewing Joe's portfolio, the gentleman said, "You know, we could use [you]. We'll hire you."

It was an unlikely start for an even more unlikely dream. Disney was just finishing *Alice in Wonderland* and embarking on *Peter Pan*; the studio needed artists skilled at drawing human figures. They were about to start training classes in a few weeks and gave Joe a job in the mail room until classes began. "I got to know everybody on the lot. Everybody. The machine shop, the carpentry shop, publicity, the power plant."

Though Joe had lucked into his job at Disney, he never took it for granted. "I thought, well I got my foot in the door and I'm not going to ever give them an excuse to fire me…. I always worked real hard and I always had the highest drawings count." Joe became a jack-of-all-trades at the studio—working on layout for *Sleeping Beauty*, helping marry animation and live action in *Mary Poppins*, working on Ward Kimball's Oscar-winning short *It's Tough to Be a Bird*, and updating the design of Donald's nephews Huey, Dewey, and Louie. He became more involved in special effects throughout the 1970s, eventually earning an Oscar nomination for *The Black Hole*.

Now after all these decades at the studio, Joe was being presented with the chance to lead the most ambitious animated film since he joined: *The Black Cauldron*. Joe was excited to get to work on the story, but he didn't want to replace any of the directors on the film. He considered *The Fox and the Hound* codirectors Art Stevens, Ted Berman, and Rick Rich to be his friends. He and Art had been colleagues for the last thirty years. However, both Ron and Tom Wilhite, the vice president of creative development, began pressuring Joe to accept the role of producer. They told him, "If you're not going to do it, we don't know who is going to do it." It was only after Joe consulted with Art, Ted, and Rick and got their blessing that he agreed to take over.

When Joe took on the role of producer in May 1980, his first job was to wrestle with the numerous treatments and storyboards that had been created for *Cauldron* over the last several years. As he was reviewing the existing work on *Cauldron*, Joe began to see a connection between himself and the main character Taran. He recalled the feeling he had days after Pearl Harbor, when he had been so eager to join the war effort, and it reminded him of the film's hero pig keeper, who naively sees war as a game. Having lived through the Battle of Iwo Jima, Joe wanted the character's journey to reflect his own evolution.

"There's nothing glorious about being in battle," Joe told an interviewer. "There's something weird about grown men hunting each other down with guns and hand grenades."[495]

Like Joe, those most drawn to *The Black Cauldron* at Disney were members of the Greatest Generation, who saw that even a morally justified war could lead to inhumanity. When Lloyd Alexander had dreamed up Prydain, he drew his inspiration from the last peaceful place on Earth before encountering the war-ravaged remains of continental Europe. Otto Englander, who lost his extended family in the Holocaust, tried to enlighten the public about the war's psychological impact on returning veterans. Woolie Reitherman was awarded the Distinguished Flying Cross and an Air Medal with two bronze Oak Leaf Clusters for his service in the China Burma India Theater. Despite such heroics, his son Bruce recalls that Woolie's feelings about his service were complex, and that he rarely mentioned the wartime experiences or achievements that so clearly had left an indelible mark on his life and character. Rosemary Sisson served on the enormous support team for D-Day but lamented how the war had robbed her generation of their youthful innocence. Mel Shaw concluded, after seeing the suffering of civilians in Southeast Asia, that "War transforms mankind into the cruelest creature on the face of the earth, and it seems to me that we never learn from history."[496] Though none of these filmmakers necessarily set about to turn *The Black Cauldron* into Disney's most implicitly antiwar film, it may have been the natural product of their collective experiences.

As the Reagan era was celebrating a certain kind of indestructible zero-sum masculinity represented by Arnold Schwarzenegger and Sylvester Stallone, *The Black Cauldron* offers an alternative hero—a scrawny, awkward teen who abandons his fantasies of being a celebrated warrior in exchange for his friend's life. In *The Black Cauldron*, the villainous Horned King is not killed off by this hero, but instead by the all-powerful weapon of war they had both been seeking—the titular cauldron.

Critic Gene Siskel chafed, calling Taran "simpering" and a "dullard;" he compared him to "insufferable goodie-goodies" that only "a twerp" could like.[497] Yet Joe Hale wanted to create a hero who was potentially more relatable to the film's intended teenage audience—one that faced the pressures of adolescence and occasionally stumbled. "So much pressure is put on kids these days to succeed. Everyone cares who won the gold medal in the Olympic Games but nobody cares about the guy who came in one-hundredth of a second off," he told an interviewer. "I wanted to tell kids, 'Even if you don't make the first team, that's OK.'"[498]

Joe's approach is in keeping with the spirit of the books. In Lloyd Alexander's introduction to the Chronicles of Prydain, he writes, "Most of us are called to perform tasks far beyond what we can do. Our capabilities seldom match our aspirations, and we are often woefully unprepared. To this extent, we are all Assistant Pig-Keepers at heart."[499]

With Joe at the helm of *Cauldron*, he had one year to settle the outstanding issues surrounding the film before animation began. "I wanted to do a musical," said Joe. Every Disney animated film until this point had songs; several Disney songs won or were nominated for Oscars. As he looked at the first sequence, he imagined Taran singing about wanting to be a brave warrior, instead of doing farm chores. He also considered a villain song for the Horned King explaining why he was so evil ("how would you like to be a four-year-old with horns?"), and a song for the half-beast sidekick Gurgi explaining how he was lost and alone in the world. Ron explained he didn't want to make this a musical because the movie had to appeal to teenagers: "Somebody who had gone through the demographics came to the conclusion the people who were keeping the studios alive were kids from 14–18 or something. They were buying 90% of the tickets and they wouldn't go see a Disney film for anything. So, the whole idea of *The Cauldron* was to make a non-traditional Disney film that would appeal to a whole different audience."

Later in production, the idea of adding songs came up again. Frederick Loewe, the composer of *Camelot* and *My Fair Lady*, offered to write a closing song for the film. Once again, Ron's answer was no. "For some reason, [Ron] did not like musicals," said Joe. *The Black Cauldron* would be the first Disney film without songs, though Elmer Bernstein's score notably featured Cynthia Millar on the ondes Martenot, an instrument Millar says made a great contribution to the film thanks to both its playfulness and its "very frightening sound."

Joe and the directors asked some of the Nine Old Men to contribute character designs for *Cauldron*. Milt Kahl and Marc Davis sent in designs to guide, and hopefully inspire, the young animators. Eric Larson continued to train new recruits throughout *Cauldron*'s production (as did veteran artist Walt Stanchfield, whom animator Mark Henn cites as another key mentor for his generation). Although none of the Nine Old Men animated on *The Black Cauldron*, six of the nine—Woolie, Marc, Milt, Frank, Ollie, and Eric—were involved in its story, design and production, with Eric Larson listed in the final credits as an animation consultant.

In June 1980, Ron Miller was elevated to president of Walt Disney Productions, with Card Walker serving as CEO and chairman of the board.[500] At forty-seven years old, Ron knew he had to improve the output of Disney films, which he viewed as the heart of the business. He wanted to find films that connected with adult audiences. A few months earlier, he and Card met with top Paramount executives Barry Diller and Michael Eisner, who were trying to finance two films currently threatening to go over budget: the musical *Popeye* and the special-effects fantasy *Dragonslayer*. *Popeye* had been conceived when producer Bob Evans couldn't get the rights to the Broadway smash *Annie*. *Popeye* was the first major film role for Robin Williams and was directed by Robert Altman. Altman opted to shoot the film in Malta, but it proved to be a disastrous mistake. Bad weather shut down production for the better part of a month, forcing the film to go several million dollars over budget.[501]

According to *Dragonslayer* screenwriter Hal Barwood, "Disney was brought in by the Paramount execs because the approx. $12 million budget seemed iffy with all the visual effects we contemplated. (They were right!) I don't have any idea why Ron Miller responded, but I'm glad he did, because otherwise that movie would have been another wonderful screenplay in our writers' trunks." What may have attracted Disney to this second project was the association of George Lucas via his special effects company Industrial Light & Magic. *Dragonslayer* underperformed at the box office, though its high-cost special effects were nominated for an Oscar and have been praised in recent years by Guillermo del Toro and George R.R. Martin.[502]

In hindsight, it may seem like a questionable decision to back these two costly productions, but at the time, Paramount seemed to be the studio that could do no wrong. The output of other Hollywood studios in the late 1970s is best defined by screenwriter William Goldman's famous quote from his book *Adventures in the Screen Trade*: "Nobody knows anything.... Not one person in the entire motion picture field *knows* for a certainty what's going to work." Ron Miller and Disney weren't alone in releasing a string of films that failed to connect with mass audiences (*Herbie Goes Bananas, The Last Flight of Noah's Ark, Condorman*). Yet while other studios were flailing, Paramount had a string of hits under Barry Diller and Michael Eisner: *Saturday Night Fever, Grease, Heaven Can Wait, Up in Smoke, The Warriors, Meatballs,* and *Star Trek: the Motion Picture*.

"The secret sauce was youth," said former CalArts teaching assistant and Paramount story editor David Kirkpatrick. "It was catering to the under 25 crowd."

Diller and Eisner got their start together at ABC Television in New York, where they helped turn around the third-place network. Eisner had a hand in bringing about popular programming across the entire ABC schedule: *Schoolhouse Rock, The Jackson 5ive, All My Children, One Life to Live, Happy Days, Starsky and Hutch,* and *Welcome Back, Kotter.* Diller became chairman and CEO of Paramount in 1974 and in time, hired Eisner as president. In his oral history for the Television Academy's The Interviews series, Eisner described his strong working relationship with Diller: "We started within a couple months of each other at ABC, at exactly the same age, a couple months apart. So, we knew how to communicate. We had a shorthand...we generally agree on what's good and what's bad, what's commercial, what's not commercial, what's worth doing." He added, "If we didn't get along or agree on something we always did it in private. We had a good public united face to everybody."[503]

At Paramount, Diller had a young assistant named Jeffrey Katzenberg. Katzenberg was a teenage phenom in New York City politics, working for Mayor Lindsay's administration. "I was the youngest employee ever on the payroll of the City of New York," Katzenberg later said. As he gained influence and responsibility under Mayor Lindsay, he found it hard to go back to school and skipped college. "So in 1973, [I] found myself working for Barry Diller as his assistant, go-fer, at Paramount." Katzenberg said Diller was the most important mentor of his career. "He took this incredible interest in me and invested in me and moved me from department to department so that I really learned the business. Nobody does that anymore."[504]

Katzenberg said it was a very different time in the movie business than today. "The studios were becoming stronger again, the types of films were very diverse and there was much more personalization in terms of films and filmmakers. You know, these three kids walked in my office one day when I was at Paramount and projected a little film on my wall and talked about a movie called *Zero Hour* and how they wanted to make a parody of it. And that turned into *Airplane.*"[505]

In 1980, Paramount promoted Katzenberg to senior vice president of production under Don Simpson, and then in 1982, he was promoted to president. "When Jeffrey stepped into Don's job, it became a very different place. Very locked down. Jeffrey really wasn't a story guy but he knew that notes were important. So I worked very closely with Jeffrey then on notes," said Paramount story editor David Kirkpatrick.

Around the time of the *Popeye-Dragonslayer* deal in 1980, Michael Eisner also joined the board of CalArts. He called it a "refreshing contrast" to the intensity of the movie business.[506] He soon got to know both Roy E. Disney and Diane Disney Miller, who were also members of the board. Diane and Michael's wife Jane joined forces to help plan a benefit for the Los Angeles Children's Museum, which coincided with *Popeye*'s premiere at Mann's Chinese Theatre.[507] All fifteen hundred guests were invited to walk the red carpet, including the many children in attendance. Thanks to Paramount, the list of A-list attendees was starrier than the usual Disney premieres of the age: Barry Diller, Cheryl Tiegs, *Popeye* producer Bob Evans, Ali MacGraw, Cher, Hugh Hefner, Peter Falk, Neil Diamond, James Caan, Henry Winkler, Marsha Mason, Neil Simon, and of course Robin Williams, Shelley Duvall, and Robert Altman.[508]

When Disney released *Popeye* overseas, the film was trimmed to reduce its musical elements.[509] *Popeye* did better-than-remembered business, but cemented Altman's reputation as a rogue director who didn't work well within the studio system. Going into the 1980s, Paramount decided to deemphasize the riskier success factors of 1970s Hollywood—namely, the whims of iconoclasts and critics—and instead focused on the surefire combination of glamorous young stars and popular music. The Paramount of Diller, Eisner, and Katzenberg was redefining success in the movie business while Disney was struggling to keep up.

Chapter 15

In the summer of 1981, Diane Disney Miller decided to host a CalArts fundraiser at the Disney lot to coincide with the release of *The Fox and the Hound*. Jane Eisner joined in on the planning. Instead of a formal black-tie gala, they organized a Western-themed benefit. Among the people reportedly in attendance were Robert Blake, Universal's Lew Wasserman, 1920s star Rudy Vallée, and John F. Kennedy Jr.[510] The last of the Nine Old Men who had worked on *The Fox and the Hound*—Woolie, Frank, Ollie, Eric—smiled, standing alongside the emerging generation of new animators.[511] Guests were treated to midway-style games, cold chicken, roast beef, cookies, and popcorn. Tim Burton won a stuffed Bambi doll playing the milk can toss. Ron Miller sat in a dunk tank and was a good sport when onlookers hit a bullseye, getting him soaking wet. Some of the junior animators were invited to draw caricatures of the guests. It was the epitome of "Downhome Disney" – an intangible kind of handspun magic.

Sue Mantle DiCicco and Mike Gabriel were now officemates on the first floor of the Animation Building. As Mike recalled it, "Sue volunteered [for the party], typical fearless Sue, and she duded up: straw cowgirl hat, cowgirl boots, plaid shirt and tight jeans. As I toiled away in our shared office working on my scene after hours the evening of the wrap party, I heard some boots clicking down the hallway. Sue opened the door and had a nice gin and tonic cocktail for me that she had brought all the way from the free bar at the party." After that night, Sue and Mike dated for a while. "We got along really well and enjoyed the same sense of humor," Mike said. Although they eventually broke up, office romances were not uncommon at Disney Animation. Some led to lifelong relationships, including that of Jerry Rees and Rebecca Lodolo Rees.

A very different office pairing—one that was purely professional—was happening elsewhere in the Animation building. Tim Burton and a new recruit from West Germany, Andreas Deja, were put in a room together to help develop concept art for *Cauldron*. Andreas had grown up loving *The Jungle Book* and was greatly influenced by the work of Milt Kahl. He knew he wanted to work at Disney and when he heard they were making *Cauldron*, he read Lloyd Alexander's books and began sketching characters for the film. The Disney style just seemed to come naturally to Andreas. He submitted his *Cauldron* work to Disney and was hired in 1980. "One of the problems was there was no one there that really did the Disney style characters," said Joe Hale. "Until Ed Hansen brought in a portfolio of Andreas Deja, and I looked at his drawings and boy, he had the Disney style right down pat. And I said, 'Get the kid over here. He's ready to go. Hire him right now.'"

Years later, Andreas wrote that he and Tim got along well, but their design approaches were radically different. Andreas's *Cauldron* characters looked traditionally "Disney," even becoming more homogenized once he arrived in Burbank. On the other hand, Tim's designs—more than three hundred total pieces of concept art—were strange and otherworldly. Ron Magliozzi, who organized the first major exhibit of Tim's art for New York's Museum of Modern Art in 2009, said Tim's *Black Cauldron* concepts were the first important body of his professional work. "We can do a whole show on [just] *Black Cauldron*.... Every single piece is worthy of exhibition. Some day, I'm sure someone will do it." Magliozzi says many of Tim's signature themes as an artist were explored in those *Cauldron* concepts: his use of black and white, creatures as characters, and body modification. "There's a lot of sexual energy and frustration in *The Black Cauldron* stuff. I find it very erotic," referring to

Tim's use of body modification. "It's probably one reason they thought it was not Disney like."

Jorgen Klubien, whose many credits for Disney include *The Nightmare Before Christmas*, said, "[Tim] has like the sweet Disney-esque take on the old Universal horror movies. That's basically Tim's genius."

Tim's colleagues at the time remember his exploration of the villainous Horned King. In some of Tim's concepts, the character is fighting a losing battle with his mental health—listening to hand puppets, who are offering competing advice; as he becomes more insane, his horns grow and multiply. Tim's concept for the three witches in the film had them morph into a table-and-chairs set. His peers loved his wildly imaginative art. However, management felt it was too idiosyncratic to replicate.

A compromise was proposed to have Andreas try to "Disney-fy" Tim's work, but the resulting work lost the appeal of Tim's art. Andreas would go on to become one of the most famous animators of the Disney renaissance, supervising villains like Gaston, Jafar, and Scar. He later said, "I can't help imagining what I would do today with Tim's concept in animation. I think I would go to town and have a ton of fun."[512]

Disney began assembling the voice cast for *The Black Cauldron*. For the villainous Horned King, Disney hired Oscar-nominated British actor John Hurt (*Midnight Express*, *The Elephant Man*) who was also starring in Disney's Cold War thriller *Night Crossing* (1982), based on the real-life story of two East German families who escape Communism in a hot-air balloon. Hurt was enthusiastic about *The Black Cauldron*. In a 1982 interview, he said, "Just looking at the sketches and what little footage has already been accomplished has excited me [to] no end, and even my wife doesn't recognize the sound I make in it."[513]

For the role of the young hero Taran, Disney selected teen actor Grant Bardsley. Casting young teenagers on a multiyear production was always a risky proposition since puberty could wreak havoc on the recording process—a problem that plagued Disney's *The Sword in the Stone* (1963). Disney reached out to an acting teacher who worked with Grant's mother Pennie to make sure his voice hadn't changed since his audition. Pennie assured her colleague that Grant's voice was "still very light" and he was hired. Grant began recording when he was thirteen and finished three years later—miraculously, his voice remained consistent throughout the process. Grant and Pennie flew from the U.K. to Los Angeles every Easter break and summer vacation to record his dialogue. Grant proved to be a quick study, nailing most of his reads quickly—as long as it didn't involve stage laughter, which was his weakness.

"They bent over backwards to make sure we had a good time," said Grant's mother Pennie. "I don't think we paid for a meal." As their visits continued, the studio agreed to fly the whole family over so Grant and his siblings could visit Disneyland.

As the only member of the cast or crew in the film's target demographic, Grant thought the film "was wonderful but as a thirteen-year-old to sixteen-year-old, I probably would not have gone to see it myself because I wasn't into fantasy. Strangely enough at that time, I was much more of a *Star Wars* kid as were the kids I knew," said Grant. Still, he liked the film's darker elements. "John Hurt's voice was fantastic."

Grant recorded most of his lines playing against either his mother or the film's directors. Grant said director Art Stevens was a "great leonine bloke with a mane of white hair, very deep voice and very charming." Art and the other directors would play the scenes with "total commitment. It was fun to see them doing that." Still, Pennie sensed growing conflict at the recording sessions between Art Stevens and codirectors Ted Berman, Rick Rich, and producer Joe Hale. Art seemed to be pushing cuter, more traditionally Disney elements while the other filmmakers seemed committed to keeping a more consistently darker tone.

For the role of Princess Eilonwy, Disney was interested in bringing back former Disney child star Hayley Mills. They even filmed a 1981 television special where Mills visits the studio to speak with the filmmakers about the part. Ultimately though, British voice actress Susan Sheridan was cast as Eilonwy. "I think they really wanted someone like Hayley Mills to play the part," said Sheridan, "but she didn't sound like a child anymore." Even though Sheridan was just a year younger than Mills, her vocal performance was convincingly youthful. "When you play children's voices, no one should know you're an adult," said

Sheridan. In fact, her voice was so convincing that Disney was prepared to send a chaperone to bring her to the U.S. until she told them she was thirty-four. She tried to perform with a Welsh accent befitting the film's setting, but she quickly learned the filmmakers couldn't understand the dialect, so she instead settled on an upper middle-class British accent.

Rosemary Sisson sat in on recording sessions to smooth out the language barrier between the Brits and the Yanks—finding the right mix of phrases and pronunciations to please both audiences. A key word of concern was "bauble." In the U.K., the word "bobble" means pompom, so the preferred emphasis in the recording session was 'BAWH-ble'. (It would be Rosemary's last involvement with *Cauldron*; when she saw the film during a U.K. screening in October 1985, she was disappointed her credit was merely "additional dialogue," despite recognizing most of her storyline.)[514]

According to Pennie Bardsley, Wilfrid Hyde-White (Colonel Pickering in 1964's *My Fair Lady*) was originally set to play the wizard Dallben. She said Hyde-White was replaced after a recording session with Grant because his performance seemed to lack warmth. Producer Joe Hale asked Susan Sheridan if she could think of anyone to play the roles of Dallben as well as the bard Fflewddur Fflam. British actors Freddie Jones and Nigel Hawthorne were in town filming the Clint Eastwood film *Firefox* and staying at her hotel. They both were cast in *Cauldron* at Sheridan's suggestion.

For the role of the Horned King's reptilian henchman Creeper, Joe Hale auditioned a CalArts student named Phil Fondacaro. Phil was majoring in design, minoring in theater and music—a true multidisciplinarian, which would have made Walt proud. One of the animation students recommended Phil audition for the movie due to his unusual voice, which has a high-pitch growl. Phil didn't have professional experience and was very nervous until he saw the designs and got to know the character's manic but eager-to-please personality. "I love the film. I love the darker side," said Phil, who at 3' 6" categorizes himself as a little person. "It's more of a challenge to try and make 'little people' be evil, it's a little more difficult, a lot more challenging. I enjoy that challenge.

Creeper has been one of my pieces that I've been able to do that and pull it off." Phil Fondacaro went on to have a lengthy career in fantasy and horror films including *Return of the Jedi, Willow, Troll,* and the Disney television movie *Fuzzbucket.*

Rounding out the cast was comedian John Byner, who played two roles—the mischievous man-beast Gurgi and the grumpy fairy Doli. Byner was a regular presence on late-night television thanks to his vocal impersonations. For Gurgi, he played a version of his long-running, high-pitched character Felix Fossididdi. John was asked if he could come up with another voice for the smaller role of the fairy Doli. "I threw something at them and they liked it."

Originally rounding out the cast was comedian Jonathan Winters, in the role of King Eidilleg of the Fair Folk. Animator Ron Husband worked with director Art Stevens on the Fair Folk sequence and remembers one wonderful and riotous lunch where Jonathan Winters entertained them, grabbing Ron's sketchpad and doing his own drawings. Throughout *Cauldron's* development, the Fair Folk sequence threatened to be tonally incongruous with the rest of the film. Early designs had the fairies living in a Smurf village of mushroom houses. Later, a disco-era aesthetic creeped into the concept art. The version with Jonathan Winters, under the supervision of Art Stevens, would have presumably added some humor to the proceedings. Yet as funny as Winters was, Joe Hale was concerned his voice was too recognizable for adults in the audience. The episodic nature of the scene threatened to grind the story to a halt, and Winters' delivery made it feel like a different movie. Hale ultimately replaced Winters with character actor Arthur Malet and he overhauled the entire sequence, which was already partially animated.

John Musker was set to make his directorial debut as the fourth codirector on *Cauldron.* "I was at odds with some of the other directors who were in their 60s and whose sensibilities were different from mine, which is steeped in television, pop culture, Monty Python and fast-paced, improvisational Chicago humor. I was considered a malcontent."[515] Musker attempted to incorporate Tim Burton's outré designs into the film but ultimately failed. "I couldn't convince the powers that be that the Disney umbrella was broad enough that you could retain sincerity and conviction in the acting and the performances, but the characters didn't have to look a certain way."[516]

Glen Keane was working with Musker to make the film more surreal—including adding an M.C. Escher influence to the witches' sequence. "At a certain point, I remember Joe [Hale] said, 'Glen, I don't think we need you on this movie.' I said, 'Well, I think I can really contribute a lot in some way.'" Glen said Joe's reply was, "No, no, I don't think so." Recent CalArts graduate Mark Henn was surprised when he too found himself on the outs with *Cauldron*'s management without ever getting an explanation.

John Musker said he and animator/story artist Ron Clements "hated *Black Cauldron* and [management] hated everything we did on it. So we were banished."[517]

Ron Miller was concerned that some of Disney's most promising talent were being pulled off *Cauldron*. He felt artists should be reassigned to a different director before being pulled off the film, which he was concerned wasn't always happening.[518] He also began looking for other outlets to keep these exiled artists engaged, worried that more young people would depart. The first project for these other animators was *Mickey's Christmas Carol*, a holiday featurette directed by Burny Mattinson. It would be Mickey Mouse's first return to the big screen in thirty years and it became a showcase for animators Glen Keane, who animated Scrooge and (Willie the Giant as) the Ghost of Christmas Present, and Mark Henn, who was assigned to Mickey Mouse. Musker and Clements were assigned to start a new feature, *Basil of Baker Street*, which would later be renamed *The Great Mouse Detective*.

Perhaps burdened by its ambitions, production on *Cauldron* seemed to be embroiled in unintended conflict. Art Stevens had been excited for the film's climax, where he envisioned a danse macabre with the Horned King being pulled into the cauldron. However, Art's vacation coincided with one of John Hurt's semiannual vocal sessions so Joe Hale tweaked the scene to capitalize on Hurt's availability. Joe said, "I wrote some dialogue for that sequence, which was used in the final production, in case the danse macabre sequence didn't work out for us. Vance Gerry did some story sketches and the changes were cut into the work reel. When Art returned from vacation and found out that we had recorded this dialogue before I had the opportunity to explain to him the reason I did this, he found out about it, he got very upset with me and decided to retire." Joe said other factors played into Art's decision including his age and health, as he had suffered a series of small strokes before the vacation. "After he retired, I invited him to the studio for lunch and screened the picture for him and he forgave me and we remained friends after that," said Joe. Art's sudden departure left Ted Berman and Rick Rich as the film's two credited directors.

Despite the turmoil, other artists made a sincere effort to elevate *Cauldron*. Animator Phil Nibbelink and layout artist Guy Vasilovich were given free rein to come up with a thrilling action sequence where the hero Taran is trying to save his pig Hen Wen from flying dragonlike Gwythaints. "Ted Berman, who was the director, just kind of left Guy and I alone for a year," said Phil. "We just threw everything we had at it, just went crazy trying to make it as punchy as we could." They used hand-drawn animated backgrounds to give the scene a visceral quality. Like the bear fight in *The Fox and the Hound*, it aimed to bring modern cinematic language to Disney Animation. "Animated backgrounds were certainly nothing new. I mean, they were doing animated backgrounds back in the earliest days of *Plane Crazy* and *Steamboat Willie*.... Back in the day, it was sort of a new and wild thing that we were doing," added Phil.

"We spent six months just doing that one sequence," said animator Lenord Robinson, who worked with Phil on the Gwythaint chase. "While it's a very short sequence, it definitely was something the picture needed."

To blow off steam on *The Black Cauldron*, the young crew found new ways to entertain themselves. "One of the all-time funniest things we would do in the early eighties was what we called The Eddie Shows," Mike Gabriel explained. Artist Mike Giaimo had gotten hold of life-size cardboard cutouts of 1950s and '60s stars like Marlon Brando, Doris

Day, Zsa Zsa Gabor, and Eddie Fisher. Each cutout had a mouth that could be made to look like it was moving. "Mike [Giaimo] had a speaker box outside his office window playing loudly to all employees walking into work past his office, an old record of Howard Keel and Ethel Merman singing "Anything You Can Do I Can Do Better." He had set up the two cutouts of Eddie Fisher and Doris Day and was [puppeteering] their mouths to the words of the song. Rapid fire. "No you can't." "Yes I can." "No you can't." "Yes I can." It was hilarious and got a great reaction from all of us. I was dumbstruck at how funny and quirky cool that worked." The Eddie Show became a semiannual event, with Fourth of July editions, Christmas engagements, and even a *Sound of Music* edition with Doris Day as Maria. "John Lasseter would work the line gathered around the window, hand out showtime pamphlets, and set up a video and shoot each performance. We had so much fun creating these Mickey and Judy type simple prop shows each season.... Honestly, the spirit of just creating a fun show together and putting some real effort into the entertainment value of each song, each prop, each new idea.... I remember driving home every year on the long LA freeway drive to Huntington Beach for Christmas at home, always right after the Eddie Show was over and always feeling sad that I have to leave my studio life for a week. I felt more like I was leaving my family, not going to see my family," said Mike Gabriel. That sense of family extended beyond the workplace as the artists chose to spend their time off with each other, going on trips together to Lake Tahoe or the Grand Canyon.

Like some of his peers, Tim Burton's time on *Cauldron* also ended in frustration. His designs for the dragon-like Gwythaints imagined the creatures' heads as hands, which could detach themselves from their bodies. It proved to be the straw that broke the camel's back.[519] Mike Gabriel said director Art Stevens insulted Tim by drawing a line and on one end was Tim and on the other was Andreas Deja. He made a mark near Andreas' side and said, "This is where we are going to be going with the designs for the film, Tim, you need to start thinking in that regard." Andreas' designs would be the ones which influenced the film.

According to the daughter of *Black Cauldron* codirector Ted Berman, he too told Tim that "he was way too talented to be there at Disney. He had such a unique style and such a unique talent that he needed to be making his own films."

Tim's colleagues remember his dejection when he was moved off *Cauldron* after a year of work. "It's like letting him really find his true self and then telling him that that's not a good thing is awful," said Jerry Rees. Nevertheless, Tim Burton was able to look back at the unusual opportunity he had and acknowledge its importance to his development. In 2013, he told *The Hollywood Reporter* that "to be left in a weird vacuum was great for me—slightly frustrating. It was still amazing.... I got to sit in a room for a year and just draw things for *Black Cauldron*—whatever I wanted to draw.... Even though it was a strange time in the company's history, I got a lot of interesting, strange opportunities to just explore things."[520]

Tim's art had caught the attention of Ron Miller's VP of creative development Tom Wilhite, a small-town Iowa native now in his late twenties. Wilhite gave Tim the chance to develop new projects for Disney: a stop-motion short *Vincent*, a Disney Channel show *Hansel and Gretel*, the live-action featurette *Frankenweenie*, and some early ideas that would lead to *Tim Burton's The Nightmare Before Christmas*. Wilhite came to Disney in the late '70s, after being plucked from obscurity to handle PR for Groucho Marx.[521] He had also managed *Rocky*'s underdog Oscar campaign.[522] When he came to Disney, he ran the 1978 campaign around Mickey Mouse's fiftieth birthday—which the company decided would officially be celebrated on November 18, the release date of *Steamboat Willie*.[523] But Wilhite was more than a PR flack. He was a risk-taking creative executive, willing to take leaps of faith on untested projects and raw talent, including Tim Burton and John Lasseter. He became the architect of Ron Miller's strategy of winning back younger audiences.

"I give so much credit to Tom Wilhite, a young man who came out of publicity, who brought a number of films to my attention. And he was right on," said Ron Miller. "I had a lot of respect for Tom."

Tom's biggest claim to fame would be greenlighting *Tron*. The film was the brainchild of independent animator Steve Lisberger and became a groundbreaking work featuring Jeff Bridges, but its real star was its effects—the most extensive use of computer animation at the time. "I give a tremendous amount of credit of my doing *Tron* to Tom Wilhite," said Ron. Jerry Rees and fellow Disney animator Bill Kroyer joined the film to help storyboard its computer animation. According to Jerry, Steve would later say his purpose in making *Tron* was to neutralize the threat of computers being used as instruments of war, by instead pushing their development toward artistic expression.

"It was such a handcrafted film. Even though computers were involved, we had to lead the computer by the hand for every frame. I even did stop-motion for some of the computer animation scenes to get the motion to work," Jerry said.

"*Tron* certainly had some serious breakthroughs, but they were on the bleeding edge of what the technology could do. I remember the big computerized face in the movie took a supercomputer to create—you could probably do the same thing on a cell phone today. All of the light cycles were hand drawn in 3D space. There was no software to do any of that at the time," said David Mattingly who also worked on the film. For a time, it seemed *Tron* was the live-action film that could change Disney's fortunes with movie audiences.

In July 1982, just days before *Tron* opened in theaters, an analyst working for Montgomery Securities told clients to sell Disney stock. He had just seen a preview screening for the new film and felt it was a "seriously flawed disjointed story" and spoke negatively about the computer animation.[524] *Tron* was prejudged to be a disappointment and a sign that Disney was not able to turn around its film department. *Tron* was in trouble before its opening weekend.

Disney ended up taking a $10 million write-off on *Tron*.[525] *Tron* may have lost money, but it helped Disney make some inroads with the young adult demographic Ron had been chasing. Over time, *Tron*'s pioneering effects earned it new fans and it continues to be a property that Disney revisits in its parks and films.

Disney had two takeaways from *Tron*. The first was the importance of a high-quality big-screen experience during the rise of home video. 70 mm film releases—often paired with Dolby sound—were boosting the box office of 1982's summer films. Movies as disparate as *Star Trek II: The Wrath of Khan* and *Annie* earned 20 percent of their revenue from just a few dozen high-end prints; the same was true for *Tron*, which had forty-three prints in 70 mm.[526] Second, *Tron* had a popular arcade game, which *The Arizona Daily Star* called a representation of the video game "at its most sophisticated, complex, varied and challenging."[527] It helped keep *Tron* relevant among gamers. Learning lessons from *Tron*, Disney decided to release *The Black Cauldron* in 70 mm and work with Sierra Games to create an adventure-style computer game based on the film, giving Sierra's video game designer Al Lowe the creative freedom to develop the game how he saw fit.

Just weeks after *Tron* opened, Don Bluth released his first feature, *The Secret of NIMH*. It had been nearly three years since he left Disney. "The critical reception was great," said *NIMH* producer John Pomeroy. "The financial one was a tragedy. MGM did not understand how to market an animated feature film." He called *NIMH*'s inability to find a theatrical audience an "absolute heartbreak," given how much their group had risked with their high-profile departure.

That summer, both *Tron* and *The Secret of NIMH* were competing against Steven Spielberg's *E.T. the Extra-Terrestrial*, one of the most critically acclaimed and commercially successful family movies ever released. Adjusted for inflation, *E.T.* is still the fourth-highest grossing movie of all time and was the top-grossing film of the 1980s.[528] It cemented Spielberg's reputation as the most powerful brand in Hollywood, and he was hailed as the new Walt Disney.

A few weeks after *NIMH*'s disappointing release, John, Don, and Gary got a call from Spielberg. "I want to come over and meet you guys," he told the trio, according to John. "I can't believe what you guys did. I thought this art form was dead." At the end of a three-hour meeting, Spielberg told them he wanted to find a property they could collaborate on. They eventually settled on a story of a Jewish family of mice fleeing

Russia and immigrating to America, called *An American Tail* (1986). The CalArtians may have dismissed Don Bluth as a Walt wannabe, but their hero Steven Spielberg chose him as his first collaborator in the field of animation.

As production on *The Black Cauldron* seemed to be hitting its stride in the summer of 1982, the union representing the animators went on strike. The primary target was not Disney, but producers of Saturday morning cartoons who were sending work overseas to save money, but the whole industry was impacted. "I could see the writing on the wall," said *Cauldron* cel painter Carolyn Guske, who had also worked at Filmation. "Stuff was going overseas and we were losing our jobs."

The strike's impact on the Disney staff varied greatly. When Ruben Aquino joined the animation training program weeks before the strike, he initially felt intimidated by the talent of his peers. He used the strike to improve his rough animation tests. Some animators claimed "Financial Core" status, a loophole that allowed them to return to work.[529] On the other hand, animator Cyndee Whitney was increasingly worried about her financial well-being. She had a young son, whom she hoisted up in the backyard to use as reference for *Cauldron*'s Fair Folk sequence. As the strike dragged into its ninth week, Whitney reached a breaking point. "I was about to lose my house," she said. Whitney was trying to hold strong but at the next union meeting, she told a local television reporter, "I want to go back to work," echoing the waning morale of strikers. The strike ended the following Monday. Coming just a year after President Reagan weakened the dominance of organized labor by firing eleven thousand striking air traffic controllers, the animation strike was settled without the guarantee to protect U.S. jobs. It also forced Disney to shuffle its release schedule, pushing *Mickey's Christmas Carol* to December 1983[530] and contributing to *The Black Cauldron*'s ballooning budget.[531]

In October 1982, the same month the animation strike ended, Disney finally opened EPCOT Center at Walt Disney World. It was Walt's last major dream to come to fruition. Walt envisioned EPCOT as a utopian city—an answer to the urban decay of the 1960s, but also an attempt to make a better world for his family. One of Walt's unlikely inspirations for EPCOT was Ron and Diane's former neighborhood near Ventura Boulevard, where a nearby vacant lot was littered with debris. Diane later told an interviewer, "He saw no reason why things shouldn't be maintained at the most attractive level and be functional."[532] Yet over the course of the 1970s and without Walt's guidance, the plans for EPCOT became less of a community and more of a permanent world's fair. At a cost of $1 billion, it was a big, bold addition to the Disney portfolio, with pavilions featuring future technologies and cultures from around the world. In April 1982, Ron told a group of investors that EPCOT would turn Walt Disney World, already the top vacation destination in the world, from a two- or three-day destination to one where visitors would spend a full week; it ultimately changed how many people vacation.[533] When EPCOT opened six months later, Walt Disney World attendance jumped more than 80 percent in its first year of operation.[534]

In Search of Excellence is widely considered to be one of the most influential business books published in the last half century. Released in 1982, the bestseller looks at best practices across top companies. In the book, Disney managers are praised for their human touch. It quotes marketing executive Red Pope, who studied the company and said, "How Disney looks upon people, internally and externally, handles them, communicates with them, rewards them, is in my view the basic foundation upon which its five decades of success stand.... I have come to observe closely and with reverence the theory and practice of selling satisfaction and serving millions of people on a daily basis successfully. It is what Disney does best."[535]

Walt Disney Productions had learned many lessons from the aftermath of Walt's passing. Perhaps the most important was the need to have an orderly line of succession in its executive ranks. With EPCOT fulfilling the last of Walt's ambitions, Card Walker was ready to turn over Walt Disney Productions to Ron Miller. In February 1983, Ron Miller was elected chief executive officer of Walt Disney Productions—a planned handoff from Card Walker, who would step down after the April opening of Tokyo Disneyland, the first overseas Disney theme park.[536] Three years earlier, Walker inherited the role from Donn Tatum who stepped down as CEO, also at the age of sixty-seven.[537] Ron Miller was finally at the helm of the company Walt said he would someday run.

Ron partnered with Ray Watson, who had been a company director since the mid-1970s and would serve as chairman of the board. If age were the only factor, Ron would perhaps be running the company until he turned sixty-seven in the year 2000; the new millennium was seventeen years away but seemed much farther in the future. With Ron now in control, he was free to steer the company into modernity.

Months after assuming the role of CEO, Ron laid out his philosophy and goals for the company in an op-ed for *Variety*, which was celebrating its fiftieth anniversary as Disney was celebrating its sixtieth. His vision was deeply rooted in the values established by Walt and Roy while very much focused on the future. He knew the electronic revolution was shifting the ground underneath Hollywood, but he believed Disney was well positioned to meet the moment. He wrote, "...All technology can do is change the systems of delivering the entertainment, not the entertainment itself. Clothes, cars, gadgets and lifestyles have changed over the years, but emotions have not and entertainment plays to the emotions. People want to laugh, to cry, to love and that's the heart of our business."[538]

Ron knew the Disney name evoked a deep emotional connection with its audience around the world. "It's a public trust we cherish and one we would never violate." Yet, he also explained the establishment of a second film label to release more mature movies, which would broaden Disney's audience. He touted Disney's efforts to engage in emerging sectors including cable television, home video, video games, and computer software while still investing in feature films and television. He explained how the Animation Department, now double in size, would increase its output to one film every other year. That would soon yield results such as *The Black Cauldron*, *The Great Mouse Detective*, and the live-action/ animated film *Who Framed Roger Rabbit*, for which Ron had secured the story rights in 1981.[539] He cited advancements in filmmaking technology used for EPCOT Center—experimental techniques involving the use of 3D technology and computer animation—which could also be used in upcoming feature films. He was proud of the new subscriber-driven Disney Channel, which thanks to three hundred thousand customers and a reach of nearly one thousand cable systems across eight million homes, he called "the single most successful launch in the history of pay television." The fact that 20 percent of Disney Channel subscribers didn't have children under thirteen showed its appeal beyond young kids. He concluded the piece saying, "The name Disney plays a prominent role in every facet of the entertainment business and I'm proud to say that we've been pioneers in many of them, and still are. So, as in the past, we're prepared for the future and whatever it has to offer. I'm confident 50 years from now, a successor of mine will be just as enthusiastic in the 100th anniversary edition of *Daily Variety*—in whatever form it is then appearing."[540]

Chapter 16

Ron Miller had spent the better part of the early 1980s experimenting with films he thought could appeal to modern audiences. He decided to release a teen comedy *Midnight Madness* (1980) without the Disney label. The 1983 Margot Kidder spy caper *Trenchcoat* also tried to downplay its Disney connection. *The Devil and Max Devlin* (1981), starring Bill Cosby and Elliott Gould, was a PG-comedy about Satan. 1982's *Tex*, based on S.E. Hinton's novel and starring Matt Dillon, was a PG-rated mature teen drama. They all failed at the box office though *Tex* earned some critical acclaim. In the wake of these and other disappointments like *Night Crossing* (1982) and *Something Wicked This Way Comes* (1983), Ron Miller and Disney desperately needed a hit.

Disney's experiments with attracting mature audiences were about to finally turn a corner with the unlikely live-action hit *Never Cry Wolf*. The film was based on Farley Mowat's 1963 book and had a script by screenwriters Jay Presson Allen (*Cabaret*), and Curtis Hanson (*L.A. Confidential*). However, it was director Carroll Ballard who was the real star of the film for Ron. "Without him, it had a chance of being a typical commercial picture," Ron said. "But with his particular genius, the beautiful stylized look he brings, it can be much more."[541] Ballard had just completed his masterpiece *The Black Stallion* for United Artists. Ron was impressed by *Stallion* and wished it had been a Disney release.[542] To attract Ballard for *Never Cry Wolf*, Ron agreed to do something unusual for Disney. He stepped back and gave Ballard total control of the production.[543] It was the way the rest of Hollywood had treated major directors since the late 1960s. However, Ballard's *Never Cry Wolf* would stretch Disney's patience in the three years it took to complete.

While Ballard was developing the film at Disney in 1980, he met animator Glen Keane, who was a big fan of *The Black Stallion*. Glen asked Ballard about the bear fight scene he was animating and asked Ballard how he would improve it. Ballard indicated he'd animate it from three different angles. The specifics of Ballard's suggestion would have been painstakingly difficult in animation, but the advice gave Glen "the feeling that there was this freeform approach that Carroll approached his directing. So I did a lot of exploring and thumbnailing, then committed to movement from one shot to the next." Glen said Ballard helped him think cinematically to realize the scene's kinetic potential.

Unlike in animation, it's harder to control nature in live action filmmaking. Set in the Canadian Arctic, *Never Cry Wolf* culminates in a scene where hundreds of caribou are herded by wolves. It is a dramatic piece of filmmaking, but it proved to be incredibly hard to shoot. Ballard, like the film's character, found himself stuck between the whims of nature and the greed of animal poachers. He was given just eleven days to film with a herd of domesticated reindeer before their antlers would be harvested and sold overseas as aphrodisiacs. The reindeer ran away on the first day of shooting and didn't return before the antler harvesters wanted them back. Ballard would have to wait until the following year when the right conditions returned to get another chance at completing the scene—at a cost of $50,000 a day.[544]

Ballard came home from Canada in the summer of 1981 and began assembling a cut of the film that ran about five hours. He whittled it down to three and a half hours before screening it for Disney executives. "I guess it was at the end of that screening that I realized that this was not going to be a smooth flight," Ballard told *The New York Times Magazine*, which chronicled the film's troubled postproduction.[545] Presumably, much of that first cut was silent since the main character is alone for long stretches, so Ballard went back to add narration and remove another hour.[546] He continued to play with the film's editing throughout 1982, but it continued to get negative audience response.[547] Ron told Ballard that if he wasn't finished with a suitable cut of the film by January 1983, he'd take the film away from him.[548] With his back against the wall, Ballard needed a new path forward. He found inspiration from a demo album of ambient jazz music called *Vapor Drawings*, by musician Mark Isham.[549] Isham was hired to create a score that fused native Alaskan and new age music. The haunting score created an isolating yet inspiring ambiance to match the mood of the film. *Never Cry Wolf* now miraculously began to click with audiences. *Never Cry Wolf* was originally budgeted at about $5 million, but by the time it was completed three and a half years later, it had cost about $12 million.[550]

Disney had to be careful with the film's marketing. If animals featured too prominently, people could mistake it for a Disney nature documentary. If it overemphasized Disney's name, it could seem like a kid's film. The lead actor Charles Martin Smith was not a big star who could draw an audience. Instead, the poster for *Never Cry Wolf* shows Smith against the Alaska landscape, binoculars in hand. The poster also carries a fifty-word description explaining the Lupine Project—the real-life premise of the film. Remarkably, it worked. *Never Cry Wolf* was arguably the best reviewed Disney movie since Walt had died and it became a sleeper hit—earning more than $27 million over the course of its run.[551] It was the proof Ron had been waiting for. The public was ready for a new kind of Disney movie.

Ron decided it was time to introduce his concept for an alternate movie label to release different kinds of films. "I bit the bullet," Ron said. He replaced Tom Wilhite with Dick Berger from 20th Century Fox. "I said, 'Dick, we've got to stand up. What we've got to do is come up with a system that we can tell all those people out there that are true Disney diehards that we're going to continue making the product, the Disney product as we have in the past, but we are going to let them know in certain cases, we are going to embark on making films that are going to appeal to a much broader audience. We will put our own label on it'—which was Touchstone. And in some cases, if not all cases, it's probably going to have a PG rating, but that's telegraphing to you people [that] there might be something in that film that is outside of the typical Disney film.' The first film that we did was *Splash*."

The director attached to *Splash* was a former child actor who had worked with Ron Miller at Disney years earlier. Ronnie Howard, the teenage star of Disney's *The Wild Country*, was now the up-and-coming director Ron Howard of *Night Shift*. (Even after the future Oscar-winning director became one of the most famous filmmakers in the world, Ron Miller would continue to refer to him as "Ronnie" for decades to come.) *Splash* is a literal fish-out-of-water romantic comedy about a New York bachelor who falls in love with a mermaid. Ron really liked the script and he went next door to Dick Berger's office to discuss greenlighting this mermaid comedy.

Ron said, "Dick, I'm reading a damn property here that I really think is phenomenal. And we've got Ronnie Howard who'd direct it. It could be our first Touchstone film.'"

Dick wasn't sold. "Ron, I gotta be honest. I saw that at 20th Century Fox and I turned it down."

"Well, I think maybe you should really read it again. I'm strongly in favor."

After rereading the script, Dick threw his support behind the project. Ron remembered Dick saying, "'If you want to go with it, let's go. I'll support it a hundred percent. It's a good film. It's got a good team,' Brian Glazer and Ronnie Howard. So we went forward and it became a Touchstone film." *Splash* began filming in April 1983,[552] with a cast that included Daryl Hannah as the mermaid Madison, John Candy and Eugene Levy in supporting comic roles, and a television actor who had yet to star in a major film—Tom Hanks.

If Touchstone were to succeed, Ron Miller knew he needed the support of Disney shareholders. In February 1984, the annual stockholders meeting was held at Walt Disney World in Florida. Several hundred people were in attendance as Ron addressed the group.[553] "I explained that we had done a film directed by Ronnie Howard and it's a little bit off color. It has to appeal to a broader audience. I said, 'We're going to run it for you right afterwards. And I will be in the reception room and if you want to complain, if you want to hit me over the head, I'm there.' And I was there. The screening went so well. I knew it was a winner." He says of the three thousand people who were there, only two came up to him to express any reservations about the film.

When *Splash* opened on March 9, 1984, it was the long-awaited game changer Ron needed. It was one of the top ten highest-grossing movies of 1984[554] and launched Tom Hanks's career as one of the world's top movie stars. *Splash* was also nominated for a Golden Globe for Best Picture—Musical or Comedy, as well as an Academy Award for Best Screenplay. It is also credited with popularizing the girl's name Madison, based on Daryl Hannah's character.[555]

Despite *Splash*'s success, the original goal for Touchstone was not to churn out comedies. When Disney took out full-page ads in newspapers across the country to explain what Touchstone was, it promoted the label in this way: "All across America, moviegoers want mature entertainment. But they don't want violence. They don't want exploitation. They don't want tasteless themes. They want quality. They want standards...while Walt Disney Pictures will continue to create *timeless* classics, our new TOUCHSTONE Films will create *timely* entertainment. Films about contemporary romances. Social issues that shape American values. Exciting adventure movies. Family dramas. And more."[556] The first film mentioned in the ad was not *Splash*, but *Country*. *Country* was actress Jessica Lange's passion project, which she brought to Disney in 1983. She had just won the Supporting Actress Oscar that year for *Tootsie* and was also nominated for Lead Actress in *Frances*. A double Oscar nomination in a single year is a rare phenomenon, and at the time of Lange's win, it hadn't happened in forty years—not for Bette Davis, Katherine Hepburn, or Meryl Streep. That recognition gave Lange considerable clout in the industry and she used it to not only star in *Country* but produce it.

Lange was inspired to make the film after reading about farmers impacted by the economic recession of the early 1980s, and seeing parallels to the Great Depression. "I had an idea—not even a story, just a concept. I couldn't even articulate it," Lange told an interviewer. "Of course, when you're hot, you don't have to articulate."[557] Lange was indeed hot within the industry. She had earned considerable respect for her acting abilities and her romance with playwright Sam Shepard drew comparisons to Marilyn Monroe and playwright Arthur Miller.[558] Lange and Shepard fell in love on the set of *Frances*, and the pair would be appearing together as costars in *Country*.

While shooting the film in Iowa—away from the glare of Hollywood—Lange and Shepard began to imagine a more conventional life together. He proposed marriage to her in the wintry climate of Waterloo. He described the proposal like this: "I swept her outside into the cold wind & snow & popped the question. We jumped up & down together like little kids, giggling in the snow."[559] (Lange and Shepard were partners for more than twenty-five years and had two children together, though they never officially married).

Whereas other real-life screen couples sometimes use the intrigue surrounding their relationship to further their own celebrity, Lange and Shepard were more interested in drawing attention to the ongoing farm crisis of the 1980s, the worst economic catastrophe to hit American farmers since the Great Depression.[560] The roots of the farm crisis began in the late 1970s, when the Fed began raising interest rates to battle high inflation.[561] The situation got worse when the Soviet Union invaded Afghanistan, and in retaliation, President Carter imposed a grain embargo. Some believe that move may have ultimately damaged American farmers more than the Soviets.[562] Overnight, some U.S. farmers found themselves with harvested crops that could no longer go overseas, while the U.S.S.R. looked to Ukraine and other parts of the world to replace U.S. commodities.[563] President Reagan ended the embargo after taking office,[564] but interest rates continued to soar, while land values and commodity prices fell. Many farmers, especially in Iowa, found themselves overleveraged. The bottom fell out when the USDA's Farmers Home Administration (FmHA), which had previously provided FmHA loans to riskier lenders, began foreclosing on hundreds of farms.[565] This was the backdrop against which *Country* was set.

Country was not an easy shoot. Production was halted after a couple weeks of shooting in Iowa, when Lange realized her vision for the film didn't match that of director/writer William Wittliff. "Jessica just didn't like what she was seeing in the dailies," Shepard told an interviewer.[566] Lange replaced Wittliff with Richard Pearce, who had cut his teeth as a cinematographer on documentaries like *Woodstock* and *Hearts and Minds*.[567]

She explained the decision by saying, "Two people see something entirely differently. It's amazing. You're running on parallel lines.... At a certain point, there was no coming together anymore. Communication just kind of fell apart."[568]

Country resumed filming at the end of October 1983, near the end of the harvest season. The delay and subsequent reshoots cost Disney an extra $2 million, bringing the cost of *Country* to $10 million.[569] The additional time in Iowa allowed Lange and Shepard to have a lived experience there, observing the plight of the farmers and the impact of the crisis on the wider community. Given Iowa's economic crisis, it may be encouraging to hear that half of the film's budget was going toward the local economy[570]—a case where Hollywood excess was improving the lives of people in need.

Extensive changes were made to the script, cutting expository dialogue and reducing Wilford Brimley's role as Lange's father. More agency was also given to Lange's character.[571] Shepard was reported to have handled most of the rewrites.[572] Disney stuck by Lange through all the changes, even though when Ron Miller visited the set, he found Shepard to be "very aloof" toward him.

Some of the film was shot back on the Disney lot in Burbank. Effects animator Esther Barr remembers walking through a soundstage made to resemble Iowa cornfields—presumably for a scene where the family is caught in a tornado. "That was really wild to walk into a soundstage and just have rows and rows of corn," Barr remembered. "I was pretty excited to be working on the lot."

Country was in production at the same time as two similarly themed movies: *The River* about struggling farmers in Tennessee, and *Places in the Heart*, set in Texas during the Great Depression. Lange and Disney decided to move up the release date of *Country* to stay competitive against these other movies.[573] Nevertheless, critics began to lump these three together as "save the farm" movies.[574]

Country was the capstone in Ron Miller's efforts to make serious, mature movies. If the complaint about Disney post-1966 was that the company was hampered by a "what would Walt do?" mentality, *Country* disproved that. It was not a film Walt would do; it was the film Walt could *never* do. It was the contemporary social issues picture he worried would alienate audiences, with content too dark and too political for Walt. It was Disney's *To Kill a Mockingbird*.

As if to drive home the point that *Country* was not a standard Disney film, the opening sequence features both a teenager's unused condom and a cereal bowl with Looney Tunes characters.

Despite Richard Pearce's documentary background, *Country* doesn't quite match the authenticity of something like the Italian neorealist films shot against the ruins of postwar Europe, but it did try to capture what was happening on the ground in Iowa in its own Hollywood way. The film's climax shows an auction where the townspeople refuse to buy the family's repossessed assets; it mirrors similar protests that happened throughout the country in the 1980s.[575] The scene strives for a documentary-style vérité.

Country also doesn't shy away from the ways the farm crisis was causing mental health problems for families dealing with the loss of their homes and careers. In the film, viewers see Sam Shepard's character descend into alcoholism and domestic violence, while their friend dies by suicide after losing his family's farm. During an eighteen-month period from 1983 to 1985, a survey covering a third of Iowa counties found at least eleven farm-related suicides and 256 foreclosures.[576] A study of just five states (Wisconsin, Minnesota, North Dakota, South Dakota, and Montana) showed more than nine hundred farmers died by suicide over the course of the farm crisis.[577]

Still, the film sparked debate about how realistic its portrayal of farming was. Critic Pauline Kael wrote, "I know there are people who will applaud *Country* for the worthiness of its subject and the seriousness of its tone. But *Country* isn't a serious treatment of its subject," calling it a feminist *The Grapes of Wrath*.[578] In *The Des Moines Register*, columnist Lori Erickson poked holes in the film, including the assertion that Jessica Lange "doesn't look like any farm wife I've ever known."[579] The column prompted several letters to the editor complaining about the crass generalization and defending the movie. Robin Saunders of Ames, Iowa, wrote, "The film is not only entertaining; it is an accurate and moving dramatization of the current fight of the American farmer to retain the family farm. When President Reagan asks, 'Are you better off now than you were four years ago?' not everyone can say 'yes.'"[580] Reagan himself saw the film at Camp David in October 1984. He wrote it was "blatant propaganda message against our Agri. Programs."[581]

Country premiered at the opening night of the 1984 New York Film Festival, making it only the fifth American film to do so. It was a buzzy slot, which in preceding years had launched the Oscar-winning film *Chariots of Fire* and the zeitgeist favorite *The Big Chill*.[582] Lange's performance was widely acclaimed and earned her another Academy Award acting nomination—the first acting nomination for a Disney film since *Mary Poppins*.

Over the course of the next year, *Country* would have an impact far greater on the farm crisis than its box-office grosses would suggest. The film failed to break even in theaters, due in part to the cost of the production's false start.[583] Yet when *Country* was released on VHS in the spring of 1985, it proved to be a popular rental[584] before it was then licensed to HBO that fall. As more people saw the film at home, producer and star Jessica Lange used *Country* as a platform for change. In May 1985, Lange testified in front of the House Democratic Caucus Task Force on Agriculture, joined by Sissy Spacek, who starred in *The River*, and actress Jane Fonda. Her dramatic testimony earned an extended round of applause, which is extremely unusual at a congressional hearing.[585] It helped put the national spotlight back on the farm crisis, which was otherwise playing out in communities far from the media centers of New York, Washington, D.C., and Los Angeles. It was only weeks later that top musicians joined forces for the very first Farm Aid concert—a star-studded festival that was conceived by Bob Dylan, Willie Nelson, Neil Young, and John Mellencamp. Lange was signed on to emcee Farm Aid, though ultimately her participation was limited to a prerecorded public service announcement.[586] Lange's advocacy ultimately paid off. On December 23, 1985, President Ronald Reagan—who had dismissed *Country* as "propaganda" a year earlier—signed the bipartisan-approved Food Security Act.[587] It was the first major legislative step to stop the farm crisis.

It had been more than two decades since Walt told Ron he wished he could make a movie like *To Kill a Mockingbird*. Ron had now accomplished more than that. Ron had created a new vision for Walt Disney Productions—the most dramatic reimagining of Walt's legacy in decades. The invention of Touchstone had led to *Splash*, the hit comedy for modern audiences, and *Country*, the socially relevant drama that went on to have a tangible impact on American politics. The trifecta would be complete with *The Black Cauldron*, a film that showed animation was not just for children. Walt had always seen more promise in Ron than perhaps any other person had. Now, Ron was reciprocating by fulfilling the great expectations Walt had thrust upon him.

Splash opened on Friday March 9, 1984. It resulted in the best opening for any Disney film ever up to that point. It proved to be the zenith of Ron's tenure as the head of Walt Disney Productions. In his greatest moment of triumph, Ron's long-standing rivalry with his cousin-in-law Roy E. Disney came roaring back—suddenly, and with a vengeance. On that same Friday that *Splash* was being released in theaters, Roy E. Disney announced he was resigning from Disney's board of directors.[588] His calculated departure captured headlines, not just overshadowing Ron's accomplishment but also triggering a series of events that nearly brought an end to the company founded by brothers Walt and Roy Disney.

Chapter 17

"Clearly what I had done for the last seven years had not had much effect on the company,"[589] Roy E. Disney said, reflecting on Walt Disney Productions since his departure in 1977. Upon leaving Disney, Roy used his Disney stock as collateral to start his own business—an investment firm called Shamrock, named for his sailboat. "Shamrock became pretty much an end in itself because it was a small business that had a tremendous amount of growth potential," said Roy. "The first thing we did was to buy a broadcasting company that owned seven radio stations and three TV stations around the country. And we bought it cheap because it was in dreadful shape. And we had to go sort of take care of business with all these stations and broadcast properties. Which was great fun. I mean, you know, it was a people business."[590]

Roy also followed through with his ambition to make an independent film—a documentary about sailing, which was his passion. "In Southern California there's this famous race, yacht race from Newport Beach down to Ensenada every year…you could call it the Woodstock of sailing. And so I thought, why not just go out and shoot this like it's one of our nature films. So we rounded up four boat owners who were willing to bring a cameraman along. And we did a lot of interview footage with the skippers of the boats and with their wives and their crew and with race officials and we had cameras and helicopters and chase boats all over the race course. And we shot something like 160,000 feet of 16 mm film over about a 48-hour span."[591]

Roy personally funded the documentary *Pacific High* to a tune of $500,000, and it was released in 1980. He hoped his documentary would popularize sailing and maybe win an Oscar.[592] However, *The Los Angeles Times* gave it a scathing review, saying the film was "tedious." "We get to know little more about these yachtsmen than what we see, which is that they are a group of amiable, healthy-looking Caucasians in the 30 to 50 range. Oh yes, they tend to be male chauvinists when it comes to racing," read the review.[593] *Pacific High* had one unusual claim to fame, as the first R-Rated movie from anyone in the Disney family, thanks to a few obscenities.[594] Roy remained proud of the film, though it was not a great success. "We almost got it nominated for Best Documentary. But I think they all felt it didn't have enough 'social significance.' Sorry. I rolled my eyes on that. It was a good movie."[595]

As Roy pursued other endeavors, he faded into the background on the Disney board. He rarely voiced his objections, except when Walt Disney Productions paid Walt's family company Retlaw more than $40 million to acquire his uncle's name and likeness.[596] Still, he later said he was increasingly concerned about Ron's leadership. "If you look at the financial data from those years, the company was on a pretty heavy downhill slope. There was really no creativity within the company at all."[597]

The large investments in EPCOT and the Disney Channel, combined with the $21 million loss on *Something Wicked This Way Comes* and the delay of *Never Cry Wolf*, were taking its toll on Disney's earnings.[598] Takeover rumors circled after the company's fall 1983 earnings report showed profits down 7 percent for the year.[599] It did not help Ron's position that he and Diane had recently separated after thirty years of marriage.[600] Walter Miller said raising seven children had strained Ron and Diane's relationship. "It changed a whole lot from being this magical childhood, the innocence of it, to them having a whole lot of children that were getting older and they were overwhelmed.... There wasn't a whole lot of great communication in the household." Despite the separation, Diane never publicly wavered in her support of Ron's leadership.

In the winter of 1984, immediately following the stockholder meeting where Ron introduced *Splash*, Roy began to devise a plan to get control of the company away from Ron. "Frank [Wells], and Stanley [Gold], and I met in New York right after [the] Board Meeting that we'd attended in Florida. And sort of cooked up this plan, that I would resign and given all of the potential scenarios that could follow that, then Frank would be partnered with us in some way or another and would love to have a part in running the company."[601] Roy would call this group his "Brain Trust."[602]

Wells suggested they bring in Michael Eisner from Paramount to help run the company. "He's hot. He's got a track record. You do everything you can to get him and I'll help."[603] Ron had previously tried to bring Eisner into the Disney fold, but he seemed content running the top film company in Hollywood. Since Eisner's first brush with Disney during the *Popeye-Dragonslayer* deal, Paramount had only grown more successful with smash hits like *Raiders of the Lost Ark*, *Beverly Hills Cop*, *Flashdance*, *An Officer and a Gentleman*, and Best Picture winners *Ordinary People* and *Terms of Endearment*. Barry Diller, Michael Eisner, and Jeffrey Katzenberg were becoming as famous as Paramount's film stars. The business titans would be profiled later that year on the front cover of *New York Magazine*.[604]

The Brain Trust decided the best course of action was for Roy to resign from the board—an opening salvo in his fight to control Disney. On Friday, March 9, 1984, Roy submitted his letter of resignation. He did not give any reason for why he was stepping down after seventeen years. Chairman of the board Ray Watson was concerned about the optics of Roy's departure; other than Ron, Roy was the only Disney family member on the board, and he was also the largest shareholder.[605] With blood in the water, the company was suddenly a more attractive target for Wall Street sharks. Mickey Mouse was about to meet Gordon Gekko.

Roy's machinations attracted the attention of Reliance chairman Saul Steinberg, a corporate raider who wielded enormous influence in the business world by threatening hostile takeovers. Steinberg was reportedly not particularly concerned about Disney's future, but instead saw value in the company's assets—including its Florida land holdings and its film business.[606] As with other corporate raiders of the age, Steinberg's reputation preceded him; chatter about his interest in a struggling company often drove up the stock's price. Most companies would sooner buy back his stock at a higher rate than risk liquidation, leaving Steinberg with a considerable profit by simply going away. This maneuver would become known as greenmail.

Between March and May 1984, Steinberg's company Reliance bought more than four million shares of Disney stock making Steinberg the largest shareholder, overtaking Roy E. Disney.[607] Stanley Gold and Roy had dealt with Steinberg before. They had just reached a settlement with him that January, after he backed out of a deal with Shamrock to sell a television station. Stanley asked Roy who he'd rather have run Disney: Ron Miller or Saul Steinberg. Roy said, "I'm not especially crazy about either of them. But if that's the choice, I'll take Saul Steinberg."[608] In truth, Roy was hoping to take over the company himself. Roy testified at a later civil trial that he contacted "junk bond king" Michael Milken about financing his own takeover bid of Disney.[609] The estimated $2.5 billion required to take over the family company would likely have required Roy to sell off parts of the company. He ultimately didn't want to see Walt Disney Productions get torn apart, with its film library acquired by another studio or its theme parks sold to a hotel company.[610] Steinberg would likely follow a similar strategy to pay back his takeover attempt.

Their backs against the wall, Ron and Ray Watson hastily scrambled a strategy to save Disney. One of the first steps recommended by Disney's financial advisers was to increase executive compensation, in a show of support for the company's current leadership and to raise salaries to industry standards.[611] Ron's annual compensation was $375,024—or about $1 million adjusted for inflation.[612] He also enjoyed additional perks such as the use of the company jet and free Disneyland passes for his family. With Diane's family wealth, the Millers had few financial complaints. Yet by comparison, Paramount's Barry Diller earned a base salary of $550,000 and additional bonuses that raised his total compensation to more than $2 million—making Diller the top-paid executive in the country.[613] Disney agreed to raise Ron Miller's salary to $500,000 and increased other executive salaries. Ron and Ray Watson were also guaranteed compensation for the next five years, no matter what happened—i.e., "golden parachutes".[614]

Ron and Ray Watson's next step was to look for companies that they could purchase with Disney stock. The acquisitions would dilute the power of any individual shareholder.[615] They felt the two most attractive companies were Arvida, a real estate company with thousands of acres in Florida,[616] and Gibson, a greeting card company which could offer possible synergies with Disney characters.[617] In less than two weeks, Ray Watson and Ron put together a deal to purchase Arvida for $200 million in Disney stock.[618] It gave Arvida's owners, the Bass brothers, a 6 percent stake in the company.[619] Steinberg's holdings were diluted to 11.1 percent,[620] but that didn't seem to deter him. Meanwhile, Roy was infuriated since he felt Disney overpaid for Arvida.[621] (Disney sold Arvida three years later for more than $400 million—twice what it had paid.)[622]

Meantime, Steinberg was assembling a team of investors, including Kirk Kerkorian of MGM, to help buy Disney. Kerkorian was reportedly fronting $75 million toward Steinberg's takeover, which would then give him the option of buying Disney's film and television assets for $447 million.[623] It was a seemingly more attractive offer for Steinberg than the $350 million Roy E. Disney said he would pay Steinberg for the film studio.[624] Steinberg vowed to bring a lawsuit against the Arvida acquisition and the impending Gibson deal, while at the same time threatening a proxy battle to gain control of Disney.[625]

Stanley Gold continued behind the scenes negotiations with Ron and Ray Watson. They invited him to the Disney lot on Friday, June 1, to discuss a path forward. They wanted Roy back on the board to show a unified front against Steinberg and other corporate raiders. At one point in the conversation, Ron asked Stanley the top question on his mind.

"Does Roy really hate me?" Ron asked. "I don't hate him."

"No, Ron, he doesn't hate you," Stanley replied, but then launched into Roy's concern about Walt Disney Productions film output under Ron and Disney's new president Richard Berger. To bring Roy back into the fold, Stanley said the board would have to be expanded to include Roy's allies.[626]

A week later, Steinberg announced a tender offer. He threatened to acquire another 37.9 percent of Disney, which would bring his total holdings to 49 percent.[627] Frank Wells and Stanley Gold rushed to Ron's Encino house to beg him and Ray Watson not to pay greenmail to get rid of Steinberg. Instead, they offered an alternative of sorts—the two sides of the Disney family could join forces in a leveraged buyout of the company.[628] It was too little, too late.

On the weekend of June 9, as Disneyland celebrated the fiftieth anniversary of Donald Duck,[629] Ron and Ray Watson secretly negotiated a stock buyback agreement with Steinberg. They agreed to pay him a fee of $325 million, meaning Steinberg would walk away $60 million richer,[630] but at least he was walking away.

The greenmail deal was controversial, but it also brought widespread outrage over the tactics of corporate raiders. A group of stockholders sued Disney and Steinberg, hoping to reverse the deal. The lawsuit wound its way through the courts for several years, before being settled midtrial in 1989.[631] Roy's Brain Trust was further aggrieved by the Steinberg payment, the purchase of Arvida, and the impending acquisition of Gibson. Stanley Gold met again with Ron and Ray Watson. He had two demands. The first was three seats on the board, for Roy, himself, and Roy's brother-in-law Peter Dailey. The second demand was hiring Frank Wells as a senior executive at Disney.[632] The board shakeup would tip the scales in Roy's favor, but if it meant an end to the existential threat against Disney, Ron and Ray would support it. The second demand was more complicated. Ron worried Frank's installation would anger other longtime executives like Dick Nunis, Ron's former USC teammate who had worked his way up to president of Walt Disney Attractions.[633] Ron was also disappointed in Wells's support of Roy since he too considered Frank to be a friend.[634] Ron valued loyalty, perhaps to a fault.

A few days later, Gold changed the terms. Instead of hiring Wells, Roy was demanding Card Walker and Donn Tatum be removed from Disney's Executive Committee.[635] Card and Donn had led Walt Disney Productions after Walt's death, but to Roy, they represented Disney's refusal to modernize. The board met and decided Card and Donn would step down from the committee, and both men agreed to it, for the good of the company. With that, Roy E. Disney, Stanley Gold, and Peter Dailey joined Disney's board.[636] The Brain Trust was now on the inside, and it was vocal in its objection to the Gibson deal.

On July 17, Roy E. Disney and Ron Miller did something that hadn't been done in a long time—they broke bread together at the Disney commissary. Ron and Roy never formed the close partnership that had once been presented as the future of Disney. They couldn't even pretend to still be the same happy family that had gathered at the White House to support Walt's legacy. But at least for this meal, joined by Ray Watson, the two men could sit in each other's company and make small talk.[637] Ron and Diane had also started to reconcile and decided to end their separation.[638] For a moment, it seemed like perhaps the worst was over. Instead, the eye of the hurricane was merely passing over Burbank.

While Ron had spent the first half of 1984 fending off hostile takeovers from his office on the third floor of the Animation Building, the artists on the first floor were toiling under the practical impact of *The Black Cauldron*'s technical ambitions. In January, Ron told Production manager Ed Hansen that he felt very good about the film, and that it was time to "settle down now and get it finished."[639] For the better part of that year, the studio seemed to be working around the clock to complete *Cauldron*.

Esther Barr had become accustomed to working twelve- to fourteen-hour days, seven days a week. She was working on some of the first computer animation ever used inside a Disney animated feature—which was used in the film for Princess Eilonwy's spherical floating bauble. "They were just graphs of a ball going around, so you didn't even have to animate the ball. You just kind of gave it positions on a graph, and then the computer did the plotting and then you told it how many frames and what to do between it," she said. "It was pretty crude." She and her colleagues often ate dinner at Jack in the Box across the street because they never got home in time for dinner.

For *The Black Cauldron*'s painted animation cels, Disney was using a new process called animation photo transfer, which would give the frames more sophisticated ink lines.[640] The Ink & Paint Department added a night shift to keep up with demand. Whereas Ink & Paint's day shift had been a female-only environment since the days of Walt, the night shift was coed. "The old Disney way was you could spend a lot of time on a cel to make it right. So I think that's kind of why they had to get a night crew is that the day crew was just not coming up to speed," said freelancer Carolyn Guske. "I think that's also probably why they hired a bunch of younger people that were used to working fast. Working at Filmation, you better turn out your 20 or 30 cels a day, whereas Disney was like 5 to 10. So it was a very different ballgame."

Background artist Donald Towns said the 70 mm widescreen format made the painted backdrops of *Cauldron* particularly cumbersome. "We had backgrounds that were probably about five feet [in] length," he said. "So if we had long shots, then it could easily take us a week, sometimes two weeks, depending on what it was."

Phil Nibbelink animated an elaborate introduction to the Horned King's henchmen. "The big scene that I'm infamous for is the scene where you're panning through the castle for the first time and you see all these guys eating. There's a [woman] dancing on the tabletop. I don't know how many characters...but I'm in that scene. I put a caricature of myself grabbing Creeper and saying 'More women.'...But that scene had so many characters, it was such a long scene. I got into real trouble with the production. I mean, everybody was angry at me.... At the time it was hard to combine levels. In those days of cels, you could only have maybe seven levels so you had to combine stuff in Xerox. But since it was panning and things were at different speeds, it was hard to combine."

Animator Ruben Aquino found himself struggling to design a seemingly endless number of Fair Folk for a crowd shot. He decided to borrow Tinker Bell's design, in the process creating one of the first Easter eggs in modern Disney animation.

In 1984, when Michael Jackson was at the height of his popularity, he reached out to Disney for a private screening of *The Black Cauldron*. Disney invited him to Burbank and showed him the film in a screening room on the third floor of the Animation Building.[641] Michael sat in the front row as Joe Hale played the work reel for him, with many scenes still in pencil form. By Joe Hale's account, Michael loved the movie—he was vocally excited as the movie played. "Ooooo, all right!" he reportedly cried out multiple times.

Michael Jackson's enjoyment added to the studio's optimism for *Cauldron*. "Everybody who has seen *The Black Cauldron* is very enthusiastic about it. It looks more and more exciting all the time," Ron told an interviewer.[642] Ron believed animation, and *Cauldron* specifically, could be the center of a new "synergism" strategy. New animated films would increase sales of videocassettes, and then subscriptions to the Disney Channel. *Cauldron* would not just spawn the usual merchandise— books, dolls, records—but also a ride at the parks and a computer video game.[643] "Animation is more important to us now than it has been for at least 20 years," Ron said.[644] Yet he was so consumed by the corporate raiders that he ceased paying close attention to the day-to-day production of *Cauldron*.

On July 18, 1984, Minneapolis-based raider Irwin Jacobs announced he was among a small group of investors who had purchased more than a million shares of Disney stock in the weeks since Saul Steinberg's greenmail attempt—giving Jacobs's team a nearly 6 percent stake in Disney.[645] Jacobs had become a Wall Street celebrity after his attempted takeover of Pabst Brewing Company, but he disliked his nickname of "Irv the Liquidator."[646] Jacobs' sudden appearance on the scene made Disney vulnerable once again.

Stanley Gold asked to meet with Ron on the studio lot on Friday, July 20. The two men sat in Ron's office. Norman Rockwell's portrait of

Diane as a little girl still hung on the wall as it had in Walt's day. Stanley asked if Roy could return to Walt Disney Productions in an executive capacity. Ron said he was open to the idea, but didn't know where Roy fit.[647] It's unclear whether this latest demand would have finally brought peace to the Disney lot, but Ron didn't seem to seriously explore the idea.

Instead, the Brain Trust found an unlikely ally in Irving Jacobs. He thought Disney was foolish to pay more than $300 million for a greeting card company, and he vowed to restructure Disney if the deal moved ahead.[648] Jacobs began to personally lobby members of the board and found that Sid Bass and Stanley Gold also opposed the Gibson deal. Jacobs's politicking worked so well that it created daylight between Ray Watson and Ron Miller.

Ray Watson realized support for the current management team was rapidly eroding. He wrote a memo to himself, blaming Ron for their current situation: "[Roy's] resignation was seen as a clear vote of no-confidence for Ron…[Ron and Diane's] marriage difficulties indicated erosion of support from the Walt side. When all of this was put in the same crucible with the investment community's suspicions that Ron got the job more because of who he was married to than for what he had done, then any kind of bad business news made the company vulnerable.… We need to resolve the [Ron Miller] issue as soon as possible."[649]

The summer Olympics were getting underway in Los Angeles. The mascot Sam, a bald eagle, had been designed by Disney artist C. Robert Moore.[650] Walt Disney Productions was supposed to help program the opening and closing ceremonies, but Disney and the Olympic Committee parted ways over budget concerns.[651] It was a disappointment for Ron since he helped organize these ceremonies for the 1960 winter Olympics, on Walt's behalf.[652] Before the Games were over, Jacobs's pressure campaign against Gibson had turned into one against Ron. Stanley began to tell Ray Watson that he and Roy would support the current management team if they got rid of Ron. At the next board meeting, a vote was held to cancel the Gibson deal, and Ray Watson called for an outside review of the company to determine the next best steps.

Afterward, board member Philip Hawley told Ron that he was likely to be asked to resign when that review came back.[653]

Ron was devastated by this news. He began to cry and left his office to gain his composure.[654] He asked Ray Watson what he should do next. "I think you ought to get a lawyer to protect your interests," Watson said.[655] Ron had trusted Watson to have his back and didn't realize that Watson had also begun to question his leadership.

On September 6, 1984, Ron Miller entered the Disney boardroom for the last time as CEO. According to *Storming the Magic Kingdom*, when he entered, no one made eye contact with him. They knew he was hurt, angry, and emotional. None of that would change his fate. The die was cast and there would be no going back. He addressed the room, "Don't you have something to say to me?"

Ron attempted to plead his case in vain. "I've given my life to this company. I've never worked anywhere else. And I've made progress with this company. I think I've taken great strides in leading it as far as it has come. I feel like this is a betrayal."[656] Not since Don Bluth's perfidy had Ron felt so double-crossed. Disney was his company, where the employees were family first, colleagues second. He openly confronted his betrayers with thinly veiled anger. He began to address each board member one at a time, demanding they give him the respect of their attention.

He then turned to Roy, the man who he felt kickstarted this whole coup. Wasn't he family? Couldn't he remember when they were united in a common purpose to support the Disney legacy—supporting CalArts or joined together at the Nixon White House? Neither said a word.[657] The betrayal was too great. They just glared at each other.

He then turned to Roy's collaborator Stanley Gold. "Don't you have anything to say, Stanley? You talk so much all the time. You're really the ringleader of all this."[658] Stanley was uncharacteristically silent. He looked down at the table, hoping this display of awkward, angry emotion would soon pass.

Ron had prepared a letter for the board, arguing that he should keep his job—talking about his accomplishments since he took over the company.[659] Touchstone. *Splash*. His strategy to turn around the film division, and in doing so, change the fortunes of Walt Disney Productions. EPCOT Center had yet to turn a profit, but it was revolutionizing how Americans vacationed. Theme parks were no longer daytrips or weekend getaways, but a resort destination where people would spend the entirety of their precious time off. The company was also expanding overseas with Tokyo Disneyland, and soon perhaps, a new park in France called Disneyland Paris. The sun would never set on the Disney theme park empire. He could have also mentioned the expansion into subscription cable, home video, and video games. He could have mentioned how he helped rebuild the Animation Department not once, but twice. He had always taken the long view, pushing Disney in new directions unlike anything the company had seen since the best days of Walt. Disney had been criticized for caring too much about "What would Walt do?" Ron was answering the question, not by living in the past but by dreaming about the future. Walt had faced periods of uncertainty, but he was never forced to deal with a hostile takeover attempt from people who ultimately cared more about their own self-interests than the long-term success of Disney. Ron felt he had saved Walt's company, preventing it from being sold for parts or merged with some larger entity. The same could not be said for Warner Brothers, MGM, United Artists, or Paramount. Hadn't Walt—the visionary, the dreamer of EPCOT, CalArts, and the entire Disney empire—wanted this man, the man he called his son, to run his studio after he was gone? None of these board members seemed to care about that. Disney was no longer a person, but a corporation. The following morning, the board voted unanimously to ask Ron to resign.[660] He submitted his resignation letter at their request.

Ron hoped other executives would step down in a show of defiance. It stung when they didn't. People who could have defended him in the press, like Card Walker or Donn Tatum, mostly stayed quiet. Ray Watson issued a statement to reporters heralding Ron for "his many fine contributions to the success of the company."[661] On the other hand, Dick Nunis, Ron's former USC teammate turned president of Disneyland

194

and Walt Disney World, let it be known that Ron's departure "will have no effect on either park."[662]

Roy E. Disney would later say of Ron's forced resignation, "It didn't make us friendlier than we had been before. But you know, it was just simply one of those things that in my view at least and in a lot of people's views, had to be done."[663]

Ron held out hope that another studio would come looking for his expertise, but that never panned out. One of the few people who seemed to show any kind of decency near the end was Michael Eisner. Around the time of the resignation, Walter Miller remembered being at home with his dad when Ron said, "Michael Eisner just called. He says he's gotta talk. This is not good." Eisner drove over to the house to say he was being offered Ron's job. As much as that may have stung in the moment, Ron would later come to appreciate what Eisner did.

"That experience, being forced to resign, was with my dad 'til the very end. It was devastating to him. And of course, there was a lot of anger involved to the very end.... He never said it, but I think not only was he angry, but it was a really embarrassing situation that devastated him for years and years and years," said his son Walter. "Being forced to resign from that studio he worked so hard at, feeling like he was stabbed in the back, being a scapegoat...he retreated from that whole world, that part of his life."

After Ron's forced resignation, Roy still needed support for his choices to run the company—Michael Eisner and Frank Wells—but there was not unanimity among the directors. Stanley and Roy tried to win over Card Walker by offering Walt's side of the family a seat on the board. Stanley offered to give up his seat in favor of Diane.[664] "My mom said 'Go to hell,'" said Walter Miller. "In a show of defiance and support for my dad, she sold all her Disney stock. She just said the hell with it." It was no small decision. Walt Disney Productions had been a major part of Diane's life since birth. Walt showed Diane his approval for the man she loved by welcoming him into the family and into the company. Walt Disney Productions was still an important link to her father and her childhood. Yet she was now willing to give it all up.

Diane turned down the board seat. It was then offered to her sister Sharon, who accepted.[665]

"Everything changed," said Walter Miller, including for the Miller family. Walter had been working for a Disney Channel production and shooting footage for the Mexico pavilion in EPCOT with his brother Chris. "When that happened, when that went south, Chris and I hopped into my Volkswagen Vanagon to get away on a month long ski trip across New Mexico and Colorado, and that was the end of it."

Eventually Roy's choices to run Walt Disney Productions won out. On Saturday September 22, 1984, the board installed Michael Eisner as chairman and CEO and Frank Wells as president.[666] "They were brought in as equals. And that was why it worked," said Roy.[667] Roy and his Brain Trust celebrated all they had accomplished over the last six months with a victory lunch. As the meal was wrapping up, Michael Eisner realized that despite everything that had just transpired, he didn't know Roy's endgame.

Eisner turned to Roy and said, "You know, we never talked about this. What do you want to do now?"

Roy responded, "Why don't you let me have the animation department?" He added, "I think I'm the only guy who knows how it works, 'cause I grew up around it. And I think I'm the only guy that knows all the people involved and the mechanics of it, you know, and what it takes to make an animated film. I've never made one but I know how you do it."

Eisner's answer was simple.

"Great, do it."[668]

Chapter 18

On Monday September 24, 1984, Michael Eisner and Frank Wells showed up to the Disney lot for the first time in their new roles running the company. Walt's old office would now belong to Eisner. Ron's scripts—including his copies of *Black Cauldron* treatments from Lloyd Alexander and Rosemary Sisson, and Charles Embree's original story analysis—were sent back to the Story Department.[669] The Disney family arranged for other items to be returned, including Norman Rockwell's portrait of Diane.

Eisner and Wells called an all-employee meeting that afternoon so they could reassure the rank-and-file workers that a bright new day was ahead for Disney. It was held on the abandoned backlot of *Something Wicked This Way Comes*—the film that was reported to have lost $21 million in 1983, sending Disney stock tumbling just months before Ron Miller's forced resignation.[670] The two men—tall, manicured in well-tailored, expensive suits—looked every bit the part of a Hollywood executive. It was a clear contrast with the typical Disney uniform of cozy cardigan sweaters.

"They were 100% different than what we had ever had there. Good or bad they were completely different. Out of place. They looked like lawyers landed on a little league baseball field," said Mike Gabriel. "It was clear one of us was going to change, either us or them. It was us."

197

"They were standing up there with their microphone and they were already talking like it's Wall Street," said animator Tony Anselmo. "I could just see these were not artists. You guys are Suits. This is not good. I don't trust these guys as far as I could throw 'em. These are bad guys. This is not good. But we had Roy, who we knew took animation and he would protect us. And he did. He really did."

"I often thought back to that moment of being told we would all be safe in our jobs," said Mike Gabriel. "Within a year or two most in that crowd had been let go, and we in animation were thrown off the lot and placed in crummy Glendale warehouses.... My only solace is I wasn't fooled then and wasn't surprised now. These guys were sharks and they ate meat for a living and never slept, they swam all through the night to stay alive. This was the big leagues now and these guys were lethal."

In truth, an exodus of animation talent had begun near the end of Ron's tenure. After *Tron*'s release in 1982, Jerry and Rebecca Rees gave notice that they were leaving to develop an independent animation version of Will Eisner's *The Spirit* with Brad Bird. Ron Miller was aware that John Musker, Ed Gombert, and Randy Cartwright were also considering joining the Bird/Rees project, which was especially concerning since Musker was the codirector on *The Great Mouse Detective*. Musker was honest with management that he didn't know what the exact offer was to join *The Spirit*. With Musker's permission, Disney promoted Burny Mattinson to codirector on *The Great Mouse Detective* in case Musker did leave.[671] Ron had also shelved development on *The Brave Little Toaster* in July 1983, which was used as an excuse to terminate another first-year CalArts Character Animation student, John Lasseter, whom management felt was underperforming. Glen Keane had asked to switch to freelance status in early 1984 to focus on a children's books series.[672] Tim Burton left after completing the 1984 live-action short *Frankenweenie*. Sue Mantle DiCicco left Disney around the same time as Tim; the two friends shared a hug and wished each other well as they left for new pursuits.

Still, the experiment to save Disney Animation that had begun in 1971 had largely worked. In the first 12 years since CalArts opened its doors, Disney hired fifty-five artists from the school.[673] As of 1983, three out of the seven animation directors, two of the eight story artists, and ten of the forty-four animators working at Disney were all CalArts alum.[674] The studio now had a young group of animators trained in the tradition of Disney animation, who were also brimming with fresh ideas and ambitions. Michael Eisner, Jeffrey Katzenberg, and Roy E. Disney would soon tap into this spirit to create some of the most beloved animated films of all time, but in the first days of the new regime, the problem facing them was finishing *The Black Cauldron*.

Board chairman Ray Watson reached out to Roy E. Disney on September 21. Dick Berger had planned to book Radio City Music Hall to premiere *The Black Cauldron* and the live-action film *Return to Oz* in the summer of 1985. However, Watson needed Roy's assurance that *Cauldron* would be ready. Watson was concerned delays on the expensive film could potentially incur high interest costs if it needed more time to be finished. He wrote Roy wanting to know if it would be ready by summer and if not, what the additional financial burden would be. Irwin Jacobs was still threatening a takeover and Disney couldn't afford the continued perception of being vulnerable. (The Bass brothers finally bought out Jacobs on October 4, finally ending the immediate threat of a hostile takeover that had consumed the company for most of 1984.)[675]

Michael Eisner asked Jeffrey Katzenberg to leave Paramount to join him at Disney as president of Motion Pictures and Television. On Katzenberg's first day on the lot that October, he went to Michael's office on the third floor of the Animation Building. Katzenberg showed up excitedly with a buck slip of all the items on his to-do list. "I was meant to look after movies and television and Disney Channel and all of home video and all of that stuff," Katzenberg said. "I had all these great things I wanted to go do."[676]

As the meeting wrapped, Eisner stopped Katzenberg before walking out the door.

"Jeffrey, one thing I forgot, before you leave," Eisner called him back in.

"What's that?"

"Come over here, I wanna show you something." Eisner pointed to a building across the lot. Eisner was probably pointing at the Ink & Paint building, where the animation cels were photographed and painted. "You see that building over there?"

"Yep."

"Do you know what they do there?"

"No, I have no idea."

"That's where they make the animated movies. And that's your problem,"[677] Eisner said. Eisner felt the Animation Department needed additional executive management beyond Roy. Eisner believed that Disney had talented employees—he just needed to identify them. He said in an interview, "In any institution there are great people. You just have to find them. You can't walk in and say they're all idiots; they're not. Some people need leadership, some people need people to follow them—but they're there."[678]

Joe Hale and Roy E. Disney held a screening of *The Black Cauldron* for Michael Eisner and Frank Wells on the Disney lot. According to Joe, Eisner showed up with his family in tow and when Wells wasn't on time, Eisner insisted on starting without him. As the film was underway, Wells finally showed up with a bag of potato chips. "Frank sat there while the picture was running, talking and eating potato chips all the way through it," remembered Joe. Neither executive seemed to be paying attention. Joe can't remember if Katzenberg was at that same screening, but he did remember how much the new executive hated the film. Decades later, Katzenberg still has a Pavlovian reaction to *Cauldron*: "It's a horrible movie, a horrible movie.... I watched the movie and just said, my God, we can't release this in this way."[679]

"[*Cauldron*] was a group of people trying to reinvent the brand, and they thought the way to do it was to do something very aggressive and more adult," Katzenberg recalled. "It was just a mess."[680]

Katzenberg insisted the film be revised in editing—giving notes to Joe including a shot replacement in the introduction to the Horned King. Joe—along with several others who have recounted the story but were not in the room—interpreted that to mean that Jeffrey thought there was unused footage to cover the shot, which could simply be spliced into the film. Joe Hale said he and Roy tried to explain that animated films were not edited like live-action films. Due to the laborious nature of animation, there was no extraneous footage. However, animator Tad Stones, who also was not in the room, believes Jeffrey was simply misunderstood and just wanted them to rework the scene from another angle. "What he was saying is this shot isn't dramatic enough… we need a better shot with more power. He was treating it like an actual movie made of shots and angles and visual storytelling."

Katzenberg also insisted to Roy and Joe that they needed to cut ten minutes out of *Cauldron*. "I don't want this picture running over an hour and 20 minutes," Katzenberg demanded. "If it goes over an hour and 20 minutes, I'm going to fire you." Was Katzenberg serious? "He was kidding of course, I think," Joe added, with just a touch of uncertainty. They started to discuss how to improve the film when Katzenberg again said, "Cut 10 minutes out of it." He then got up and left.

Roy and Joe tried to make cuts without ruining the integrity of the film. They got about four minutes out of it. They ran it again for Katzenberg but before they got very far, he asked, "Did you cut 10 minutes out of it?"

"No," Roy said.

"I said cut 10 minutes out of it," and with that, Katzenberg stood up. Joe and Roy tried to reason with him.

"They said, you can't edit an animated movie," remembered Katzenberg. His response, "Yeah, you can. I'll show you. Just watch me."[681]

Katzenberg proceeded to take matters into his own hands. He asked for the film to be brought to an edit room so he could supervise his own cut of the film. "I started editing the movie, and honestly, like the entire studio went completely nut crazy. Meltdown time," recalled Katzenberg.[682]

Roy called Eisner, asking him to stop Katzenberg.

"What are you doing?" Eisner asked his protégé.

"I'm trying to fix this piece of shit, what do you think?" replied Katzenberg.[683] Eisner would later call *Cauldron* "lugubrious"[684] and he let

Katzenberg move forward with the edits. Eisner had created creative friction by allowing both Roy and Katzenberg to be in charge of the Animation Department. Joe Hale felt stuck in the middle, as the two wrestled for control of *The Black Cauldron*. Joe liked Roy from his days working on documentaries. Up until this point, Disney still was a small family company where practically everyone knew each other. Although Disney had its share of egos in the past, rough edges were fairly uncommon.

Katzenberg was a contrast in style from previous Disney leadership. He was brash—a product of New York City politics, where he worked as a teenager before landing at Paramount. When your Hollywood colleagues are Barry Diller, Michael Eisner, Don Simpson, and Bob Evans, you don't get to the top by being meek. Katzenberg has publicly said he has "a big ego" and is "really, really competitive."[685] He was not afraid to let his views be known, even if it made him unpopular. "When Eisner and Katzenberg came in, it was like *The Sopranos*," Joe said. Still, Joe and the other animators felt protected because of Roy.

On November 17, 1984, Disney invited two sets of recruited audiences to screen a work print of *The Black Cauldron*. The first audience was the "traditional Disney family audience" with kids under twelve. The age range of the second group was twelve to forty-nine, the original intended "mature" audience for *Cauldron*. The film itself was unfinished. Some sequences had gone through the ink and paint process, but other scenes were still in rough pencil test animation, which not all audience members appreciated.[686]

Overall, the reaction from both groups was fairly positive but the mature audience gave *Cauldron* better scores overall, with 22 percent saying the film was excellent and 76 percent saying the film was either very good or better. This kind of response from adults was considered above average for a Disney film of that era. All sectors were "enormously impressed" with the animation, which had "an almost three-dimensional quality." The adults generally found the story to be predictable and thought Princess Eilonwy was too "old-fashioned" and the hero Taran was a "wimp." Still, they liked "the combination of real suspense and sophisticated fantasy." Meanwhile, the family audience generally responded favorably to "the highly effective mixture of adventure, humor and 'scariness.'" 18 percent of parents from the traditional Disney audience said the film was excellent, and 70 percent said the film was very good or better. Parents were more likely to tell someone else *The Black Cauldron* was a "must see" than the mature audience.[687] Although there were silver linings in these audience surveys, Joe Hale said the reaction had already dropped from an earlier screening in Atlanta that occurred before the new regime started tinkering with the film. Seventy-nine percent of that earlier Atlanta audience said the film was excellent or very good, and 50 percent said they would definitely recommend it.

In the later survey from November 1984, audiences liked the humorous sidekick Gurgi and the henchman Creeper. However, they felt some of the subplots went unresolved, and reaction to the bard Fflewddur Fflam was "at best, lukewarm." The biggest split between the family audience and the mature audience was a scene where Fflam is transformed into a frog and is temporarily lost in a witch's bosom. "The adult audience found it to be humorous. The 'family audience' was somewhat concerned that this sequence might be inappropriate—and possibly even tasteless—for young children."[688] Both parents and adults in the survey group wrestled with the question: what age was too young for *The Black Cauldron*? It was something both demographics considered on their own—after all, weren't Disney movies meant for kids? Both groups felt the film was "too intense" for kids under six. This created a huge problem for Disney, whose research showed the primary audience for Disney cartoons was kids six or under, backed up by analysis of a recent rerelease of *The Jungle Book* which primarily played to kids under six (and presumably, their parents).[689] Four key scenes were cited as being problematic: the flying Gwythaint dragons chasing the pig Hen Wen, the Horned King in the "creepy" castle, the Cauldron Born marching out of the castle to destroy the world, and the Horned King's abuse of his henchman Creeper. The survey results conclude, "In terms of marketing *The Black Cauldron* it thus becomes mandatory to expand the Disney audience."[690]

Selling adult animation was, and to some degree remains, an uphill battle. Ralph Bakshi, who pioneered the market, recently acknowledged how hard it is. "The market for adult animation got slightly better, but sex and cursing was what they thought it was all about, when what adult animation really meant was animating America, its social problems and history. The cursing and sex was really in the films to get the idiots to show up."

Under Ron Miller, it probably would have been the marketing department's top priority to figure out how to build Disney's adult base ahead of *Cauldron*'s release. However, new studio executives are rarely held to the priorities of a previous regime. In fact, it would be counterintuitive to expect them to follow the same path since, presumably, if the old regime had the right outlook, they would still be in power. Rather than try to sell adults on *Cauldron*, it was easier to make the film slightly more palatable to kids who dragged their parents to see it. Hence, Katzenberg's attempt to "fix this piece of shit."[691]

In the 1980s, nothing said control in Hollywood more than who got to control the "final cut" of a film. Just a decade earlier, directors had ruled the roost. In the 1970s, the auteur theory, which said the director was the author of the film, was taking hold in the American imagination, making celebrities out of the once anonymous role. The auteur theory seemed to be confirmed by the popularity and idiosyncratic style of directors like Robert Altman, Francis Ford Coppola, Stanley Kubrick, Elaine May, Sam Peckinpah, Gordon Parks, Sidney Poitier, Martin Scorsese, and Steven Spielberg. For many, their fame and success helped them gain more control over the "final edit" of their films than had ever been allowed under the old Hollywood studio system.

By the 1980s, the pendulum began to shift back in favor the studio, as ambitions, egos, and in a few cases, drugs, led to spiraling, out-of-control productions that failed to resonate with the public. The most infamous was *Heaven's Gate* (1980), Michael Cimino's follow-up to his Oscar-winning film *The Deer Hunter* (1978). Films go wildly over budget and bomb almost every year—but few disasters have had such sweeping ramifications for the movie industry as *Heaven's Gate*. The three-and-a-half-hour roller-skating Western had lost more than $40 million—or about $160 million adjusted for inflation.[692] In 1981, United Artists, the studio behind *Heaven's Gate*, told *The Los Angeles Times* it would never allow "final cut" to go to a director again unless it was contractually obligated.[693] That edict wasn't enough to help United Artists. They lost more money than they could spare and soon, the company was bought out by Kirk Kerkorian, the man who owned MGM and one of the corporate raiders who tried to take over Disney.[694]

After *Heaven's Gate*, it became more common for studios and producers in the 1980s to recut a director's film, especially if it was dark, experimental, or didn't offer a Reagan-era happy ending. Among the more famous casualties of the period are Ridley Scott's *Blade Runner* (1982),[695] Terry Gilliam's *Brazil* (1985),[696] David Lynch's *Dune* (1984),[697] and Jonathan Demme's *Swing Shift* (1984).[698] Under Ron Miller, Disney had its share of live-action films that were recut—most notably, the revised ending of *Watcher in the Woods* (1980). However, it was exceedingly rare for Disney animated features to be recut so dramatically this late in production. (Walt had trimmed a fully animated song from *Snow White* for pacing, but it can be argued he was the auteur of that film).

Over time, as a growing audience of cineastes became interested in the backstories of films like *Brazil* and *Blade Runner*, the studios eventually learned they could try to make a few more dollars on older films by offering director's cuts—a trend that hit its zenith in the early days of DVDs. Many directors were happy to get another crack at letting the world see their films as intended. Yet that never happened with *The Black Cauldron*, leading to wild speculation about what graphic footage was edited out. For curious fans of *The Black Cauldron*, two of the unanswered questions surrounding the film are: What exactly was deleted, and would it have been a stronger movie if it remained uncut?

If a full working print of the film exists, it has yet to come to light. However, an unearthed work reel of the last third of the film gives new insight into how the film may have turned out if not for the edits forced by Katzenberg. The reel shows sequences 9.1 (where Taran trades his sword for the cauldron) through the end credits, which still list Art Stevens as the third director.

Immediately upon watching the work reel, one encounters the first of many cuts—and it's small but significant. In the final cut of the film, Fflewddur's harp and Gurgi's "crunchings and munchings" are offered to the witches so Taran can keep his sword. In the work reel, Eilonwy also steps in, offering to sacrifice her most important possession—her magic bauble. It's a minor moment and arguably redundant, but it keeps Eilonwy in the center of the narrative. It also shows the witches are not impressed with minor magic, like harps or baubles. They only deal with serious sorcery, making Taran's sword—which can fight on its own—a true find.

After Taran relents and trades his sword, the witches' cottage disappears and the Black Cauldron erupts from the ground. In the theatrical release, the witches suddenly appear in the clouds, laughing at Taran and company. Orddu says, "I say, what funny little ducklings! Don't they know the Black Cauldron is indestructible!" Taran has been duped. However, the work reel shows Taran struggling to destroy the black cauldron—picking up a large branch, a substitute for the sword he just lost. He swings it at the cauldron, but it is no match for its evil power and it breaks in two. He tries again by picking up a small boulder and chucking it at the cauldron. But again, it cannot be damaged, and the rock crumbles. Eilonwy, Gurgi, and Fflewddur join in—they push up against the cauldron, hoping to at least shake it from the ground. But it still won't move. Finally, a dejected Taran says "It's no use, it's hopeless. It won't budge." It's ultimately a richer scene, making the witches' con more deceitful and showing Taran as a more active hero.

The work reel also shows us additional moments of humor and romance—two things some of the film's detractors say are missing. When the witches disappear, Taran and his friends are left in the Marshes of Morva, dejected and powerless. It is at this point when Doli, the fairy who helped them find Morva, decides he has had enough and leaves the group. In the work reel, an angry Fflewddur shouts out, "And don't hurry back, you oversized tooth fairy." Gurgi adds in: "You dragonfly!"

It's a small laugh, but a temporarily relief before the darkness that is to follow.

When Doli leaves, Taran is filled with self-doubt. In the work reel, he says "Without my sword I am nothing, just an assistant pig keeper." Eilonwy tries to cheer him up. "Look, you're Taran," she says as she puts her arm on his shoulder. "You were Taran before you had the sword and you are Taran now. You are somebody." As she reassures him, she puts both hands on his face and gently makes him look into her eyes. Fflewddur and Gurgi watch from the log, caught up in the moment. "You must believe in yourself. I believe in you," she says. Taran, focused only on Eilonwy, is surprised and flattered that she still respects him after he has failed yet again. He replies back, "You do? Thank you, Eilonwy, and I think that you are…"

He starts to stammer as he can't find the words to tell her how he feels. He awkwardly pulls his hands out of hers, but she grabs them again. As he looks for the right words to say, she closes her eyes and moves in for a kiss. An overexcited Gurgi kisses Fflewddur, ending the tender moment between the potential lovers.

In the theatrical release, this scene plays like this:

Eilonwy: Look, you are somebody! You must believe in yourself. I believe in you.

Taran: You do? And I think that you're…

(Taran accidentally grabs her hands and then pulls away)

Taran: Uh, I mean…

(Fflewddur and Gurgi are on screen hugging each other, watching Taran and Eilonwy)

Taran (off-camera): That is…

Eilonwy (off-camera): Yes, Taran?

(Gurgi kisses Fflewder, everyone laughs)

It may not seem like a big loss, especially on paper. However, by shortening this delicate moment between the teenage leads, this scene loses its romance. It also has a cascading effect on the rest of the film; it makes Taran and Eilonwy's relationship seem more platonic than the awkward teenage romance it is intended to be. Ultimately, the work-print scene is one of the better depictions of adolescent insecurity and vulnerability within the Disney canon.

In Ron Miller's films—like *Tex*, *Country*, and *Ride a Wild Pony*—young people are rarely the fully formed and overconfident, and ultimately, two-dimensional kind of teens made popular in other films of the era like *The Breakfast Club*. They are learning how to make their way in the world, and more often than not, they are shaped by the events that happen to them rather than shaping the events themselves. This may be seen as a negative from a narrative perspective, but for many young people, it may ultimately be truer to life.

The edits to the climax of *The Black Cauldron* have been subject to the most speculation. Some fans assume that since the Cauldron Born undead sequence is already frightening and grotesque, it must have been heavily edited. Online chatter is that the film could have ultimately received a PG-13 or even R rating without these cuts.[699] Yet what is ultimately revealed by the work reel is that the final version of the film is relatively unchanged with one major exception. When an undead soldier lunges toward a henchman, the henchman's flesh melts away until all that is left is his skeletal remains. When Eilonwy says "Oh! It's horrible" in the final film, this is what she is referencing. The scene was animated by Phil Nibbelink, who says it took him weeks to animate the close-up of the warrior falling to the ground and then having his flesh bubble until it boils off the bone. "They looked at my shot, which had just been finished. They say, 'Cut it out. My three year old couldn't, wouldn't be able to see a shot like that.'" It's hard to say whether this moment would have changed the film rating to PG-13. The PG-13 rating was still a relatively new category in 1985, largely brought about by complaints about Paramount/Spielberg's 1984 film *Indiana Jones and the Temple of*

Doom.[700] Then again, if Disney had really wanted to cater to the mature audience, the PG-13 may have helped.

The final section of the workprint worth discussing is the very end of the film. After the Horned King is defeated by Gurgi's self-sacrifice and the heroes are back safe on shore, the cauldron bubbles up from the sea. Taran breaks down—falling to his knees, crying out for his lost friend Gurgi. "Why didn't I stop him?"

Fflewddur tries in vain to reassure him. "Taran, now stop it please. It wasn't your fault. It's alright. Come on, there you are." In the workprint, it is more clear how much Taran is hurting from the apparent death of his friend and how much he blames himself. There have been many resurrections in Disney films, dating back to *Snow White*, but up until this moment, it was rare for an animated character to grapple with the complex emotions, including self-blame, which can accompany grief.

What the work reel comparisons ultimately show is "death by a thousand cuts." There were no major sequences gone, few shocks or surprises about what was left on the editing floor. Joe Hale remembered another sequence that was trimmed down—when the pig Hen Wen is being pursued by the flying Gwythaint dragons. Prior to the cuts, every time Joe Hale watched the scene, it made the hairs on his neck rise but that changed after the edits. "I think they cut only one scene off of that but it ruined the whole thing," he says.

Animator Mike Gabriel worked on *Cauldron*, but is no fan of the film. "I truly can't stand to watch it. It makes me nauseous," he said. Yet he ultimately agrees that "the last-minute editing Jeffrey did to try and save it, didn't help. It just made it feel more disjointed than it was before the cuts."

Looking back on it all, Ron Miller was dry-eyed about *Cauldron*'s fate: "In all fairness to those guys, Eisner and Katzenberg, they wrote the whole damn thing off. All they wanted to do is get it out there and get rid of it. There was no hard work or love or anything on their part because they totally, they were totally unfamiliar with the property. They looked at it, made some criticisms, and made some corrections and made some changes. [They said] 'Let's get it out there, and take our loss and we'll write it off.' And they did."

For all of Eisner and Katzenberg's concerns about *Cauldron*, they were ready to capitalize on the film in case they were wrong. In January 1985, they asked Joe Hale to develop a possible featurette for the film's breakout stars Gurgi and Creeper, which could move into development if audiences demanded more.[701]

As late as June 1985, a month before *Cauldron*'s July 1985 release, a continuity script shows the film was still not 100 percent finalized. At the end of the film, there was to be a late-add narration over a shot of the heroes walking off into the sunset: "Taran, Eilonwy, and Gurgi, are they myths or dream and where does the black cauldron still lie hidden? Who will ever know the truth?"[702] For any concerns about story holes in *The Black Cauldron*, questioning if the main characters you just watched for eighty minutes were real would probably not have gone over well with any audience. This last-minute attempt to explain away any inconsistencies in the edits was wisely cut just before the film was printed for distribution.

Lloyd Alexander hadn't actively followed the *Black Cauldron*'s progress, but he was aware the film was due to be released in July 1985. He reached out to Disney in June, saying a friend had seen a recent screening and told him he would love the final film.[703] Lloyd hadn't visited Disney since 1980; given all that had transpired there, it may as well have been a lifetime ago. Still, he was warmly invited to *Cauldron*'s New York debut at Radio City Music Hall, which once upon a time was where Disney premiered some of its most important films. The Radio City audience was first treated to a forty-minute stage spectacular that pitted Mickey against *Sleeping Beauty*'s Maleficent—and along the way featured *Fantasia*'s dancing brooms, Mary Poppins, and even the pink elephants from *Dumbo*.[704] The Rockettes were there too—though when the show was first announced, Disney made the mistake of excluding the dancers, leading to a PR nightmare of picketing Rockettes before a compromise was reached.[705] As incongruous as it may seem to follow a Mickey Mouse revue with skeletal warriors trying to take over the world, few in the audience that night seemed to mind. When the end credits rolled and the lights came up, Joe Hale noticed Lloyd Alexander had been sitting behind him the whole time.

"I was wondering how you were going to make *The Black Cauldron* and take the story and make a film out of it," Lloyd said to Joe. "I loved it, but you didn't really use my story."

Joe replied, "Remember this, Mr. Alexander, however you feel about the story or how anybody feels about it, we may have changed it in the picture, but your books are going to be exactly the same."

Lloyd Alexander appreciated Joe's statement and he was genuinely enthused about the film he just saw. He wrote Joe later that week.

> Dear Joe: Oh wow, where to start? I didn't know which was more exciting—the picture, which was marvelous, or finally meeting you in person so I could congratulate you on the very premises of Radio City! The picture was brilliant, I was dazzled and delighted. You and everyone concerned worked marvels. As for your Creeper, he was a splendid conception, a gem in himself.... In short, it turned out to be a great festive occasion in every way. (I'll ignore the trip home through rain, thunderstorms, gridlock and the Lincoln Tunnel—that's all become trivial!) [706]

Gridlock of a different kind was impacting multiplexes in the summer of 1985, making it one of Hollywood's worst summers at the box office in this era.[707]

After *Jaws* ushered in summer blockbusters in 1975, Hollywood had focused on creating summer tentpoles. *Star Wars*, *Raiders of the Lost Ark*, and their sequels became major summer events, which propped up the studios with record profits and repeat business. However, Hollywood went into 1985 with no major tentpoles, and as a result, the whole circus collapsed. Only a few films, specifically *Back to the Future* and *Rambo: First Blood Part II*, were major hits.

Back to the Future director Robert Zemeckis told an interviewer, "You didn't know you had a really great hit until your fourth weekend. We had a thing called 'legs' in those days. You opened your movie and your movie opened strong, then your movie did its magic. You could let the picture build, you could add screens and all these wonderful things. In our fourth weekend, we outgrossed the sequel to Mad Max. Then we knew we had a movie that would play all summer long."[708]

That summer, Hollywood made the fatal mistake of releasing more than forty-five movies.[709] Multiplexes were popular but still relatively new, and fifteen-plus-screen megaplexes had yet to come along. As a result, few films were able to stick around long enough to gain "legs." Instead, they had to prove themselves quickly or get bumped to accommodate the next wave of films, which in turn, would get only a couple of weeks to prove themselves. That summer, Disney—which released *Cauldron* as well as the box-office disappointments *Return to Oz* and *My Science Project*—was at a distinct disadvantage. Up until this point, exhibitors viewed Disney as a boutique studio. It released only a small number of movies compared to Paramount and Universal, which at the time were known as "volume studios." "From the exhibitor's point of view, Disney was always a minor supplier," producer Steve Tisch told *The Los Angeles Times* in 1985. Tisch had unique insight—his family helped run Loews Theatres and he was working with Eisner and Katzenberg on the upcoming Touchstone comedy *Big Business*. "It is critical that they now establish credibility with the theater owners."[710]

Dick Cook, then senior vice president for domestic distribution, agreed. "In the past, Disney was unable to develop a solid relationship with the theater owners because we did not have a consistent flow of product. We might have a Christmas release but we didn't have one before or after the holiday."[711]

The Black Cauldron opened widely on July 26, 1985. It earned just over $4 million dollars that weekend, which UPI called "good but not spectacular." It was fourth in the box office charts behind *National Lampoon's European Vacation*, *Back to the Future* and a rerelease of *E.T.*[712] By its second weekend, it earned $11 million total but slipped to fifth place, faring slightly better than *E.T.* and the new Sesame Street film *Follow That Bird*.[713] By its third week, *Cauldron*'s showtimes were largely limited to discounted matinees and it fell off the Top 10.

The Black Cauldron underperformed at the box office, earning about $21 million total[714] against a budget that was reported to be between $25 million[715] and $30 million.[716] (In recent years, the claim has risen to over $40 million, coinciding with unfounded rumors that the entire Animation department was almost shut down).[717] However, the film generally received positive reviews and even a few raves. Roger Ebert gave the film three and a half stars out of four,[718] as did *Newsday*'s Peter Goodman.[719] Rex Reed said, "...as kiddie films go, it's pretty sophisticated stuff... the result is a film of great charm, energy and imagination..., *The Black Cauldron* is one Disney feature even Uncle Walt might have been proud of."[720] Critic William Royce put it on his list of the top ten films of 1985, saying "The finest achievement of Disney's animation crew in recent years flew right over the heads of most of the kiddies (not to mention reviewers). A classic tale of good and evil, strength and weakness that deserves a permanent place in the hearts of children of *all* ages."[721] Almost all critics cited the film's animation as a strength, even if some of the mixed reviews felt the story wasn't as strong as it could be.

Just days after *The Black Cauldron*'s release, a conference was held in Los Angeles to discuss the recent boom in children's entertainment, specifically in the home video market. In attendance were the heads of Sunbow Productions (*Transformers*, *G.I. Joe*), Marvel Productions (*Muppet Babies*, *Spider-Man*), Family Home Entertainment, and NBC's chief of children's programming. One conclusion reached was that revenue, the real measure of success, was not tied to quality. Instead, the group concluded name recognition of characters, often reinforced by toys and television shows, was an increasingly vital factor in children's programming. Kathryn Galan, who helped distribute *The Smurfs and the Magic Flute* and *Here Come the Littles* for Atlantic Releasing, said "It's a sad fact but it appears to be true that *Care Bears* and *He-Man*, which are not great movies will outdraw movies like *Return to Oz* or *The Black Cauldron*...which are of tremendous quality."[722]

Chapter 19

In 1986, Walt Disney Productions officially changed its name to The Walt Disney Company.[723] It was a signal of the changing times at Disney. Michael Eisner was quickly becoming a celebrity CEO with the golden touch. For the first time in its history, the company surpassed $2 billion in revenue.[724] The theme park business was strong, and television and film production was booming. Eisner promised to churn out twelve to fifteen live-action films a year,[725] the vast majority under the Touchstone label that Ron developed.

To accommodate the increased live-action production, the executive team decided as early as January 1985 to move the Animation Department off the Burbank lot and into temporary workspace in Glendale.[726] For many staffers, it was demoralizing to have the department kicked out from the building bearing its name. Animation rooms were needed to create production offices for Disney's new movie idols, like Bette Midler, who was starring in a string of Touchstone comedies.[727] Roy E. Disney swore that the animators would return to the lot in a few years, though it would ultimately take a decade before he was able to keep his promise. In February 1986, Disney Animation left the Burbank studio that Walt had specifically designed around the animation process five decades earlier. Some of the artists expressed their frustrations by drawing cartoons about the relocation. In one, two gravediggers at Forest Lawn Cemetery are working near the tombstone of Walt Disney. One says, "There's that sound again, Fred! Like something is spinning faster and faster!"[728]

"Our last day at the studio lot, our last Friday before reporting Monday in our unfinished Glendale offices…we tore the place apart," said animator Mike Gabriel. "A lot of us kicked holes in the walls, threw coffee on the walls, wrote 'messages' on the walls, and did our skinny animator lame best to leave some minor damage to express our disgust for having to leave *OUR* animation building that Walt Disney built for *US*, not you Paramount executives! Read the sign above the entrance door! Animation! We left angry and jilted, and always wished to return."

The move to Glendale, coming on the heels of the regime change and the lackluster reception of *The Black Cauldron*, seemed to be the final straw for some department veterans, including Joe Hale and Ted Berman. Ted Berman's daughter Cathy remembered her father's decision to leave Disney. "This was a new era beginning, and I think he felt that it wasn't really for him," she said. "For the first time ever in his entire career at Disney, he was called into a Saturday meeting with Jeffrey Katzenberg. And his dog was there. And my father said, 'OK, the studio has changed. This is just a different place. There were never Saturday meetings.'"

Eric Larson, the last of the Nine Old Men still with Disney, retired after the Glendale move.[729] Mark Henn stopped by Eric's office in Glendale in those final days and Eric showed him a picture of the Disney animation team back in Walt's heyday—at the Hyperion Studio in the 1930s. Eric said to him, "I look at all these people here [in the photograph], and I look at your generation. And I think that you guys are every bit as talented as the people that I'm looking at in this photograph."

"He enjoyed working with younger people and passing on all of his knowledge," said Mark, who would go on to enjoy a forty-three year career at Disney animating Simba in *The Lion King* and many of the modern Disney Princesses.

Despite all the upheaval since Ron left in 1984, many artists took comfort in knowing that Roy E. Disney was looking out for their best interest. Roy had grown up around the Animation Department, and he wanted to see it return to its former glory. "When Roy came in there with Eisner and Katzenberg he said, don't you dare touch animation, it's the crown jewel of Disney, keep it around, keep it alive, keep it going and let's do something with it. So really credit goes all to Roy Disney for really saving the animation department at that time," said Hendel Butoy, who was promoted from animator to director for Disney Animation's first sequel, *The Rescuers Down Under.*

Although Roy gets a lot of credit for keeping the traditions of Disney animation alive, Eisner and Katzenberg were intrigued by the possibilities of the medium early in their tenure. Eisner's early ideas included a *Fantasia II*, featuring the music of Andrew Lloyd Webber's *Cats*, and a dog-based rip-off of *Catcher in the Rye* called *Dufus*.[730] Katzenberg, however, was interested in developing new fairy tales, including mining the Grimm fairy tales that hadn't already been turned into features.[731]

Disney's corporate metabolism was speeding up, fueled in large part by Eisner and Katzenberg's ambitions to grow the film studio and, by extension, the company. Yet the new generation of animators was also hungry for new challenges. "I think there had been the time period, during *The Black Cauldron* years, which were long years, where there was no pressure, there was no deadline, there was no incentive to get the work done," said Peter Schneider, whom Roy installed in the new role of president of feature animation in 1985. Schneider had no previous background in animation, but had worked with CalArts president Bob Fitzpatrick on the Olympic Arts Festival.[732] He said he met some resistance when joining Animation but that many animators were happy to be challenged to meet tighter deadlines while still upholding Disney's standards. Schneider told the team, "We will make mistakes but they are going to be our mistakes, so go to it."

George Scribner, an animator who was suddenly promoted to the role of director, said he embraced management's new approach. "[I took the attitude] that these guys had made a lot of movies. You may not have liked them, but they had made a lot of movies that made a lot of money and understood storytelling."

Other changes took some by surprise, including layoffs, which had become exceedingly rare when Ron Miller was trying to grow the Animation Department. Rick Farmiloe said when he finished working on

The Great Mouse Detective (1986), he was told his assignment had been completed—meaning he was being laid off. "Disney didn't have layoffs," said Farmiloe. "When the new guys came in, that was the way it was. It was like, you guys aren't working. We don't have a film for you to go onto right now. We're not going to keep paying you to do nothing." He was brought back three months later for his next assignment, but he no longer took his employment at Disney for granted.

In 1986, the combined force of Don Bluth and Steven Spielberg provided the first significant challenge to Disney Animation in decades, with the release of *An American Tail.* The film had a robust marketing plan with tie-ins from McDonald's and Sears, and an Oscar-nominated Billboard number-two song,[733] "Somewhere Out There." *An American Tail* became the highest-grossing animated film at the domestic box office with $47 million.[734] That was almost double the box office of Disney's *The Great Mouse Detective*, which earned $25 million earlier that year.[735] (*The Great Mouse Detective* earned only $4 million more than *The Black Cauldron*, but had been far cheaper to produce). *An American Tail* reawakened the public's interest in animation, as did Disney's heavily promoted 50th anniversary rerelease of *Snow White* the following summer, which earned about as much as *An American Tail.*[736] *Who Framed Roger Rabbit*, the live-action/animated hybrid that marked the first collaboration between Spielberg's Amblin and Disney's Touchstone, became a blockbuster, earning $156M in 1988.[737]

An American Tail's success seemed to open Katzenberg's eyes to the financial potential of animation. "Jeffrey took Frank and Ollie's book [*The Illusion of Life*] and went to Hawaii, read it, came back just totally on fire for animation," said Glen Keane. "Jeffrey suddenly started pulling on all the levers that he could, bringing in Bette Midler and Billy Joel [for *Oliver and Company* (1988)]. And it was this whole new feeling of what Disney animation could be."

With Katzenberg fully committed to the success of Feature Animation and a team of ambitious artists who had been trained in the traditions of the Nine Old Men, Disney finally achieved a popular renaissance that rivaled Walt's golden age: *The Little Mermaid* (1989—$84 million),[738] *Beauty and the Beast* (1991—$145 million),[739] *Aladdin* (1992—$217 million),[740] and *The Lion King* (1994—$312 million).[741] "[Jeffrey] was a big part of how these films turned out so well, no question," said Mike Gabriel, who added that Katzenberg's drive to make everyone better—along with his detailed story notes—shaped these modern classics. "His determination to have every second of the film be entertaining to the audience made us all work harder to make something where every second mattered."

Many factors ultimately contributed to the success of these films—including basic supply and demand, as the beginning of the millennial generation finally increased the U.S. birth rate from mid-1970s lows.[742] The Disney renaissance would also not have been possible without the leadership of Michael Eisner, Jeffrey Katzenberg, and Roy E. Disney. Yet, credit is also due to the years-long development of the next generation of Disney animation throughout the 1970s and 1980s. This commitment started under the Nine Old Men and continued with the development of the Character Animation program at CalArts and followed through at Disney, during Ron Miller's tenure.

These efforts changed the fortunes of Disney, and the wider animation industry. When Jeffrey Katzenberg left Disney in 1994, he started DreamWorks Animation. DreamWorks films have since earned $6 billion in theaters, and won the first Oscar for Best Animated Feature for *Shrek*.[743] Pixar—eventually acquired by Disney—was cofounded by first-year CalArts Character Animation student John Lasseter, who also brought in former colleagues Joe Ranft and Brad Bird as well as CalArts alumni Pete Docter and Andrew Stanton. Pixar created its own golden age of animation with *Toy Story, A Bug's Life, Toy Story 2, Monsters, Inc., Finding Nemo, Cars, The Incredibles, Ratatouille, WALL-E, UP*, and *Toy Story 3*. Like DreamWorks, Pixar's films have also earned $6 billion in theaters.[744]

To keep Disney Animation alive after Walt's death required an unusual mix of ingredients: raw talent and skilled artistry, tradition and innovation, youth and experience, reverence for the past and a dissatisfaction with the status quo, the incubation of talent and an impatience with being held back. At times, egos clashed and tensions boiled over. Ultimately, the alchemy needed to reanimate the medium was brewed in a Cauldron.

Epilogue: Ever After

For *The Black Cauldron*'s thirtieth anniversary in October 2015, Disney held a special screening at Hollywood's El Capitan Theatre. A spry ninety-year-old, Joe Hale returned to introduce the film as part of a panel discussion before it was screened in 70 mm for the first time in years. As the end credits rolled and the lights came on, Joe rose to extended applause. It was the closest thing to a happy ending for *The Black Cauldron* since 1985. From 1985 until 1998, the film was largely unavailable for public viewing; at the time of its 1998 VHS debut, it was the last Disney animated film to receive a home video release. *Cauldron* may just be beginning to enjoy a small cult following, much like *Fantasia* had to wait thirty years before finding its unlikely audience.

Ron Miller never saw the final cut of *Cauldron*, but he was satisfied with the last version of the film he saw. "That was a big film. It was an expensive film and it was a very challenging film. For the most part, I think they did a damn fine job. I'm proud of them."

The Black Cauldron ultimately marked a significant transition for Disney—a passing of the torch from the Nine Old Men to a new generation of animators. The conflict over the film's edits also highlighted the contrast between what was Ron Miller's Walt Disney Productions and what would become The Walt Disney Company of Michael Eisner, Frank Wells, Roy E. Disney, and Jeffrey Katzenberg. The perceived failure of *The Black Cauldron* helped feed the narrative that Ron Miller's

219

tenure was a fiasco, and that the company was saved by Roy E. Disney. Yet, Michael Eisner has always been generous in his assessment of Ron Miller over the years, crediting him for attempts to modernize the company. In 1985, he told interviewer Jane Pauley, "I really didn't think anything was wrong at Disney. Most of it was right."[745] Still, there's no denying Eisner led a period of rapid growth at Disney that even Walt could not have imagined.

Within ten years of Eisner's arrival, Disney's revenue surpassed $8.5 billion and the company had greatly expanded its global reach.[746] This was fueled by the expansion of Disney theme parks, Touchstone Pictures, and of course, the Animation Department. Still, former Disney chairman Ray Watson said if Disney had not been besieged by corporate raiders in 1984, "...the company probably would have come out fine. I don't think it could have grown to the extent that Michael Eisner has grown this company, but...it wouldn't have been hard to raise prices in the parks, which were underpriced, and do a lot of things that they did when they came in too."[747] For some who survived the transition from Ron Miller to Michael Eisner, the growth was exciting, but there was also a sense that "downhome Disney" had disappeared.

Nowadays, industry experts warn against treating employees like "family," which is how Ron saw Walt Disney Productions.[748] The current recommended model is that of a performance-focused sports team. The average worker now spends about four years with one employer, and the median tenure of workers ages twenty-five to thirty-four is less than three years. Older workers may have a tenure closer to ten years.[749] It's increasingly rare to find anything like the forty- to fifty-year careers of the Nine Old Men—lifers with a vested interest not just in the current success of the company, but dedicated to its future preservation through training and mentorship of young employees. Yet nearly every artist who trained at Disney in this era has a shared reverence for the veterans who mentored them. Of course, the departure of the Bluth group exposed the near-fatal assumption that those being trained would in turn remain blindly loyal to Disney management—including multiple female animators who felt undervalued in an era when gender discrimination was more overt throughout the industry.

Today, it is also hard to imagine any organization making an equivalent long-term talent investment to what Disney did in the early 1970s to grow its Animation Department—both internally and via CalArts. The expectation was not a three- to five-year return on investment, but rather one designed to yield results in a decade and beyond. Yet, there was ultimately great value in taking the long view. The films directed by CalArts graduates for Disney and Pixar (acquired by Disney in 2006) and/or remakes of films directed by CalArts graduates have grossed more than $27 billion worldwide in their theatrical releases.[750] That does not include the additional revenue these movies have brought to the company through merchandise, parks, and other outlets. The $45 billion Disney Princess industry[751] owes much of its intellectual property to the characters animated by two CalArts grads who entered the animation training Program: Glen Keane and Mark Henn. Their combined characters include Ariel, Belle, Jasmine, Pocahontas, Mulan, Tiana, and Rapunzel.

After the forced resignation, Ron and Diane Miller focused their energy on growing Silverado Vineyards, their Napa Valley-based independent company. At President Reagan's first summit with Soviet leader Mikhail Gorbachev held in Geneva in November 1985, a 1983 Silverado Chardonnay was served with dinner, playing a small role in lubricating the discussions that helped end the Cold War.[752] Silverado would remain family owned and operated throughout Ron and Diane's lives, meaning Ron would never again have to answer to shareholders.

In the mid 1980s, Ron had to undergo emergency quadruple bypass surgery after his cardiologist performed a routine stress test. Years of bad habits—smoking, stress, drinking, and a diet of pickled pigs feet and BLTs—had taken their toll. Diane was by his side as he recovered and for the rest of their lives, she helped him maintain a healthier lifestyle. With the couple fully reconciled, their marriage seemed to grow stronger with age. Ron began to put his Disney days in the rearview mirror. In

2010, he said "I moved on and forward and into a lot of different things. Life has been good."

Ron Miller would never claim to be the creative visionary that Walt was. It's why he said Walt's death "was the end of something that will never be seen again." He didn't have all the answers—and at times, he fumbled. Yet, he also helped Disney survive at a time when the larger culture was abandoning traditional values in entertainment. He also remained committed to Walt's dream of CalArts and helped it develop a symbiotic relationship with Disney. In trying to honor Walt's memory, he also took risks—the biggest was the one Walt himself was too afraid to try: turning Disney into a contemporary brand without alienating its base. The success of *Splash* proved this strategy could work, which is why the Eisner regime inherited a Disney better positioned for the future. *Country*'s legacy is now largely forgotten, but the conviction of star/producer Jessica Lange helped it play a small but significant role in the 1980s farm crisis. It was the closest Ron ever got to fulfilling Walt's dream of making a film like *To Kill a Mockingbird*. The other film in Ron Miller's unofficial trilogy is *The Black Cauldron*. It's easy to dismiss *Cauldron* as the New Coke of Disney Animation—i.e., a 1985 rebrand quickly rejected by consumers—yet the film's ambitions helped push Disney Animation toward modernity.

As the years passed, Diane and Ron began a series of legacy projects to honor Walt—in part to differentiate the man from the Disney company. In doing so, Diane became the public face of Walt's family. One of the first major projects was the construction of the Walt Disney Concert Hall in Los Angeles. The venue was originally commissioned in 1987; Lillian Disney put $50 million of her own money toward the Frank Gehry–designed building. Yet for several years, it looked like progress was stalled, and by 1994, it seemed like it might shut down completely. However, in 1997, the Walt Disney Company stepped in to provide a much-needed $25 million infusion and Roy E. Disney personally donated another $5 million. Diane was appreciative of her cousin's goodwill and she publicly downplayed any previous tension. "We have different lives. We go different ways" she told *The Los*

Angeles Times, adding "I don't think I ever lost any esteem or respect for my cousin."[753]

Diane was also instrumental in keeping the project true to Frank Gehry's intent, even as others involved threatened to bring in another firm to keep costs down. Diane reportedly put her foot down at the idea of anyone other than Gehry being involved in the plans saying, "My father taught me that the creative people were the most important, and the creative person in this project is Frank Gehry."[754] When the Walt Disney Concert Hall opened in 2003, it was widely acclaimed as an architectural masterpiece—its near-perfect acoustics nearly as impressive as its deconstructivist silver exterior. It has since become one of Los Angeles's most recognizable landmarks and has been called one of the top ten most important buildings in the history of the United States.[755]

Roy E. Disney and Diane would continue to help each other with projects that honored their fathers. She asked her cousin to participate in a documentary *Walt: The Man Behind the Myth* and when the same production team had trouble getting access to certain archival material for an interactive CD-ROM, Roy pulled some strings at Disney on Diane's behalf.

On November 30, 2003—a month after the Walt Disney Concert Hall opened—Roy E. Disney resigned as chairman of the Feature Animation Division and from Disney's board of directors, citing "serious differences" with Michael Eisner. It was nearly twenty years since he had last left the company, but history was threatening to repeat itself. Roy's resignation letter, filed with the SEC, cited personal disputes with Eisner among his many reasons for stepping down. He wrote, "For whatever reason, you have driven a wedge between me and those I work with even to the extent of requiring some of my associates to report my conversations and activities back to you. I find this intolerable."[756]

Roy launched the "Save Disney" campaign, in which he complained about "[the perception] that the Company is rapacious, soul-less, and always looking for the 'quick buck' rather than long-term value which is leading to a loss of public trust." He also complained about Michael

Eisner's lack of a succession plan. With blood in the water once again, it looked like Disney could be at risk of a hostile takeover. One of the key differences between Roy's 1984 resignation and his 2003 "Save Disney" campaign was that the internet and cable news now helped amplify Roy's message. Roy's efforts against Eisner were far more public facing than what transpired with Ron two decades earlier.

Walter Miller said, "I recall during the Save Disney time, Roy reaching out to my mom on a few occasions, trying to get my mom on his side, which she wanted no part of, given the history. She was in no hurry to support Roy Edward." Yet Diane finally decided to break her silence when an outside company made a $54 billion offer for Disney. Even though she had largely walked away from the company after 1984, she did not want to see her father's legacy vanish. Instead, she granted an interview to *The Los Angeles Times* about Michael Eisner and the "Save Disney" campaign.

Diane said, "It's time [for Michael Eisner] to step down and let someone else come in for the future." Given her reputation for discretion, her words carried enormous weight. However, she also made it clear she was not happy with Roy's ongoing media campaign against Eisner, which she called "vicious." A true diplomat, Diane offered a path forward for all parties. "Roy loves the company as much as I do, and he wants to see it remain independent too. But what he has done put it in jeopardy."[757] She called for an orderly but timely succession, allowing Eisner a dignified exit. Twenty years later, Diane was now trying to give Michael Eisner the grace Ron had been denied. Her well-timed words cooled temperatures. The following summer, as Disneyland marked its fiftieth anniversary, Diane made a rare public appearance at her father's park to celebrate the milestone. She stood with Michael Eisner and his chosen successor, Bob Iger.

When Roy E. Disney died of stomach cancer in 2009, a memorial was held for him at the El Capitan Theatre in Hollywood. Roy had become a beloved figure in the animation industry, thanks to his steadfast support of Disney Feature Animation. Hundreds of people showed up to pay their respects. Bob Iger used the occasion to announce that the building that now housed Feature Animation on the Disney lot would be renamed the Roy E. Disney Animation Building—acknowledging his pivotal role in restoring Animation's importance at Disney.[758] CalArts would also call Roy its "staunchest advocate."[759]

That same year, Diane opened the Walt Disney Family Museum in San Francisco. At first, Ron seemed reluctant to revisit his past despite being supportive of Diane's vision. "My dad and my mom and I were up to our necks in this project. And my dad was at all the meetings," said Walter Miller. Through museum events, Ron slowly began to reconnect with the filmmakers and artists he had worked with thirty years earlier. It wound up being a therapeutic experience for Ron. "That kinda brought him out of his shell as far as recovering from really being disgraced by the forced resignation, by all the bad press," said Walter.

Diane died on November 19, 2013, after sustaining injuries from a fall at home. She was just one month shy of her eightieth birthday. "It devastated my dad. It just was completely out of the blue," Walter Miller said. By this point, Ron and Diane had been married for sixty years, and the grieving process was especially hard for Ron. "For three years, he kind of walked around as a zombie. Everything made him emotional," said Walter.

After Diane's passing, Ron got more involved in the Walt Disney Family Museum—as much to keep her legacy alive as Walt's. Rich and Kathleen Greene had become close with the Millers while working on the legacy projects. Rich called Ron to check in on him after Diane's passing. "[Ron] would say to me, 'Richard, I'm sitting here and I'm looking around. It's all the stuff Diane put together. I just want to be in the room with things Diane loved.'"

Ron Miller passed away on February 9, 2019, at the age of eighty-five. The cause of death was congestive heart failure. Upon Ron's demise, Bob Iger put out a statement saying, "His life and legacy are inextricably linked with our Company and the Disney family because he was such a vital part of both, as our CEO and Walt's son-in-law. Few people had Ron's understanding of our history, or a deeper appreciation and respect for our Company, and he shared it generously with anyone who wanted to know more. I was fortunate to have known him, and even luckier to have called him a friend."[760]

Michael Eisner also paid tribute, calling Ron a "serious good guy." He said, "For my entire career, I have had great respect and fondness for Ron."[761]

Some obituaries remembered Ron for pushing Disney in new directions—the groundbreaking computer animation of *Tron*, Touchstone's *Splash*, the advent of the Disney Channel, and the pursuit of Disney theme parks abroad. Some of his other accomplishments went unnoticed, like his involvement in EPCOT; the expansion into home video and video games; the critically-acclaimed film *Never Cry Wolf*, which brought Disney back into the cultural conversation; the socially conscious *Country* and its role in the 1980s farm crisis; and the rebuilding of the Animation Department.

Just before he died, Ron Miller said the biggest risk he took in his life was becoming CEO of Disney. In 2010, Ron Miller reflected on his time at Disney, saying, "I think I had the ability to recognize a good story and a good cast. I don't think I was ever difficult to work with, as far as the people were concerned. I was honest and to the point. I think we had a lot of fun making films."

At the time of Ron's death, The Walt Disney Company employed two hundred twenty-three thousand people around the world, and its total assets were valued at approximately $194 billion.[762] It was consistently listed as *Fortune*'s most admired media company in the world. The following year, CEO Bob Iger announced he was stepping down at the age of sixty-nine, after a fifteen-year reign of significant growth and major acquisitions including Pixar, Marvel, Lucasfilm and 20th Century Fox.[763] Yet Iger was called back into action in 2022, when his successor Bob Chapek was forced out after a rocky two-year tenure.

The question of succession, a recurring issue for the company, was once again rearing its head. Also of concern were a string of films perceived to be box-office disappointments—including animated films *Strange World* and *Wish*. To some investors, the Walt Disney Company appeared vulnerable again. Nelson Peltz's Trian Fund Management held a reported $3 billion in Disney stock, which gave Peltz the political capital to publicly challenge Iger and Disney's board. Peltz said he felt "Disney has lost its way over the past decade," blaming the board for the stock's underperformance.[764] Peltz launched a high-profile bid to get three seats on Disney's board.

Much had changed at Disney and on Wall Street since the events of 1984.

Corporate raiders are now called activist investors, and public perception has softened around their position in the food chain. "Back in [the 1980s], they were considered buccaneers and amoral and destructive of industries," said John Taylor, author of *Storming the Magic Kingdom*. "[Now] It goes on all the time. I'm reading about it practically all the time in *The Economist*." For his part, Peltz was reported to prefer the euphemism "constructivist" to "activist investor."[765]

The 2024 proxy vote prompted Disney to launch a $40 million coordinated effort to prevent nominees from Nelson Peltz's Trian Group and hedge fund Blackwells Capital from being elected to their board.[766] Disney received several significant endorsements in the battle to keep the company true to Iger's vision—among them, JPMorganChase CEO Jamie Dimon and former Disney CEO Michael Eisner. *Star Wars* creator George Lucas also backed Iger, saying, "Creating magic is not for amateurs."[767] Lucas's endorsement was both symbolically and mathematically significant, since he became the largest single shareholder after Disney's acquisition of Lucasfilm.

However, perhaps the most meaningful support was the coordinated endorsement from the families of Walt and Roy O. Disney. Walter Miller, who was voted in as the Walt Disney Family Museum's president of the board in the fall of 2023, was happy to support Iger. He and his siblings had been contacted by Roy E. Disney's daughter, Susan Disney Lord. The second cousins had begun to reconnect and both sides of the Disney family saw the importance of presenting a unified front to help Iger.

Walter explained, "[My sister] Tammy and I received a[n] email from Susan Disney asking if we would join her side of the family in signing a joint letter of support from both Walt and Roy's families.... Tammy had the insight that we should draft our own letter of support, as the Walt Disney family, and one that was much more succinct...and most importantly with a mention of our mother."

On the same day, two letters were publicly distributed from the families of Walt and Roy O. Disney. The letter from Roy's family, signed by Susan Disney Lord, Abigail Disney, Tim Disney, and Roy P. Disney, read:

> As the grandchildren of Roy O. Disney, we grew up with a front row seat to the magic that fuels the remarkable company he and his brother Walt Disney built together. We spent our childhoods on the studio lot watching movies get made. We explored Disneyland with the creative geniuses behind the happiest place on earth. We saw the passion Walt and Roy had for creating life-long [sic] memories for children and families, and the infectious joy they got out of the work they did. From Mickey and Minnie, to Snow White and Mary Poppins, Disney is not a company that makes widgets—it makes magic. And it takes a special group of leaders with a deep respect and understanding for this tradition to develop the kinds of incredible experiences—whether in a theme park, at a movie theatre, or in your own home—that touch people's hearts.
>
> Bob Iger, his management team, and the Board of Directors are faithful to this magic. They understand that the longevity of The Walt Disney Company isn't only the result of smart business decisions; it is rooted in the strong emotional connection Disney continues to forge with generations of people from around the globe.

We may not agree about everything, but we know that our grandfather would be especially proud of what Disney means to the world today. We also know that, like us, he would be very concerned by the threat posed by self-anointed "activist investors" who are really wolves in sheep's clothing, just waiting to tear Disney apart if they can trick shareholders into opening the door for them.

What concerns us most about these hedge-fund-backed opportunists is that they have little to no knowledge of what Disney truly means to people like you. They haven't made any arguments for why they should be entrusted with the keys to the kingdom our family built. To the contrary, their "I alone can fix it" mentality makes clear that they are not interested in preserving the Disney magic, but stripping it to the bone to make a quick profit for themselves. We're old enough to remember the bitter episode four decades ago when another corporate raider, Saul Steinberg—who, as it so happens, was good friends with one of the current activists, Nelson Peltz—launched a hostile takeover attempt of Disney and threatened to break apart the company. He was defeated, much as these activists must be defeated today.

This is not a company of interchangeable parts. It is home to thousands and thousands of dedicated employees who share the same passion Walt and Roy had for bringing hope and happiness to people through the magic of storytelling. Disney is lucky to be led by people who are looking to the future while drawing guidance from our cherished past. As The Walt Disney Company charts its path forward, it is imperative that the strategy Bob Iger, his management team, and the Board of Directors have implemented is not disrupted by those motivated by nothing more than their own self-interest. Disney stories are filled with heroes and villains. We know who the villains are in this story, and we know they cannot be entrusted with protecting this company's rich legacy or guiding its bright future.[768]

The letter from Walt's grandchildren shares a similar sentiment but as Walter says, "without all the pixie dust sprinkled all over it." Walt's family wrote:

To the Shareholders of The Walt Disney Company,

As the family of Walt Disney, we support The Walt Disney Company management and its Board of Directors, and oppose the nominations put forth by Nelson Peltz.

The integrity in the name of Walt Disney has always been a priority to our family. Our mother—Diane Disney Miller, Walt's eldest daughter—created The Walt Disney Family Museum to ensure that the history of her father's life and those involved in the creation of his dreams would be honored and remembered. We still believe in this brand of integrity and storytelling.

Bob Iger has grown this company in a modern world, and he continues to maintain a balance of creativity and profit. It is still a company based on the desire to entertain and explore. There have been challenging times, but this current management has adjusted and grown through those challenges. We are never without gratitude and pride for our grandfather and being a part of this family, and we will always cherish the memories and the life that we had with him. With this gratitude, it matters to us what the company does and how Walt Disney is represented.

As such, we support Bob Iger and The Walt Disney Company Board.

Sincerely,

Walter Elias Disney Miller, Tamara Diane Miller, Jennifer Miller-Goff, Joanna Sharon Miller.[769]

On April 3, 2024, Iger was handed a decisive victory against Peltz. According to *The Hollywood Reporter*, individual shareholders supported the sitting Disney team 75 percent to 25 percent.[770] Walter and his siblings were glad to have contributed to Iger's triumph. He said, "None of us really are major shareholders but we do care about the company's legacy and that it isn't broken up or taken over by a billionaire that knows nothing about running an entertainment empire the likes of the Disney Company."

Few shareholders or business reporters understood the true significance of the Disney family endorsements. With the passing of Ron Miller and Roy E. Disney, the long-simmering tensions between the two men were fading into history. The second cousins, all older than their fathers were in 1984, were not as close as they might have been if their fathers had been friendlier with each other, but they were moving beyond the conflict of the previous generation to support the legacy of their grandfathers. Those legacies had been motivating factors in their parents' lives as well. The families of Walt and Roy O. Disney were spiritually reunited in purpose, as they had been more than fifty years earlier, in the days and months "after Disney."

Endnotes

1   "Streaming Unwrapped: Streaming Viewership Goes to the Library in 2023," Nielsen, January 29, 2024, https://www.nielsen.com/insights/2024/streaming-unwrapped-streaming-viewership-goes-to-the-library-in-2023/.

2   Margaret Jones, "The Mouse That Built an Empire," *The Sydney Morning Herald*, May 1, 1966, 47.

3   Bob Thomas, *Building a Company: Roy O. Disney and the Creation of an Entertainment Empire* (Hyperion, 1998), 293.

4   Ed Sullivan, "Little Old New York," *New York Daily News*, November 7, 1966.

5   "All's Well After Walt Disney's Lung Surgery," *Port Huron Times Herald*, November 23, 1966.

6   "Disney Fine After Lung Operation," *Chico Enterprise-Record Mid-Valley News*, November 23, 1966, 25, and "Walt Disney Loses Lung," *The Times*, San Mateo, November 23, 1966, 36.

7   Didier Ghez, "Bill Anderson (1911-1997)," in *Walt's People, Volume 17: Talking Disney with the Artists Who Knew Him* (Theme Park Press, 2015), 153–172.

8   Orbin Melton, memo, "Thursday, December 15, 1966," December 15, 1966. Sold at auction.

9   Melton, "Thursday, December 15, 1966."

10 "Death Takes Walt Disney, Who Made Millions Happy," *The Van Nuys News and Valley Green Sheet*, December 16, 1966.

11 Bob Thomas, *Building a Company*, 297.

12 Jones, "The Mouse That Built an Empire."

13 "Dual Blow Jolts Market." *The Daily Oklahoman*, December 16, 1966, 31.

14 Arelo Sederberg, "Walt Disney Shares Up 9 3/8 points on NYSE," *The Los Angeles Times*, December 17, 1966, 7–8.

15   "Dual Blow Jolts Market."

16   UPI, "Disney Projects to Continue Uninterrupted Despite Death," *Santa Maria Times*, December 16, 1966, 6.

17   Sederberg, "Walt Disney Shares Up."

18   "1966 Walt Disney Productions Annual Report," 30, *www.disneydocs.net/disney-annual-reports.*

19   Robert. B. Frederick, "'Sound' Blows 'Wind' off No. 1," *Variety*, January 4, 1967, 9.

20   Frederick, "'Sound' Blows."

21   "Bill Anderson (1911-1997)," in Ghez, *Walt's People.*

22   "Cache Native Is Top Disney Aide," *The Herald Journal*, July 23, 1961, 7.

23   "Bill Anderson (1911-1997)," in Ghez, *Walt's People.*

24   "Bill Anderson (1911-1997)," in Ghez, *Walt's People.*

25   Harry Tytle, *One of "Walt's Boys": An Insider's Account of Disney's Golden Years* (Airtight Seels Allied Production: 1997), 189–190.

26   "'Jungle Book' in Disney Processing Two Years and Another Year to Go," *Variety*, December 15, 1965, 7.

27   "Bill Anderson (1911-1997)," in Ghez, *Walt's People.*

28   "Story Meeting on *Aristocats*," December 28, 1966, Walt Disney Archives (WDA).

29   "Story Meeting on *Aristocats*."

30   "Story Meeting on *Aristocats*."

31   "Story Meeting on *Aristocats*."

32   Tytle, *One of "Walt's Boys,"* 196.

33   Bob Thomas, "Disney Studios Carry On," *Tucson Daily Citizen*, June 24, 1967, 21.

34   Katherine Barrett, Katherine Greene, and Richard Greene, *The Man Behind the Magic: The Story of Walt Disney* (Viking Books for Young Readers: 1998), 137.

35   United States Census Bureau, "1950 Census. California, Los Angeles, Los Angeles, 66-2363," via ancestry.com.

36   United States Census Bureau, "1950 Census. California, Los Angeles, Los Angeles, 66-2363," via ancestry.com.

37   Janet Reilly, "The Interview with Ron Miller: Life in the Magic Kingdom," *Nob Hill Gazette*, December 4, 2018, https://www.nobhillgazette.com/people/the_interview/the-interview-with-ron-miller-life-in-the-magic-kingdom/article_6ef745fc-9d9d-5abc-8867-0b8abdc67ef6.html.

38   Reilly, "The Interview with Ron Miller."

39   United States Census Bureau, "1950 Census. California, Los Angeles, Los Angeles, 66-2363."

40   Reilly, "The Interview with Ron Miller."

41   Richard Hubler, "Ron Miller," Unpublished. Richard C. Hubler Collection, Box 14, Folder 53, Ron Miller, May 28, 1968, 1–21.

42 "The Luckiest Generation," *LIFE Magazine*, 28 June 1954.

43 Reilly, "The Interview with Ron Miller."

44 Alicia Carrillo, ed., *El Rodeo '53—University of Southern California Yearbook* (The Associated Students of the University of Southern California, 1953), 235–247.

45 Carrillo, *El Rodeo '53.*

46 Carrillo, *El Rodeo '53.*

47 Prescott Sullivan, "Cal Drops Ball, Game to USC, 32-20," *San Francisco Examiner*, October 25, 1953, 38.

48 Prescott Sullivan, "Cal Drops Ball."

49 Russ Newland, "Trojans Smash Cal's Bowl Hopes 32-20," *The (Santa Ana) Register*, October 25, 1953, A8.

50 Reilly, "The Interview with Ron Miller."

51 Eleanor Barnes, "Girl Baby Rival of Mickey Mouse as Dad Honored," *Illustrated Daily News, Los Angeles California*, December 19, 1933, 11.

52 Barnes, "Girl Baby."

53 Mary Angel, "A Day in the Mickey Mouse and Silly Symphony Factory," *Grimsby Evening Telegraph*, January 22, 1934, 4.

54 Angel, "A Day."

55 Richard Hubler, "Ron Miller," Unpublished. Richard C. Hubler Collection, Box 14, Folder 53, Ron Miller, May 28, 1968, 1–21.

56 Diane Disney Miller, "Memories of Christmas Past," The Walt Disney Family Museum, December 25, 2010, https://www.waltdisney.org/blog/memories-christmas-past-diane-disney-miller.

57 Dorothy Ducas, "The Father of Snow White," *St. Louis Globe-Democrat, This Week Magazine*, June 19, 1938, 7.

58 Richard Hubler, "Diane Miller," Unpublished. Richard C. Hubler Collection, Box 14, Folder 53, Diane Miller, June 11, 1968, 5–50.

59 "One Hour in Wonderland," IMDb, https://www.imdb.com/title/tt0251912/.

60 Carrillo, *El Rodeo '53.*

61 "Kappa Alpha Theta," USC Panhellenic, https://www.uscpanhellenic.com/kappa-alpha-theta.

62 "They're Sold on the U," *The Salt Lake Tribune*, November 24, 1951, 15.

63 Reilly, "The Interview with Ron Miller."

64 Reilly, "The Interview with Ron Miller."

65 Richard Hubler, "Ron Miller," Unpublished. Richard C. Hubler Collection, Box 14, Folder 53, Ron Miller, May 28, 1968, 1–21.

66 Richard Hubler, "Diane Miller," Unpublished. Richard C. Hubler Collection, Box 14, Folder 53, Diane Miller, June 11, 1968, 5–50.

67 Richard Hubler, "Ron Miller," Unpublished. Richard C. Hubler Collection, Box 14, Folder 53, Ron Miller, May 28, 1968, 1–21.

68 Richard Hubler, "Diane Miller," Unpublished. Richard C. Hubler Collection, Box 14, Folder 53, Diane Miller, June 11, 1968, 5–50.

69 "Diane Disney and Ex-Football Star at USC Married," *Santa Barbara News-Press*, May 10, 1954, B2.

70 "Ron and Diane Get Married," The Walt Disney Family Museum, May 8, 2017, based on 1956 Diane Disney interview with Peter Martin https://www.waltdisney.org/blog/ron-and-diane-get-married.

71 Richard Hubler, "Ron Miller," Unpublished. Richard C. Hubler Collection, Box 14, Folder 53, Ron Miller, May 28, 1968, 1–21.

72 Richard Hubler, "Ron Miller," Unpublished. Richard C. Hubler Collection, Box 14, Folder 53, Ron Miller, May 28, 1968, 1–21.

73 Richard Hubler, "Ron Miller," Unpublished. Richard C. Hubler Collection, Box 14, Folder 53, Ron Miller, May 28, 1968, 1–21.

74 Jack Geyer, "New York Defense Halts Rams, 20-10," *The Los Angeles Times*, September 2, 1956, 1, 7.

75 "Rams Official Season Schedule," Los Angeles Rams, https://www.therams.com/schedule/1956/.

76 Richard Hubler, "Ron Miller," Unpublished. Richard C. Hubler Collection, Box 14, Folder 53, Ron Miller, May 28, 1968, 1–21.

77 Barrett, Greene, and Greene, *The Man Behind the Magic,* 137.

78 Richard Hubler, "Diane Miller," Unpublished. Richard C. Hubler Collection, Box 14, Folder 53, Diane Miller, June 11, 1968, 5–50.

79 Richard Hubler, "Diane Miller," Unpublished. Richard C. Hubler Collection, Box 14, Folder 53, Diane Miller, June 11, 1968, 5–50.

80 Richard Hubler, "Ron Miller," Unpublished. Richard C. Hubler Collection, Box 14, Folder 53, Ron Miller, May 28, 1968, 1–21.

81 Barrett, Greene, and Greene, *The Man Behind the Magic,* 147.

82 Warwick Charlton, "Disney's Genius Included Casting, Too," *The Honolulu Star-Advertiser*, January 18, 1967, C12.

83 Bob Thomas, "Walt Disney: Perfect Picture of Anyone's Uncle," *The Miami Herald*, December 20, 1966, C18.

84 Bob Thomas, "Walt Disney: Perfect Picture."

85 Richard Hubler, "Ron Miller," Unpublished. Richard C. Hubler Collection, Box 14, Folder 53, Ron Miller, May 28, 1968, 1–21.

86 Richard Hubler, "Ron Miller," Unpublished. Richard C. Hubler Collection, Box 14, Folder 53, Ron Miller, May 28, 1968, 1–21.

87 Phyllis Battelle, "With Disney Gone, the Sparkle Fades," *The Record*, December 19, 1966, B1.

88 Richard Hubler, "Diane Miller," Unpublished. Richard C. Hubler Collection, Box 14, Folder 53, Diane Miller, June 11, 1968, 5–50.

89 Richard Hubler, "Ron Miller," Unpublished. Richard C. Hubler Collection, Box 14, Folder 53, Ron Miller, May 28, 1968, 1–21.

90   Bob Thomas, *Walt Disney: An American Original* (Disney Editions: 1994), 353.

91   Barrett, Greene, and Greene, *The Man Behind the Magic*, 169.

92   Richard Hubler, "Ron Miller," Unpublished. Richard C. Hubler Collection, Box 14, Folder 53, Ron Miller, May 28, 1968, 1–21.

93   *Walt: The Man Behind the Myth* (Pantheon Productions/The Walt Disney Family Foundation, 2001), DVD.

94   "The Famous, Unknown Mourn Passing of Genius Walt Disney," *The Waco Times-Herald*, December 16, 1966, 1.

95   Richard Hubler, "Ron Miller," Unpublished. Richard C. Hubler Collection, Box 14, Folder 53, Ron Miller, May 28, 1968, 1–21.

96   "'Substantial' Assets Willed by Disney," *Los Angeles Evening Citizen News*, December 22, 1966, 3.

97   David Shaw, "Poor Children View Film: 'Jungle Book' Debuts," *(Long Beach) Independent*, October 19, 1967, C7.

98   Howard Thompson, "Disney 'Jungle Book' Arrives Just in Time," *The New York Times*, December 23, 1967, L29.

99   Charles Champlin, "Disney Craft Flavor for 'Jungle Book,'" *The Los Angeles Times*, October 18, 1967, 81.

100   Edgar Penton, "Top Voices Enhance Kipling-Disney Art," *The Amarillo Globe-Times*, December 21, 1967, 38.

101   "Animals Portray Parts in Disney's 'Robin Hood,'" *Toledo Blade*, October 18, 1970, G7.

102   Jay Boyar, "He Helped Put Life into Disney Films," *The Orlando Sentinel*, March 24, 1983, E1, E4.

103   Boyar, "He Helped Put Life."

104   "Woolie Reitherman," *Disney Family Album*, 1985, Disney Channel.

105   Frank Thomas and Ollie Johnston, *The Illusion of Life: Disney Animation* (Hyperion, 1981), 159.

106   Frank Thomas and Johnston, *The Illusion of Life*, 159–161.

107   Champlin, "The Disney Days of Reitherman," *The Los Angeles Times*, August 10, 1981, 4.

108   Ghez, "The Letters from Otto Englander (1906–1969)," in *Walt's People, Volume 24: Talking Disney with the Artists Who Knew Him* (Theme Park Press, 2020).

109   Ghez, "The Letters from Otto Englander (1906–1969)" in *Walt's People, Volume 24*.

110   Ghez, "The Letters from Otto Englander (1906–1969)" in *Walt's People, Volume 24*.

111   Ghez, "The Letters from Otto Englander (1906–1969)" in *Walt's People, Volume 24*.

112   Ghez, "The Letters from Otto Englander (1906–1969)" in *Walt's People, Volume 24*.

113 Ghez, "The Letters from Otto Englander (1906–1969)" in *Walt's People, Volume 24.*

114 Ghez, "The Letters from Otto Englander (1906–1969)" in *Walt's People, Volume 24.*

115 Ghez, "The Letters from Otto Englander (1906–1969)" in *Walt's People, Volume 24.*

116 Otto Englander, "$1 Apiece for Embarrassing Moments," *New York Daily News*, 33.

117 "World War II Draft Registration Card (1940 October 16)," via *Ancestry. com*.

118 Michael Barrier, "Essays: A Day in the Life: Disney 1931," MichaelBarrier. com, March 5, 2009, http://www.michaelbarrier.com/Essays/Disney1931/ Disney1931.htm.

119 "Tragic Loss of Parents Spurs Worker," *Los Angeles Daily News*, September 11, 1943, 2.

120 "Tragic Loss of Parents."

121 "Snow White, Seven Dwarfs Entertain Screen Patrons," *Longview Daily News*, June 30, 1967, 19.

122 Robbin Coons, "Private Snafu, Army Pin-Up Boy," *Wichita Falls Times*, January 9, 1944, 9.

123 Amos Chapple, "Operation Punishment: The Nazi Bombing of Belgrade 80 Years Ago," Radio Free Europe/Radio Liberty April 6, 2021, https://www. rferl.org/a/nazi-terror-bombing-belgrade-1941-hitler-serbia/31179837. html.

124 "Tragic Loss of Parents."

125 UPI, "Yugoslav Jew Deaths Described at Trial," *Tucson Daily Citizen*, May 19, 1961, 18.

126 Edwin Schallert, "Janssen Developing New Type Music Film," *The Los Angeles Times*, April 3, 1944, 10.

127 Marjory Adams, "Movie Question Box," *The Boston Globe*, May 30, 1944, 14.

128 Ghez, "The Letters from Otto Englander (1906–1969)" in *Walt's People, Volume 24.*

129 Ghez, "The Letters from Otto Englander (1906–1969)" in *Walt's People, Volume 24.*

130 Inez Cocke, "Story Analyst Report of *The Castle of Llyr*, written by Lloyd Alexander," *Walt Disney Productions*, June 6, 1968.

131 Max Reynolds, "Gable Biography Portrays Life of Different Phases," *Cameron Herald*, November 30, 1961, 3A.

132 "Inez Cocke," IMDb, https://www.imdb.com/name/nm0168306/.

133 Cocke, "1955 Treatment, 'Phantom of the Opera,'" https://entertainment. ha.com/itm/movie-tv-memorabilia/the-phantom-of-the-opera-4-typed-

manuscript-treatments-and-outlines-for-the-hammer-films-production/a/
997027-1911.

134   "Inez Cocke," IMDb.

135   Sam Staggs, *Born to Be Hurt: The Untold Story of Imitation of Life* (*St. Martin's Press*, 2009), 365.

136   Max Reynolds, "Gable Biography."

137   Jean Garceau and Cocke, *Dear Mr. G——: The Biography of Clark Gable*, (*Muriwai Books*, 1961), 116.

138   Cocke, "Story Analyst Report of *The Castle of Llyr*."

139   Cocke, "Story Analyst Report of *The Castle of Llyr*."

140   Inez S Cocke, "Find a Grave," https://www.findagrave.com/memorial/8824 2093/inez-s-cocke.

141   "Hollywood Film Writer's Funeral Held," *Los Angeles Evening Citizen News*, October 17, 1969, B6.

142   Hamilton Luske, director, *Understanding Stresses and Strains*, Walt Disney Productions, 1968.

143   Abel Green, "Year of Violence and Mergers," *Variety*, January 3, 1968.

144   Oscars, "Short Film Winners: 1969 Oscars," YouTube video, June 10, 2015, 3:59, https://www.youtube.com/watch?v=CAMyOjp4nn4.

145   Bob Thomas, "Son-in-Law Boss at Disney Studio," *The Charlotte News*, July 10, 1969, 12A.

146   "Love Bug Day at Disneyland," on *The Love Bug* Special Edition DVD set, 2003, Disney.

147   Battelle, "'Fantasia' Returns as Big Hit," *Evening Herald*, February 4, 1970, 2.

148   Battelle, "'Fantasia.'"

149   Associated Press Image, Photo ID: 671201050, ID: 671201041, ID: 671201023, ID: 671201032. Dec. 1, 1967. Associated Press, Via https://newsroom.ap.org/editorial-photos-videos.

150   Bob Thomas, *Building a Company*, 33.

151   "Bomb in a Bank Hurts 10 Persons," *The New York Times*, January 5, 1908, 1.

152   Bob Thomas, *Building a Company*, 40–44.

153   Reading matter for sick vets army officer plea. (1923, December 31). (*Venice, Ca) Evening Vanguard*, p. 1.

154   Bob Thomas, *Building a Company*, 79.

155   Bob Thomas, *Building a Company*, 79.

156   Roy Disney interview by Jennifer Howard, November 5, 2007, for The Interviews: An Oral History of Television. Visit TelevisionAcademy.com/Interviews for more information.

157   Neal Gabler, *Walt Disney: The Triumph of the American Imagination* (New York: Alfred A. Knopf, 2008), 163.

158   Roy Disney interview by Jennifer Howard, November 5, 2007.

159   Roy Disney interview by Jennifer Howard, November 5, 2007.
160   Roy Disney interview by Jennifer Howard, November 5, 2007.
161   Roy Disney interview by Jennifer Howard, November 5, 2007.
162   Roy Disney interview by Jennifer Howard, November 5, 2007.
163   Roy Disney interview by Jennifer Howard, November 5, 2007.
164   Roy Disney interview by Jennifer Howard, November 5, 2007.
165   Roy Disney interview by Jennifer Howard, November 5, 2007.
166   Roy Disney interview by Jennifer Howard, November 5, 2007.
167   Roy Disney interview by Jennifer Howard, November 5, 2007.
168   "Miss Dailey Plights Troth to Roy Disney," *The Los Angeles Times*, June 23, 1955, 2.
169   Frances Dewberry, ed., "Roy Disneys to Visit Europe on Honeymoon," *Valley Times*, September 19, 1955, 6.
170   Roy Disney interview by Jennifer Howard, November 5, 2007.
171   Roy Disney interview by Jennifer Howard, November 5, 2007.
172   Roy Disney interview by Jennifer Howard, November 5, 2007.
173   Roy Disney interview by Jennifer Howard, November 5, 2007.
174   Bob Thomas, *Building a Company*, 312–313.
175   Roy Disney interview by Jennifer Howard, November 5, 2007.
176   Roy Disney interview by Jennifer Howard, November 5, 2007.
177   Roy Disney interview by Jennifer Howard, November 5, 2007.
178   Richard Hubler, "Ron Miller," Unpublished. Richard C. Hubler Collection, Box 14, Folder 53, Ron Miller, May 28, 1968, 1–21.
179   Richard Hubler, "Ron Miller," Unpublished. Richard C. Hubler Collection, Box 14, Folder 53, Ron Miller, May 28, 1968, 1–21.
180   "Actor John Wayne Conquered Cancer," *Wausau Daily Herald*, December 30, 1964, 12.
181   Patricia Ward Biederman, "$5-Million Encino Spread Is Gift Idea Fit for a Duke," *The Los Angeles Times*, December 24, 1985, https://www.latimes.com/archives/la-xpm-1985-12-24-me-20934-story.html.
182   Aissa Wayne, "Tour John Wayne's House in California," *Architectural Digest*, November 2008, https://www.architecturaldigest.com/story/wayne-article.
183   Biederman, "$5-Million Encino Spread."
184   Wayne, "Tour John Wayne's House."
185   Wayne, "Tour John Wayne's House."
186   Mayerene Barker, "1964—Year of Achievement Reviewed," *Valley News*, January 1, 1965, 7.
187   Biederman, "$5-Million Encino Spread."
188   "Disney Makes Appointment," *Valley Times*, November 22, 1968, 17.
189   Bob Thomas, "Ron Miller Now Disney Studio Head," *The Independent*, July 17, 1969, 14.
190   Arlene Eve, "Woodland Hills—Tarzana—Encino Meanderings," *Van Nuys Valley News*, October 10, 1968, 37A.

191 Richard Hubler, "Diane Miller," Unpublished. Richard C. Hubler Collection, Box 14, Folder 53, Diane Miller, June 11, 1968, 5–50.

192 "Schedule & Cost Report for Live-Action & Animated Features, Shorts & Television," 1969, Walt Disney Productions. Howard Lowery Auction, sold July 31, 2021.

193 "Disney Studio Brings Back the Cartoon Feature," *South Wales Argus*, June 23, 1977, 22.

194 "Bill Anderson (1911-1997)," in Ghez, *Walt's People.*

195 Bob Thomas, "Ron Miller is New Chief of Disney Realm," *The Gettysburg Times*, July 7, 1969, 3.

196 "Production Budget: The Aristocats," February 1968, Walt Disney Productions, Private collection of a Disney historian.

197 Mel Gussow, "Movies leaving 'Hollywood' behind," *The New York Times*, May 27, 1970, https://www.nytimes.com/1970/05/27/archives/movies-leaving-hollywood-behind-studio-system-passe-film-forges.html.

198 Kupcinet, Irv. (1971, April 16). Hope calls MGM Auction Biggest Grosser of Year. *The Indianapolis News*, p. 28.

199 "Production Budget: The Aristocats."

200 "The Aristocats Studio Production Document—Weekly Animation Productivity Report, 1968-1970," Walt Disney Productions, Howard Lowery Auction, sold October 22, 2022.

201 "The Aristocats Studio Production Document—Weekly Animation Productivity Report, 1968-1970."

202 "The Aristocats Studio Production Document—Weekly Animation Productivity Report, 1968-1970."

203 Woolie Reitherman, "Increased Productivity of Touchups and Ruffs on 'Aristocats'" memo, October 28, 1968, Walt Disney Productions, Private collection of a Disney historian.

204 Julius Svendsen, "Sweatbox Notes on Aristocats, 1968-1970," Walt Disney Productions. Howard Lowery Auction sold July 31, 2021.

205 Svendsen, "Sweatbox Notes."

206 Frank Thomas and Johnston, *The Illusion of Life,* 234–235.

207 "The Aristocats Studio Production Document—Weekly Animation Productivity Report, 1968-1970."

208 Card Walker, "The Aristocats Non-Critical Reaction Analysis (to First Rough Cut Screening)," memo to Woolie Reitherman, February 9, 1970, Howard Lowery Auction, sold July 8, 2023.

209 Nalina Eggert, "When Paris Was under Water for Two Months," *BBC News*, June 3, 2016, https://www.bbc.com/news/world-europe-36443329.

210 Svendsen, "Sweatbox Notes."

211 Svendsen, "Sweatbox Notes."

212 Walt Disney Productions, "Meet the Swingin' Sophisticats," ad in *Fort Worth Star-Telegram*, December 31, 1970.

213 "Love Story 1971 Gross $50 million," *Tucson Citizen*, January 7, 1972, 26.

214 "Fun-Parks Boom, yet Theatrical Films Remain Impressive Aspect for Disney," *Variety*, January 10, 1973, 4.

215 Christopher Finch, *The Art of Walt Disney: From Mickey Mouse to the Magic Kingdom* (New York: Harry N. Abrams, Inc., 1973), 318.

216 Snoop Doggy Dog, "The Aristocats," *Entertainment Weekly*, May 3, 1996, https://ew.com/article/1996/05/03/aristocats/.

217 Quentin Tarantino, *Cinema Speculation* (New York: Harper, 2022), 28.

218 Rebecca Rubin, "Questlove to Direct 'Aristocats' Remake for Disney," *Variety*, March 27, 2023, https://variety.com/2023/film/news/aristocats-remake-disney-questlove-1235565554/.

219 Didier, *They Drew as They Pleased, Vol. 5—The Hidden Art of Disney's Early Renaissance* (San Francisco: Chronicle Books, 2019), 83.

220 Woolie Reitherman, "Ideas and Comments Concerning the Future of Animation in the Disney Tradition," Walt Disney Productions, October 23, 1970. Private collection of a Disney historian.

221 Reitherman, "Ideas and Comments."

222 Walker, memo to Woolie Reitherman, "Future Animation," October 28, 1970, Walt Disney Productions. Private collection of a Disney historian. Private collection of a Disney historian.

223 Reitherman, "Ideas and Comments."

224 Don Duckwall, "Animation Talent Development Program—Prod. #7304" memo, April 16, 1971, Walt Disney Productions. Top of FormBottom of Form

225 Don Bluth, *Somewhere Out There: My Animated Life* (Smart Pop Books, 2022).

226 Bluth, *Somewhere Out There.*

227 Hal Sutherland, director, *Journey Back to Oz,* Filmation, 1972.

228 Duckwall, "Talent Development Program" memo, September 3, 1971, Walt Disney Productions. Private collection of a Disney historian.

229 Duckwall, "Talent Development Program."

230 Duckwall, "Notes from a General Review of those Who Have Been in the Talent Development Program" memo, September 21, 1971, Walt Disney Productions. Walt Disney Archives.

231 Duckwall, "Notes from a General Review."

232 Bluth, *Somewhere Out There*, 157.

233 Heidi Guedel, *Animatrix—a Female Animator* (Bloomington: 1st Books Library, 2003).

234 Guedel, *Animatrix.*

235 Bluth, *Somewhere Out There*, 158–159.

236 Bluth, *Somewhere Out There*, 168.

237 Bob King, memo to Card Walker, September 24, 1970, Walt Disney Productions, Private collection of a Disney historian.

238 MPSC Screen Cartoonists Guild, letter to Ed Prelock, December 8, 1970, Walt Disney Archives.

239 Julia Lee Brown, "Wife of U.S. Army Chaplain, Landscape Artist of Modern School, Likes Local Scenes," *El Paso Times*, October 15, 1916, 10.

240 "Chaplain Chouinard Dies; With 23D Infantry Here," *El Paso Herald*, September 16, 1918, 10.

241 Robert Perine, interview with Nelbert Chouinard and Eva Dickstein Roberts, not after 1967. Robert Perine research material on the Chouinard Art Institute, circa 1923–circa 1985. Archives of American Art, Smithsonian Institution.

242 Mary Ann Callan, "Luck or Temper, Irish Did the Job," *The Los Angeles Times*, June 14, 1953, 12.

243 Robert Perine, interview with Nelbert Chouinard and Eva Dickstein Roberts.

244 Jim Korkis, "The Birth of Animation Training," *Animation World Network*, September 23, 2004, https://www.awn.com/animationworld/birth-animation-training.; Donald H. Graham, Biography of Donald W. Graham, 2005, http://www.donaldwgraham.com/biography.html.

245 Walt Disney, memo to Don Graham, December 23, 1935, Walt Disney Productions. Reproduced for Animation Training Program Binder circa 1981. Heritage Auctions, sold January 27, 2019.

246 Walt Disney, letter to Nelbert Chouinard from Chouinard brochure, January 5, 1937.

247 Robert Perine, interview with Nelbert Chouinard and Eva Dickstein Roberts.

248 Callan, "Luck or Temper."

249 "Chouinard Art Institute," CalArts, https://calarts.edu/about/institute/history/chouinard-art-institute.

250 "The Close of Chouinard Art Institute and the Birth of California Institute of the Arts," Chouinard Foundation Library, https://www.chouinardfoundation.org/home/chouinard-cal-arts/.

251 "Mrs. Chouinard Feted on her 82nd birthday," *The Los Angeles Times*, February 10, 1961, 2.

252 Robert Perine, interview with Nelbert Chouinard and Eva Dickstein Roberts.

253 Robert Perine, interview with Nelbert Chouinard and Eva Dickstein Roberts.

254 "History," CalArts, https://calarts.edu/about/institute/history.

255 "Haldeman New Art Chairman," *Daily News-Post*, December 9, 1967, 10.

256 "The Nixon and Disney Newsletter—Part 3!" Richard Nixon Museum and Library, January 14, 2021, https://www.nixonlibrary.gov/news/nixon-and-disney-newsletter-part-3.

257 H. R. Haldeman, oral history interview, conducted by Dale E. Treleven, UCLA Oral History Program, for the California State Archives State Government Oral History Program, 1991.

258 R. Blubaugh, "Reagan Bolsters Hand on UC Tuition with 2 New Regents," *The Sacramento Bee*, 1968, 1.

259 "NYU Dean to be Prexy of New Art Institute," *Desert Sun*, December 14, 1967, 13.

260 Robert Corrigan, letter to Ron Miller, December 26, 1967 Ron Miller Collection, Walt Disney Archives.

261 Milton Esterow, "Herbert Blau Quits Lincoln Repertory," *The New York Times*, January 14, 1967, 1, 19.

262 Steve Proffitt, "Steven Lavine at CalArts: Inventing the Art of the Future Today," *The Los Angeles Times*, March 5, 1995, M3.

263 "Walt Disney Commemorative Medal Offered Public by Order of Congress," *Anaheim Bulletin*, August 14, 1969, B6.

264 White House Photo Office (WHPO), Washington, D.C., White House, March 25, 1969. Walt Disney's family members during their visit at White House to participate in the Walt Disney Commemorative Medal Ceremony. Walt Disney's family, Mrs. Lillian Bounds Disney, Mrs. Walt Disney, Mr. and Mrs. Roy O. Disney, Mrs. Diane Disney Miller, her husband and six children, Mrs. Sharon Disney Brown, Mr. and Mrs. Roy E. Disney and their four children, Mr. Jim Stewart.

265 H. R. Haldeman, letter to Robert Corrigan, April 14, 1969, CalArts Library.

266 Brian Lanker, director, *They Drew Fire*, May 2000, PBS, TV documentary.

267 Edward Reep, "Submission to Editors of Saturday Review of Literature," Edward Reep estate, January 30, 1972.

268 Reep, letter to "Marc," early spring of 1968, Edward Reep estate.

269 John Dreyfuss, "Ouster Fought by Faculty," *The Los Angeles Times*, November 15, 1969, 10.

270 Dreyfuss, "Ouster Fought by Faculty."

271 "Arts Institute to Use Cabrini Campus for One-Year Period," *Valley News*, August 28, 1970, 8.

272 William Glover, "New Concept in Education," *Belvidere Daily Republican*, December 29, 1970, 3.

273 "Count Basie First in New Theater," *The Signal*, May 17, 1972, p. 3.

274 Janice Ross, "Bill Irwin Falls on His Face and Lands Flat on His Feet," *Oakland Tribune*, May 7, 1982, H3.

275 James Real, "When You Wish upon a School," *The Los Angeles Times*, West Magazine, February 27, 1972, 16–19.

276 Dorothy Townsend, "Marcuse Vows to Continue Teaching at UC," *The Los Angeles Times*, July 26, 1968, 3.

277   Lance Gilmore, "Regents Probe Hiring of 2 Leftists at UC," *The San Francisco Examiner*, September 19, 1969, 5.

278   Drew Pearson, "Godfather of the Student Revolt Is Professor Marcuse of California," *The Tribune*, June 6, 1968, 10.

279   DeVan L. Shumway, "Reagan Hits Pact to End SCS Strike," *Oroville Mercury-Register*, February 25, 1969, 10.

280   "Why Cal Arts Rejected a Marxist," *The Signal*, January 14, 1970, 1.

281   John Rockwell, "Discord Surfaces Following Ouster of Cal Arts Provost," *The Los Angeles Times*, September 25, 1971, 8.

282   Herbert Marcuse, "Art as Revolutionary Weapon," lecture, 1970.

283   Rockwell, "Discord Surfaces."

284   "Why Cal Arts Rejected a Marxist."

285   Bob Thomas, *Building a Company*, 325–326.

286   Bob Thomas, *Building a Company*, 325–326.

287   Rockwell, "Discord Surfaces."

288   Dan Sullivan, "Blau Becomes Disenchanted with Disney's Dream," *The Los Angeles Times*, October 17, 1971, 1.

289   Reep, letter to Roy O. Disney, November 4, 1971, Edward Reep estate.

290   Bob Thomas, *Building a Company*, 321.

291   Mike Goodman, "President of CalArts Resigns; Money Plight, Dissension Blamed," *The Los Angeles Times*, May 5, 1972, F6.

292   Jules Engel, interviewed by Lawrence Weschler and Milton Zolotow, Oral History Program, University of California Los Angeles, 1985, The Regents of the University of California.

293   Arthur Millier, "Kandinsky, Art Pioneer, in Great Retrospective Show," *The Los Angeles Times*, March 1, 1936, 9.

294   Engel, interviewed by Weschler and Zolotow.

295   Engel, interviewed by Weschler and Zolotow.

296   Engel, interviewed by Weschler and Zolotow.

297   "Art News: Engle Work in White House Collection," *The Los Angeles Times*, November 21, 1965, 44.

298   Engel, interviewed by Weschler and Zolotow.

299   Engel, interviewed by Weschler and Zolotow.

300   Engel, interviewed by Weschler and Zolotow.

301   Engel, interviewed by Weschler and Zolotow.

302   Engel, interviewed by Weschler and Zolotow.

303   "They Put Cartoons, People Together," *Deseret News*, September 15, 1971, 18A.

304   "Disney Artist Drowns on Delta Tour," *Oakland Tribune*, August 29, 1971, 4.

305   Lloyd Alexander, *Something about the Author: Autobiography Series*, Vol. 19, 35–52, and earlier drafts, Lloyd Alexander papers, L. Tom Perry Special Collections, Harold B. Lee Library, BYU, 1995.

306   "Weather," *The Philadelphia Inquirer*, January 30, 1924, 1.

307   Alexander, *Something about the Author.*

308   Alexander, *Something about the Author.*

309   Alexander, *Something about the Author.*

310   Alexander, *Something about the Author.*

311   Alexander, *Something about the Author.*

312   Alexander, *Something about the Author.*

313   Alexander, *Something about the Author.*

314   Alexander, *Something about the Author.*

315   Alexander, *Something about the Author.*

316   Alexander, *Something about the Author.*

317   Alexander, *Something about the Author.*

318   Alexander, *Something about the Author.*

319   Alexander, *Something about the Author.*

320   Alexander, *Something about the Author.*

321   Alexander, *Something about the Author.*

322   Alexander, *Something about the Author.*

323   Alexander, *Something about the Author.*

324   Alexander, *Something about the Author.*

325   Alexander, *Something about the Author.*

326   Alexander, *Something about the Author.*

327   Kirk Honeycutt, "Bakshi Took On Fans, Hard Work in 'Rings' Animation," *Daily Times-Advocate*, October 6, 1978, B7.

328   Ghez, "Monday, September 17, 2012," *Disney History* (blog), September 17, 2012, http://disneybooks.blogspot.com/2012/09/on-saturday-some-documents-from-1972.html

329   Glenn Lovell, "The Lord of the Rings," *Fort Lauderdale News*, December 17, 1978, 14E–22E.

330   Charles Embree quote via Joan S. Webster.

331   "Paramount Names Two Key Story Dept. Men," *Los Angeles Evening Citizen News*, April 12, 1968, 5.

332   Charles Embree, letter to friend, December 30, 2017. From the estate of Charles Embree.

333   Alexander, *Something about the Author.*

334   Myra Livingston, letter to Jeanne-Marie, August 10, 1969.

335   "Minutes of the Last Story Meeting: Transcribed from a hidden tape recorder," February 1974, Walt Disney Productions, Private collection of a Disney historian.

336   Minutes of Story Meetings. *The Cauldron* Prod. #0128, meeting October 15, 1974, meeting October 21, 1974, and meeting October 23, 1974. Walt Disney Productions, Private collection of a Disney historian.

337 Minutes of Story Meetings. *The Cauldron* Prod. #0128, meeting October 15, 1974, meeting October 21, 1974, and meeting October 23, 1974. Walt Disney Productions.

338 Frank Thomas, *The Cauldron* Prod. #0128 meeting October 21, 1974, Walt Disney Productions. Present: Woolie, Lloyd, Milt, Mel Shaw, Ollie, Dick, Larry, Don Bluth, and Frank, who took these notes. Private collection of a Disney historian.

339 Mel Shaw, *Animator on Horseback: The Autobiography of Disney Artist Mel Shaw* (Theme Park Press, 2016).

340 Shaw, *Animator on Horseback.*

341 Shaw, *Animator on Horseback.*

342 Shaw, *Animator on Horseback.*

343 Alexander, *Something about the Author.*

344 Alexander, *Something about the Author.*

345 Alexander, letter to Kemie Nix.

346 Eric Larson, "To Those Concerned," undated 1972 letter, accessed via Bruce Reitherman collection.

347 Frank Thomas and Johnston, *The Illusion of Life,* 169–170.

348 "Cleveland Co-op Advertisement," *Emery County Progress*, December 22, 1906, 1.

349 John Canemaker, "Chapter Three—Eric Larson," in *Walt Disney's Nine Old Men and the Art of Animation* (New York: Disney Editions, 2001), 56–57

350 Canemaker, "Chapter Three—Eric Larson," in *Walt Disney's Nine Old Men.*

351 Cleon Larson, "Lord God of Hosts, Be With Us Yet, Lest We Forget, Lest We Forget," *Deseret News*, November 11, 1921, 12.

352 "Humbug and Pen Ready to Issue First Numbers," *The Daily Utah Chronicle*, November 19, 1924, 1.

353 Eric Larson, J. B. Kaufman, and Dan Jeup, *50 Years in the Mouse House: The Lost Memoir of One of Disney's Nine Old Men* (Theme Park Press, 2015).

354 Eric Larson, Kaufman, and Jeup, *50 Years in the Mouse House.*

355 W. Celon Skousen, scriptwriter, *Church Welfare in Action*, documentary, Church of Jesus Christ of Latter-Day Saints, 1948.

356 "'Church Welfare in Action'—First Documentary Film Ever Made by the Church," *Deseret News*, October 13, 1948, 24C.

357 Louella Parsons, "Disney Working to Complete 'Sleeping Beauty' for Yuletide," *Deseret News*, April 8, 1951, F3.

358 Canemaker, "Chapter Three—Eric Larson," in *Walt Disney's Nine Old Men,* 75.

359 "Sequence 8" feature on *Sleeping Beauty*, Platinum Edition, 2008, Walt Disney Home Video, Blu-ray/DVD. (Blu-ray/DVD).

360 Eric Larson, undated 1972 letter, Walt Disney Productions. Private collection of a Disney historian.

361 Eric Larson, undated 1972 letter.

362   Eric Larson, undated 1972 letter.

363   "Founder's Kin Named to Head Pratt Institute," *The Atlanta Constitution*, June 28, 1972, A20.

364   Eric Larson, undated 1972 letter.

365   "Minutes, Visual Communications Curriculum Committee," Walt Disney Productions, July 10, 1974. Private collection of a Disney historian.

366   Ken Anderson, memo, July 24, 1974, Walt Disney Productions. Private collection of a Disney historian.

367   "Minutes, Visual Communications Curriculum Committee," Walt Disney Productions, July 10, 1974.

368   "Minutes, telephone Call to Art Babbitt," Walt Disney Productions, July 29, 1974. Private collection of a Disney historian.

369   "Minutes, Visual Communications Curriculum Committee," Walt Disney Productions, July 10, 1974.

370   "1974 Walt Disney Productions Annual Report," 1, https://www.disneydocs.net/disney-annual-reports.

371   James Russell, "Uncertainty Trims Glamor from Disney," *The Miami Herald*, March 3, 1974, M6.

372   James Russell, "Uncertainty Trims Glamor."

373   James Russell, "Uncertainty Trims Glamor."

374   1973 Walt Disney Productions Annual Report, 23, *archive.org/details/wdp-annual-report-1973*.

375   1973 Walt Disney Productions Annual Report, 23, *archive.org/details/wdp-annual-report-1973*.

376   Nancy Cartwright, "Nancy Cartwright chats with Brad Bird," *Animation World Network*, June 30, 2009, https://www.awn.com/animationworld/nancy-cartwright-chats-brad-bird.

377   "In Conversation with…Brad Bird | TIFF 2018," TIFF Originals, YouTube video, June 12, 2018, 1:15:54, https://www.youtube.com/watch?v=njKzYTgKUKU.

378   Cristina Sanza, "Interview: 'Incredibles' Director Brad Bird Reflects on Working with Disney's Nine Old Men," *Inside the Magic*, December 18, 2018, https://insidethemagic.net/2018/12/brad-bird-interview-nine-old-men/.

379   "Boy's Film into U.S. Competition," *Corvallis Gazette-Times*, March 12, 1971, A2.

380   Sanza, "Interview: 'Incredibles' Director."

381   "Malango's Crew Working Well," *Corvallis Gazette-Times*, November 7, 1973, 26.

382   "Brad Bird," photo, *Corvallis Gazette-Times* June 17, 1975, 11.

383   "Brad Bird."

384   "Gorman-Margolin Exhibit to Open at Library," *The Gallup NM Independent*, December 5, 1974, 22.

385 "Wesleyan Graduate Named Luce Scholar," *Hartford Courant*, June 16, 1979, 23.

386 "Filmmaker John Musker (The Little Mermaid, Aladdin) and the Early Day at CalArts," *Skull Rock Podcast*, March 28, 2022, https://podcasters.spotify.com/pod/show/skullrockpodcast/episodes/Filmmaker-John-Musker-The-Little-Mermaid--Aladdin-and-the-Early-Days-at-CalArts-e1g9t0g/a-a5seq75.

387 "Filmmaker John Musker."

388 "Disney, Pixar Visionary John Lasseter Inducted into Whittier High Alumni Hall of Fame," *The Downey Patriot*, April 26, 2016, https://www.thedowneypatriot.com/articles/disney-pixar-visionary-john-lasseter-inducted-into-whittier-high-alumni-hall-of-fame.

389 Don Duckwall Letter to Nancy Beiman. June 13, 1975. Nancy Beiman collection.

390 Don Duckwall Letter to Nancy Beiman. June 13, 1975.

391 Jerry Rees, "A113: The Mysterious Origin," JerryRees.com, https://www.jerryrees.com/page29/page29.html.

392 "Kathy Zielinski," *The Animation Guild*, podcast, 31:12 (Part 1) and 38:51 (Part 2), https://animationguild.org/oral_history/kathy-zielinski/.

393 "AP Vault—Milt Kahl, Side 1" and "AP Vault—Milt Kahl, Side 2," *The Animation Podcast*, February 25, 2006, original recording 1976, and March 3, 2006, original recording 1976.

394 "Milt Kahl, Side 1" and "Milt Kahl, Side 2."

395 "Milt Kahl, Side 1" and "Milt Kahl, Side 2."

396 Undated Memo from Milt Kahl. Frank Thomas Collection, Margaret Herrick Library, Academy of Motion Picture Arts and Sciences.

397 Ron Clements, "The Black Cauldron Continuity Suggestions," August 21, 1976, Frank Thomas Collection, Margaret Herrick Library, Academy of Motion Picture Arts and Sciences.

398 Ron Clements, "The Black Cauldron Revised Continuity Suggestions submitted by Ron Clements," September 13, 1978, Walt Disney Productions.

399 John Culhane, letter to Frank Thomas, December 5, 1975, Frank Thomas Collection, Margaret Herrick Library, Academy of Motion Picture Arts and Sciences.

400 Frank Thomas, letter to Culhane, December 21, 1975, Frank Thomas Collection, Margaret Herrick Library, Academy of Motion Picture Arts and Sciences.

401 Benedict Lister, *Rosemary Anne Sisson: A Woman of Some Importance* (B.P. Lister, 2020)

402 Lister, *Rosemary Anne Sisson*, 46.

403 Lister, *Rosemary Anne Sisson*, 46.

404   Lister, *Rosemary Anne Sisson*, 46.

405   Lister, *Rosemary Anne Sisson*, 46.

406   Lister, *Rosemary Anne Sisson*, 46.

407   Rosemary Anne Sisson, letter to Vera, October 22, 1973, Walt Disney
       Studios, Burbank, California, in Lister, *Rosemary Anne Sisson*, unpublished
       draft of Chapter 14: The Disney Experience.

408   Aljean Harmetz, "Disney Rides Off in a New Direction With 'Pony'," *The
       Los Angeles Times*, August 3, 1975, 40.

409   Lister, *Rosemary Anne Sisson*, 130.

410   Sisson, diary entry, February 12, 1975, in Lister, *Rosemary Anne Sisson*,
       unpublished draft of Chapter 14: The Disney Experience.

411   Sisson, diary entry, February 12, 1975, in Lister, *Rosemary Anne Sisson*,
       unpublished draft of Chapter 14: The Disney Experience.

412   Harmetz, "Disney Rides Off."

413   Harmetz, "Disney Rides Off."

414   Harmetz, "Disney Rides Off."

415   Lister, *Rosemary Anne Sisson*, 133–135.

416   Sisson, diary entry in Lister.

417   Culhane, "The Old Disney Magic," *The New York Times*, August 1, 1976,
       https://www.nytimes.com/1976/08/01/archives/the-old-disney-magic-can-
       a-new-generation-of-artists-make-audiences.html.

418   Culhane, "The Old Disney Magic."

419   Ari L. Goldman, "Ward Kimball, Disney Animator, Dies at 88," *The New
       York Times*, July 10, 2002, https://www.nytimes.com/2002/07/10/arts/
       ward-kimball-disney-animator-dies-at-88.html.

420   "Ward Kimball," Disney Legends, Walt Disney Archives, https://d23.com/
       walt-disney-legend/ward-kimball/.

421   Canemaker, "Chapter One—Les Clark," in *Walt Disney's Nine Old Men*, 28.

422   Tessel, Harry. (1976, June 27). Disney's cartoon reissues keep paying off.
       (Long Beach) Press-Telegram, p. 12D.

423   Canemaker, "Chapter Eight—John Lounsbery." *Walt Disney's Nine Old
       Men*, 260–261.

424   Canemaker, "Chapter Eight—John Lounsbery."

425   Sisson, diary entry, in Lister.

426   Thomas, Bob. (1994). *Walt Disney: An American Original*. Disney Editions,
       p. 189-190.

427   Canemaker, "Chapter Five—Milt Kahl." *Walt Disney's Nine Old Men*, 156.

428   Burt Folkart, "Wolfgang Reitherman, 75: Disney Animator Dies in Car
       Crash," *The Los Angeles Times*, May 24, 1985, https://www.latimes.com/
       archives/la-xpm-1985-05-24-mn-17061-story.html.

429   "Kevin Corcoran Gets 2D Disney Star Role," *Variety*, December 26, 1957,
       1.

430   Ross A. Lincoln, "Kevin Corcoran Dies: 'Old Yeller' Actor and TV Producer Was 66," *Deadline*, October 7, 2015, https://deadline.com/2015/10/old-yeller-actor-and-producer-kevin-corcoran-dies-at-66-1201568865/.

431   "Film Production Chart," *Variety*, July 2, 1976, 6; and "Film Production Chart," *Variety*, November 5, 1976, 8.

432   "'Pete's Dragon' Opening in Bedford Area Friday," *The Times-Mail*, March 23, 1978, 17.

433   Bluth, director, *Banjo the Woodpile Cat*, 1979, DVD.

434   Sisson, diary entry in Lister.

435   Sisson, diary entry in Lister.

436   Sisson, diary entry in Lister.

437   Stephen Zito, "George Lucas Goes Far Out," *American Film*, April 1977, https://originaltrilogy.com/topic/George-Lucas-Interview-Circa-April-1977/id/12234#:~:text=George%20Lucas%20does%20nothing%20to,as%20a%20young%20people's%20movie.

438   Aljean Harmetz, "Disney Incubating New Artists," *The New York Times*, July 27, 1978, https://www.nytimes.com/1978/07/27/archives/disney-incubating-new-artists-mickey-mouse-turning-50-pompousness.html.

439   Robert L. Rose, "Disney's Answer to 'Star Wars,'" *The San Francisco Examiner*, November 28, 1977, 23.'

440   Charles Schreger, "Walt Disney Rolls Its Most Expensive Film, 'Black Hole'," *Variety*, October 13, 1978, 1.

441   Keith J. O'Connor, "Science Fiction Comes to the Big Screen," *Transcript-Telegram*, November 21, 1979, 28–29.

442   CDC/National Center for Health Statistics, "Total Fertility Rates and Birth Rates, by Age of Mother and Race: United States, 1940–2003," *Vital Statistics of the United States: 1980–2003*, National Center for Health Statistics. www.cdc.gov/nchs/data/statab/natfinal2003.annvol1_07.pdf.

443   David Weiner, "'We Never Had an Ending': How Disney's *Black Hole* Tried to Match *Star Wars*," *The Hollywood Reporter*, December 13, 2019, https://www.hollywoodreporter.com/movies/movie-news/we-never-had-an-ending-why-disneys-black-hole-lost-star-wars-1262526/.

444   Weiner, "'We Never Had an Ending.'"

445   Diane Miller, "Letters: Walt Disney," *The Los Angeles Times*, November 2, 1980, 99.

446   Kathryn Harris, "Takeover Talk Adds Pressure as Disney Tries to Snap Back," *The Los Angeles Times*, April 1, 1984, 6.

447   Harris, "Takeover Talk Adds Pressure."

448   Roy Disney interview by Jennifer Howard, November 5, 2007.

449   Roy Disney interview by Jennifer Howard.

450   John Taylor, *Storming the Magic Kingdom* (Alfred A. Knopf, 1987), 15.

451   Taylor, *Storming the Magic Kingdom*.

452   Guedel, *Animatrix*.

453   Bluth, *Somewhere Out There.*

454   All-Time Film Rental Champs. (1979, January 3). *Variety*, p. 54.

455   Mullinax, Gary. (1977, December 11). The Making of Pete's Dragon: Story was Discovered on a Shelf. *The (Wilmington) Morning News*, Entertainment, p. 3.

456   Maslin, Janet. (1977, November 4). Film: "Dragon" at music hall. *The New York Times*, p. C6.

457   Canemaker, "Chapter Three—Eric Larson," in *Walt Disney's Nine Old Men*, 79

458   Canemaker, "Chapter Three—Eric Larson," 79.

459   Canemaker, "Chapter Three—Eric Larson," 79.

460   Bluth, *Somewhere Out There.*

461   Guedel, *Animatrix.*

462   Guedel, *Animatrix.*

463   "NAACP, Walt Disney Sign Agreement," December 11, 1982, *The Atlanta Voice*, 1.

464   Bluth, *Somewhere Out There.*

465   Bluth, *Somewhere Out There.*

466   Harmetz, "11 Animators Quit Disney, Form Studio," *The New York Times*, September 20, 1979, C14.

467   Harmetz, "11 Animators Quit Disney."

468   Anthony Breznican, "The Strange True Story of Tim Burton's Normal Hometown," *Entertainment Weekly*, October 5, 2012, https://ew.com/article/2012/10/05/tim-burton-frankenweenie-hometown/.

469   Ed Orman, "Stockton Ports Defeat Fresno Cards, 8-3," *The Fresno Bee*, August 3, 1953, 8A–9A.

470   Orman, "Cards Lose to Oilers; Burton Is Hurt," *The Fresno Bee*, August 8, 1953, 2B.

471   Breznican, "Tim Burton: The Not-So-Grim Reaper," *TODAY*, January 8, 2004, https://www.today.com/popculture/tim-burton-not-so-grim-reaper-wbna3892992.

472   Breznican, "The Strange True Story."

473   Linda Mustion, "William R. 'Bill' Burton, BHS 1948," *Burbank Leader*, August 9, 2000, via BHS in Memoriam (blog), http://bhsinmemoriam.blogspot.com/2011/07/william-r-bill-burton-bhs-1948.html.

474   Amy Heibel, "His Teacher Remembers Tim Burton," Unframed: The LACMA Blog, May 25, 2011, https://lacma.wordpress.com/2011/05/25/his-teacher-remembers-tim-burton/.

475   "Tim Burton on His Life and Movies Coming Full Circle with 'Frankenweenie,'" *The Hollywood Reporter*, YouTube video, 29:54, February 18, 2013, https://www.youtube.com/watch?v=ki2CtwigsDY.

476   Geoffrey Macnab, "The Saturday Interview: Tim Burton on Cancel Culture and His *Beetlejuice* Sequel," *The Independent*, September 9, 2023, https://

www.independent.co.uk/arts-entertainment/art/features/tim-burton-beetlejuice-2-johnny-depp-disney-b2406538.html.

477 "Thoughts from Glen Keane," notes from meeting with Art Stevens, Don Duckwall, and Ed Hansen, June 26, 1979, Ed Hansen Collection, Walt Disney Archives (WDA)

478 Frank Thomas and Johnston, *The Illusion of Life*, 182.

479 Jackie McGlone, "The Charming Miss Davis," *Evening Chronicle*, September 8, 1979, 5.

480 Bob Thomas, "Smiles as Disney Fiasco Has a Happy Ending," *Manchester Evening News*, December 16, 1981, 3.

481 "Bette Davis Marks a Golden 50 Years in Film," *New York Daily News*, April 17, 1980, 9.

482 Vincent Canby, "Film: Disney Ghost Story: Haunted Landscape," *The New York Times*, April 17, 1980, https://www.nytimes.com/1980/04/17/archives/film-disney-ghost-storyhaunted-landscape.html.

483 Canby, "Film: Disney Ghost Story."

484 Rex Reed, "Disney Destroys Davis & 'Ffolkes' Is Flabby," *New York Daily News*, April 19, 1980, 8C.

485 Harmetz, "'Watcher in the Woods,' Revised $1 Million Worth, Tries Again," *The New York Times*, October 20, 1981, https://www.nytimes.com/1981/10/20/movies/watcher-in-woods-revised-1-million-worth-tries-again.html.

486 Bob Thomas, "Smiles as Disney Fiasco."

487 Bob Thomas, "Smiles as Disney Fiasco."

488 Sisson, in Lister, *Rosemary Anne Sisson*, unpublished draft of Chapter 14: The Disney Experience.

489 Thomas C. Hayes, "The Troubled World of Disney," *The New York Times*, September 25, 1983, 1, 12–13.

490 Steve Hulett, "'Mouse in Transition': When Everyone Left Disney (Chapter 7)," *Cartoon Brew*, July 26, 2014, https://www.cartoonbrew.com/wardkimball/when-everyone-left-disney-101724.html.

491 1985 Silver Screen auditors report from April 11, 1985; Ron Cayo memo from June 24, 1985. Ed Hansen Collection, Walt Disney Archives.

492 Joe Hale, Iwo Jima experience, February 19, 1945.

493 Lance Cpl. Bradley Carrier, "69th Iwo Jima Ceremony," *9th Marine Corps District*, March 31, 2014, https://www.9thmcd.marines.mil/In-the-News/Stories/Article/Article/519057/69th-iwo-jima-ceremony/.

494 Carrier, "69th Iwo Jima Ceremony."

495 Nancy Mills, "Disney Dabbles in Magic to Conjure a Blockbuster," *The Hamilton Spectator*, July 27, 1985, C1.

496 Shaw, *Animator on Horseback*.

497 Gene Siskel, "Animated 'Black Cauldron' Has a Drip for a Hero," *Chicago Tribune*, July 24, 1985, Section 5, 13.

498 M. McCreadie, "Drawing the Line," *Arizona Republic*, July 21, 1985, F3.
499 Alexander, *The Book of Three* (New York: Dell, 1980 [1964]).
500 "Press Release," Walt Disney Productions, June 3, 1980. Howard Lowery Auction, sold October 22, 2022.
501 Mitchell Zuckoff, *Robert Altman: The Oral Biography* (New York: Vintage Books, 2010).
502 Scott Campbell, "The 1980s Fantasy Film George R.R. Martin Calls 'Underrated,'" *Far Out Magazine*, February 6, 2024, https://faroutmagazine.co.uk/1980s-fantasy-movie-george-r-r-martin-calls-underrated/.
503 Michael Eisner, interview by Dan Pasternak on October 19, 2006, for The Interviews: An Oral History of Television.
504 Russell Howcroft, *DreamWorks: In Conversation with Jeffrey Katzenberg*, Australian Centre for the Moving Image (ACMI), May 23, 2023.
505 Howcroft, *DreamWorks*.
506 Michael Eisner and Tony Schwartz, *Work in Progress* (New York: Random House, 1998), 117.
507 Jody Jacobs, "Honors for a Humanitarian," *The Los Angeles Times*, September 26, 1980, 4.
508 "Popeye's Premiere," on *Popeye* 40th Anniversary Edition, 2020, Blu-Ray.
509 Champlin, "Disney World," *Arizona Republic*, June 28, 1981, E3.
510 Jacobs, "Western Theme for CalArts Benefit," *The Los Angeles Times*, July 13, 1981, 5.
511 Randy Cartwright, "*The Fox and the Hound* Wrap Party," July 1981, YouTube video, 8:37, uploaded July 2018, https://www.youtube.com/watch?v=8onL4lkpsfY.
512 Andreas Deja, "The Witches of Morva," *Deja View* (blog), August 14, 2012, http://andreasdeja.blogspot.com/2012_08_14_archive.html.
513 Tom Sullivan, "Hurt a New Man in Disney Thriller," *The Passaic Herald-News*, February 17, 1982, B6.
514 Sisson, letter to Vera, October 22, 1975, Walt Disney Studios, Burbank, California, in Lister, *Rosemary Anne Sisson*, unpublished draft of Chapter 14: The Disney Experience.
515 Dan Dinello, "Animaniac," *Chicago Tribune*, June 15, 1997, 12.
516 Dan Sarto and Jon Hofferman, "A Conversation with John Musker," *Animation World Network*, March 30, 2022, https://www.awn.com/animationworld/conversation-john-musker.
517 Sarto and Hofferman, "A Conversation with John Musker."
518 Ed Hansen, notes from meeting with Ron Miller, May 31, 1983, Ed Hansen Collection, Walt Disney Archives.
519 Deja, "Flying Hands," *Deja View* (blog), May 14, 2016, http://andreasdeja.blogspot.com/2016_05_14_archive.html.

520   The Hollywood Reporter, "Tim Burton on His Life and Movies Coming Full Circle with *Frankenweenie*," YouTube video, 29:54, February 18, 2013, https://www.youtube.com/watch?v=ki2CtwigsDY.

521   Elizabeth Perkins, "The Keswick Kid Moves His Magic to Hollywood," *The New York Times*, March 27, 1977, 3E.

522   Perkins, "The Keswick Kid."

523   Gerald Volgenau, "It All Started with a Mouse," *Fort Worth Star-Telegram*, February 20, 1978, 5B.

524   "Stock-Market Critics Irk Disney Officials," *Fort Worth Star-Telegram*, July 10, 1982, 2D.

525   Thomas C. Hayes, "The Troubled World of Disney."

526   Lawrence Cohn, "Larger-Than-Life Pix Pay Off," *Variety*, July 27, 1982, 1–26.

527   Larry Harnisch, Kenneth LaFave, and M. Scot Skinner, "Beating Video Games—Is It a Skill or Is It an Art?" *The Arizona Daily Star*, August 28, 1983; 1.

528   "Top Lifetime Adjusted Grosses," Box Office Mojo, https://www.boxofficemojo.com/chart/top_lifetime_gross_adjusted/?adjust_gross_to=2019.

529   Steve Hulett, "Financial Core and the '82 Strike," *TAG Blog*, March 24, 2006, http://animationguildblog.blogspot.com/2006/03/financial-core-and-82-strike.html.

530   Marilyn Beck, "Robards, Grier Recalled for Bradbury Film," *The Courier-Journal*, December 6, 1982, B10.

531   "Silver Screen Auditors Report," April 11, 1985. Walt Disney Archives.

532   Richard Hubler, "Diane Miller," unpublished, Richard C. Hubler Collection, Box 14, Folder 53, Diane Miller, June 11, 1968, 5–50.

533   Ron Miller, speech in Chicago to Midwest Banks, April 1982, Ron Miller Collection, Walt Disney Archives.

534   "1983 Walt Disney Productions Annual Report," https://archive.org/details/wdp-annual-report-1983/, 3.

535   Thomas J. Peters and Robert H. Waterman, *In Search of Excellence: Lessons from America's Best-Run Companies* (New York: Harper & Row, 1982).

536   Tom Furlong, "Disney Names Watson Chairman, Miller Chief," *The Los Angeles Times*, February 25, 1983, 1.

537   "Press Release," Walt Disney Productions, June 3, 1980. Howard Lowery Auction, sold October 22, 2022.

538   Ron Miller, "Disney Still Weighing Futures at 60," *Variety*, October 25, 1983, 147–152.

539   Ron Miller Collection, Walt Disney Archives.

540   Ron Miller, "Disney Still Weighing Futures."

541   Gary Arnold, "Crying, Laughing, Loving, Wolf," *The Washington Post*, October 9, 1983, https://www.washingtonpost.com/archive/lifestyle/

style/1983/10/09/crying-laughing-loving-wolf/54939c44-f438-4c47-beb3-53f749dc45f3/.

542   Wayne Warga, "It Isn't Funny at Mickey's Studio," *The Sacramento Bee*, October 25, 1980, A10.

543   Mike Hughes, "Hiring 'Black Stallion' Director Is a Big Step Forward for Walt Disney Productions," *The Courier News*, March 20, 1980, B11.

544   Bruce Brown, "Filming 'Never Cry Wolf,'" *The New York Times Magazine*, October 16, 1983, https://www.nytimes.com/1983/10/16/magazine/filming-never-cry-wolf.html.

545   Bruce Brown, "Filming 'Never Cry Wolf.'"

546   Bruce Brown, "Filming 'Never Cry Wolf.'"

547   Bruce Brown, "Filming 'Never Cry Wolf.'"

548   Bruce Brown, "Filming 'Never Cry Wolf.'"

549   Bruce Brown, "Filming 'Never Cry Wolf.'"

550   Bruce Brown, "Filming 'Never Cry Wolf.'"

551   "Disney Net Income Drops in 1st Half," *Variety*, April 25, 1984, 3.

552   "Disney 'Splash' Starts N.Y. Lensing; 4-Year Haul for Mermaid Pic," *Variety*, April 6, 1983, 30.

553   Jim Russell, "Disney Plans Theme Park in Europe," *The Miami Herald*, February 29, 1984, 4D.

554   "Domestic Box Office for 1984," Box Office Mojo, https://www.boxofficemojo.com/year/1984/?grossesOption=totalGrosses.

555   Kevin Polowy, "How a 'Splash' Joke Led to the 'Madison' Baby Name Boom," *Yahoo! Finance*, March 7, 2014, https://finance.yahoo.com/blogs/movie-news/splash-joke-lead-madison-baby-name-boom-190720175.html.

556   Walt Disney Productions, "Introducing Touchstone Films," February 24, 1984, *The Boston Globe*, 59.

557   Paul Rosenfield, "Rough Country," *The Los Angeles Times*, January 29, 1984, 1–22.

558   Rosenfield, "Rough Country."

559   Ale Russian, "Sam Shepard Revealed He Was Engaged to Jessica Lange — and How His 'Bad Behaviors' Ruined the Romance — in Letters," *People*, August 2, 2017, https://people.com/celebrity/sam-shepard-revealed-he-was-engaged-to-jessica-lange-and-how-his-bad-behaviors-ruined-the-romance-in-letters/.

560   Harry Smith, narrator, *The Farm Crisis*, documentary (Iowa PBS, July 1, 2013), https://www.iowapbs.org/shows/farmcrisis/documentary/5311/farm-crisis.

561   Patti Domm, "When Volcker Ruled the Fed, 'People Thought They'd Never Buy a Home Again,'" CNBC, December 9, 2019, https://www.cnbc.com/2019/12/09/when-volcker-ruled-fed-people-thought-theyd-never-buy-a-home-again.html.

562   Frank Morris, "Farmers Swept Up in Trade Wars Remember '80s Grain Embargo," *NPR*, August 16, 2018, https://www.npr.org/2018/08/16/639149657/farmers-caught-up-in-u-s-trade-war-s-remember-80-s-grain-embargo.

563   Dan Morgan, "Administration Is Facing Grain Embargo Backlash," *The Washington Post*, April 5, 1980, https://www.washingtonpost.com/archive/politics/1980/04/06/administration-is-facing-grain-embargo-backlash/ebeb1273-fc89-46ef-a426-e0060084d69e/.

564   Lee Lescaze, "Reagan to Lift Grain Embargo Today," *The Washington Post*, April 23, 1981, https://www.washingtonpost.com/archive/politics/1981/04/24/reagan-to-lift-grain-embargo-today/08f513e8-317a-4739-8ae8-9ba77b90efa5/.

565   Ward Sinclair, "FmHA: A 4-Letter Word," *The Washington Post*, July 16, 1982, https://www.washingtonpost.com/archive/politics/1982/07/09/fmha-a-4-letter-word/9b7c05b8-1e2e-4c88-a035-304e57f5474c/.

566   Blanche McCrary Boyd, "Sam Shepard: Cool, Natural and in Love," *Chicago Tribune*, October 7, 1984, 22. Originally published in *American Film Magazine*, October 1984.

567   "Richard Pearce," IMDb, https://www.imdb.com/name/nm0669004/.

568   Jim Brown, *TODAY*, Season 1984, episodes of January 25 and 26, 1984, NBC News.

569   Rosenfield, "Rough Country."

570   Jim Brown, *TODAY*, Season 1984, episodes of January 25 and 26, 1984, NBC News.

571   William D. Wittliff, revised *Country* screenplay, November 24, 1983. The original screenplay was written in September of 1983.

572   Rosenfield, "Rough Country."

573   Rosenfield, "Rough Country."

574   Roger Ebert and Gene Siskel, *At the Movies*, September 30, 1984, syndicated.

575   Dan Miller, "1984 Was a Very Bad Year for Agriculture," *The Gazette*, December 31, 1984, 8B.

576   Jennifer Phillips, "Lawman to Tell Congress: Farm Crisis Hurts Us, Too," *Quad-City Times*, October 22, 1985, 1.

577   "Suicide Rate for Farmers Soared in '80s, Study Says," *Tampa Bay Times*, October 14, 1991, https://www.tampabay.com/archive/1991/10/14/suicide-rate-for-farmers-soared-in-80s-study-says/.

578   Pauline Kael, "The Current Cinema," *The New Yorker*, October 1, 1984, 108–112.

579   Lori Erickson, "Where 'Country' Goes Wrong," *Des Moines Register*, October 11, 1984, 11A.

580   Robin Saunders, "Letters: Film Depicts Farm Struggle," *Des Moines Register*, October 28, 1984, 6C.

581 Ronald Reagan, "Diary Entry—10/05/1984," The Ronald Reagan Presidential Foundation & Institute, October 5, 1984, https://www. reaganfoundation.org/ronald-reagan/white-house-diaries/ diary-entry-10051984/.

582 Eugene Hernandez, "49 Years of New York Opening Night Films," *Film at Lincoln Center*, July 29, 2011, https://www.filmlinc.org/ daily/49-years-of-new-york-opening-night-films/.

583 "Country," Box Office Mojo, https://www.boxofficemojo.com/title/ tt0087091/?ref_=bo_rl_ti.

584 "Vidhits," *The Sentinel*, June 7, 1985, 10.

585 "Task Force on Agriculture," C-SPAN, May 6, 1985, https://www.c-span. org/video/?125430-1/task-force-agriculture.

586 Farm Aid, "Jessica Lange—Farm Aid PSA from 1985," YouTube video, 1:15, first aired September 22, 1985, posted March 10, 2011, https://www. youtube.com/watch?v=E6XiTjE0FVw.

587 Reagan, "Remarks at the Signing Ceremony for the Food Security Act of 1985 and the Farm Credit Amendments Act of 1985," December 23, 1985, Ronald Reagan Presidential Library & Museum, https://www.reaganlibrary. gov/archives/speech/remarks-signing-ceremony-food-security-act- 1985-and-farm-credit-amendments-act-1985#nara_banner_content.

588 John Taylor, *Storming the Magic Kingdom*, 48.

589 Roy Disney interview by Jennifer Howard, November 5, 2007.

590 Roy Disney interview by Jennifer Howard, November 5, 2007.

591 Roy Disney interview by Jennifer Howard, November 5, 2007.

592 Bob Thomas, "Disney Rebel Films Own 'Pacific High,'" *The Berkeley Gazette*, May 11, 1980, 19.

593 Kevin Thomas, "'R' Production from Disney?" *The Los Angeles Times*, March 14, 1980, 16.

594 Bob Thomas, "Disney Rebel."

595 Roy Disney interview by Jennifer Howard, November 5, 2007.

596 John Wark, "Walt Disney Name Rights Sought," *The Orlando Sentinel*, April 2, 1981, 12D.

597 Roy Disney interview by Jennifer Howard, November 5, 2007.

598 Thomas C. Hayes, "The Troubled World of Disney."

599 Phillip H. Wiggins, "Disney Net Falls 12.8% in Quarter," *The New York Times*, November 11, 1983, https://www.nytimes.com/1983/11/11/ business/company-earnings-disney-net-falls-12.8-in-quarter.html.

600 Kathryn Harris, "Takeover Talk Adds Pressure as Disney Tries to Snap Back," *The Los Angeles Times*, April 1, 1984, 1–6.

601 Roy Disney interview by Jennifer Howard, November 5, 2007.

602 John Taylor, *Storming the Magic Kingdom*.

603 John Taylor, *Storming the Magic Kingdom*, 45.

604 Tony Schwartz, "Hollywood's Hottest Stars," *New York*, July 30, 1984.

605 John Taylor, *Storming the Magic Kingdom*, 48–49.

606 John Taylor, *Storming the Magic Kingdom*.

607 *Heckmann v. Ahmanson*, Plaintiff's Memorandum of Points & Authorities in Support of Settlement of Derivative Action (filed September 14, 1989), Superior Court of the State of California for the County of Los Angeles.

608 John Taylor, *Storming the Magic Kingdom*, 68.

609 Delugach, Al, "Disney Heir Testifies Milken Helped Him Get Financing for Bid," *The Los Angeles Times*, June 28, 1989, 1–5.

610 John Taylor, *Storming the Magic Kingdom*, 90.

611 John Taylor, *Storming the Magic Kingdom*, 76–77.

612 *Heckmann v. Ahmanson*, Final Judgment and Order Approving Settlement, Awarding Attorneys' Fees and Reimbursement of Costs and Expenses and Dismissing Action (filed September 15, 1989), Superior Court of the State of California for the County of Los Angeles.

613 "Executive Pay Up 15%, Survey Says." *The Modesto Bee*, May 14, 1984, A4.

614 John Taylor, *Storming the Magic Kingdom*, 76–77.; and *Heckmann v. Ahmanson*.

615 John Taylor, *Storming the Magic Kingdom*.

616 John Taylor, *Storming the Magic Kingdom*,

617 John Taylor, *Storming the Magic Kingdom*,

618 Dave Gourevitch, "Disney Agrees to Arvida Acquisition Deal," *The Palm Beach Post*, May 18, 1984, 1.

619 Thomas C. Hayes, "Disney Agrees to Purchase Arvida," *The New York Times*, May 18, 1984, https://www.nytimes.com/1984/05/18/business/disney-agrees-to-purchase-arvida.html.

620 Sharman Stein, "Disney Plans to Buy Big Development Firm," *The Orlando Sentinel*, May 18, 1983, B1.

621 John Taylor, *Storming the Magic Kingdom*, 86–89.; and "Roy Disney Warns Against Arvida Buy," *The Fresno Bee*, May 20, 1984, D8.

622 Stephanie Tripp, "Disney Sells Arvida to JMB Realty," *The Tampa Tribune*, January 30, 1987, E1.

623 John Taylor, *Storming the Magic Kingdom*.

624 John Taylor, *Storming the Magic Kingdom*.

625 John Taylor, *Storming the Magic Kingdom*.

626 John Taylor, *Storming the Magic Kingdom*.

627 *Heckmann v. Ahmanson*, Plaintiff's Memorandum of Points and Authorities in Support of Settlement of Derivative Action (filed September 14, 1989), Superior Court of the State of California for the County of Los Angeles.

628 John Taylor, *Storming the Magic Kingdom*, 45, 125.

629 UPI. (1984, June 9). Donald Duck Marks his 50th Birthday. *Tulare Advance-Register*, p. 1.

630 *Heckmann v. Ahmanson*, Plaintiff's Memorandum of Points & Authorities.

631 *Heckmann v. Ahmanson*, Final Judgment and Order Approving Settlement, Awarding Attorneys' Fees and Reimbursement of Costs and Expenses and Dismissing Action (filed September 15, 1989), Superior Court of the State of California for the County of Los Angeles.

632 John Taylor, *Storming the Magic Kingdom*.

633 John Taylor, *Storming the Magic Kingdom*.

634 John Taylor, *Storming the Magic Kingdom*.

635 John Taylor, *Storming the Magic Kingdom*.

636 John Taylor, *Storming the Magic Kingdom*.

637 John Taylor, *Storming the Magic Kingdom*.

638 John Taylor, *Storming the Magic Kingdom*.

639 Notes from January 28, 1984, Ed Hansen Collection, Walt Disney Archives.

640 Charles Solomon, "Animation Takes a Giant Step," *The Los Angeles Times*, March 7, 1984, 2.

641 Bob Thomas, "Walt Disney Productions Returns to Animation," *The Lewiston Maine Daily Sun*, September 19, 1984, 28.

642 Bob Thomas, "Walt Disney Productions Returns to Animation."

643 Richard Sandomir, "Ron Miller, Who Rose to the Top at Disney, Then Fell, Dies at 85," *The New York Times*, February 12, 2019, https://www.nytimes.com/2019/02/12/obituaries/ron-miller-dead.html.

644 Harmetz, "Animation Again a Priority at Disney," *The New York Times*, August 27, 1984, C11.

645 "Investment Group Acquires 5.8% of Disney," *The Tampa Tribune*, July 19, 1984, F1.

646 Michael A. Hiltzik, "Irwin Jacobs Strikes Fear into Management," *The Pittsburgh Press*, October 10, 1984, C7.

647 John Taylor, *Storming the Magic Kingdom*, 184–185.

648 John Taylor, *Storming the Magic Kingdom*, 169–179.

649 John Taylor, *Storming the Magic Kingdom*, 179.

650 "Summer Leasuretime: Sam, the Olympic Eagle," *The Lompoc Record*, June 28, 1984, 4.

651 "1984 Olympics Will Not Be Mickey Mouse," *St. Louis Post-Dispatch*, July 10, 1983, 6D.

652 Bill Berry, "Timetable Is Arranged for Olympic Torch's Trip," *The Sacramento Bee*, January 19, 1960, B3.

653 John Taylor, *Storming the Magic Kingdom*, 198.

654 John Taylor, *Storming the Magic Kingdom*, 198.

655 John Taylor, *Storming the Magic Kingdom*, 198.

656 John Taylor, *Storming the Magic Kingdom*, 210.

657 John Taylor, *Storming the Magic Kingdom*, 210.

658 John Taylor, *Storming the Magic Kingdom*, 210.

659 John Taylor, *Storming the Magic Kingdom*, 211.

660 John Taylor, *Storming the Magic Kingdom*, 211.
661 Vicki Vaughan, "Ron Miller Quits Post with Disney," *The Orlando Sentinel*, September 8, 1984, B1.
662 Vicki Vaughan, "Ron Miller Quits Post with Disney."
663 Roy Disney interview by Jennifer Howard, November 5, 2007.
664 John Taylor, *Storming the Magic Kingdom*.
665 John Taylor, *Storming the Magic Kingdom*.
666 "Disney Productions Names Top Executive," *The Journal Times*, September 24, 1984, 5B.
667 Roy Disney interview by Jennifer Howard, November 5, 2007.
668 Roy Disney interview by Jennifer Howard, November 5, 2007.
669 Ron Miller Collection, Walt Disney Archives.
670 Phillip H. Wiggins, "Disney Net Falls 12.8% in Quarter," *The New York Times*, November 11, 1983, https://www.nytimes.com/1983/11/11/business/company-earnings-disney-net-falls-12.8-in-quarter.html.
671 Ed Hansen, memo, March 16, 1982, Ed Hansen Collection, Walt Disney Archives.
672 Ed Hansen Collection, Walt Disney Archives.
673 Ed Hansen, "CalArts Animation" memo, June 6, 1983, Ed Hansen Collection, Walt Disney Archives.
674 Ed Hansen, "CalArts Animation."
675 "Takeover Bid for Disney Ends," *The Cincinnati Post*, October 6, 1984, 7C.
676 Howcroft, *DreamWorks*.
677 Howcroft, *DreamWorks*.
678 Michael Eisner interview by Dan Pasternak, for The Interviews: An Oral History of Television, October 19, 2006. Visit TelevisionAcademy.com/Interviews for more information.
679 Howcroft, *DreamWorks*.
680 Howcroft, *DreamWorks*.
681 Howcroft, *DreamWorks*.
682 Howcroft, *DreamWorks*.
683 Howcroft, *DreamWorks*.
684 Eisner and Schwartz, *Work in Progress,* 172–173.
685 Howcroft, *DreamWorks*.
686 Allan Freeman Marketing and Research Associates, "'The Black Cauldron' Audience Reaction Research (Telephone Callback Interviews," November 1984, Joe Hale Estate.
687 Allan Freeman Marketing and Research Associates, "'The Black Cauldron.'" Joe Hale Estate.
688 Allan Freeman Marketing and Research Associates, "'The Black Cauldron.'" Joe Hale Estate.
689 Allan Freeman Marketing and Research Associates, "'The Black Cauldron.'" Joe Hale Estate.

690   Allan Freeman Marketing and Research Associates, "'The Black Cauldron.'" Joe Hale Estate.

691   Howcroft, *DreamWorks*.

692   Harmetz, "Former Executive Writes Inside Story of *Heaven's Gate*," *The Salt Lake Tribune*, August 2, 1985, M5.

693   Peter J. Boyer, "Who Has the Right to the Final Film Cut?" *The Los Angeles Times*, September 25, 1981, 1.

694   "MGM Buying United Artists for $380 Million," *The San Francisco Examiner*, May 22, 1981, C2.

695   Jacob Oller, "This Is the 'Blade Runner' Cut to Watch," *The Hollywood Reporter*, October 5, 2017, https://www.hollywoodreporter.com/movies/movie-news/blade-runner-original-final-cut-version-watch-1044897.

696   Terry Gilliam, director, *Brazil*, Criterion, 1985, DVD.

697   Brent Simon, "An Interview with David Lynch: David Lynch on Remastering *Inland Empire*, Revisiting His Earlier Work and the Chances of a *Dune* Do-Over," *AV Club*, April 14, 2022, https://www.avclub.com/david-lynch-inland-empire-interview-dune-restoration-1848795394.

698   Steve Vineberg, "Swing Shift—A Tale of Hollywood," *Sight & Sound*, 1991, https://www2.bfi.org.uk/news-opinion/sight-sound-magazine/features/swing-shift-making-of-jonathan-demme-directors-cut-comparison.

699   Ben Waldburger, "Release *The Black Cauldron* Restored on Blu-ray," *Change.org*, November 2, 2014, https://www.change.org/p/robert-a-iger-release-the-black-cauldron-uncut-on-blu-ray.

700   Ryan Parker, "How *The Temple of Doom* Changed the MPAA Ratings System," *The Hollywood Reporter*, May 23, 2017, https://www.hollywoodreporter.com/movies/movie-news/indiana-jones-temple-doom-changed-mpaa-ratings-system-999618/.

701   Notes from meeting with Michael Eisner, Jeffrey Katzenberg, Roy Disney, Stan Kinsey, and Ed Hansen January 7, 1985, Ed Hansen Collection, Walt Disney Archives.

702   *The Black Cauldron* cutting continuity script, June 1985, Walt Disney Productions. Howard Lowery Auction, sold June 26, 2010.

703   Alexander, memo, June 26, 1985, Walt Disney Productions, Walt Disney Archives.

704   Sherryl Connelly, "The Mouse That Roared," *New York Daily News*, June 16, 1985, 10.

705   Clarke Taylor, "Rockettes Dance Picket Line over Disney Decision," *The Los Angeles Times*, January 12, 1985, 3.

706   Alexander, letter to Joe Hale, July 27, 1985, Joe Hale papers.

707   Jack Matthews, "Studios Sing the Summertime Blues," *The Los Angeles Times*, September 6, 1985, 6.

708 Ian Nathan, "25 Years of Back to the Future," *Empire*, via tumblr, May 2010, https://empireaust.tumblr.com/post/108679102786/back-to-the-future-the-oral-history-spielberg.

709 Beck, "Me Rambo! Box Office Mine!" *New York Daily News*, August 30, 1985, C20.

710 David T. Friendly, "Team Disney—Flying High in Burbank," *The Los Angeles Times*, July 28, 1985, 22–33.

711 Friendly, "Team Disney."

712 Scott, Vernon. UPI. (1985, July 31). Chase's "Vacation" sequel packs 'em in. *The Stuart News*, p. A6.

713 AP. (1985, August 8). Sci-fi movies sell big. *The Cleveland Plain Dealer*, p. 11B.

714 Jim Harwood, "Labor Day Fails to Pump Much Needed Blood into National Bhoxoffice," *Variety*, September 4, 1985, 4.

715 Matthews, "Studios Sing."

716 Bob Thomas, "Feature-Length Cartoons Entering New Golden Age," *The Evening Sun*, November 22, 1989, A11.

717 Drew Taylor, "How the Black Cauldron Nearly Killed Disney Animation," *Collider*, August 19, 2020, https://collider.com/the-black-cauldron-disney-why-it-flopped-controversy-explained/.

718 Roger Ebert, "The Black Cauldron Movie Review (1985): Roger Ebert," RogerEbert.com, July 24, 1985, https://www.rogerebert.com/reviews/the-black-cauldron-1985.

719 Peter Goodman, "The Black Cauldron's" Stirring Fantasy" *Newsday*, July 26, 1985.

720 Rex Reed, *New York Post* review, July 26, 1985, via Walt Disney Archives.

721 William Royce, *Beverly Hills 213* article, January 2, 1986, via Walt Disney Archives.

722 Lee Margulies, "Explosion in Children's Films and TV Programs," *The Los Angeles Times*, August 1, 1985, 11.

723 Jeff Bater, "Walt Disney Co. Has Record Year," *Kingsport Times-News*, February 7, 1986, 6B.

724 Bater, "Walt Disney Co."

725 Bater, "Walt Disney Co."

726 Notes from meeting attended by Michael Eisner, Jeffrey Katzenberg, Roy Disney, Stan Kinsey and Ed Hansen, January 7, 1985, Ed Hansen Collection, Walt Disney Archives.

727 "Walt Disney Productions Telephone Directory," circa 1986 and July 16, 1982, Walt Disney Productions.

728 Ed Hansen Collection, Walt Disney Archives.

729 Canemaker, "Chapter Three—Eric Larson," 81.

730   Notes from meeting attended by Michael Eisner, Jeffrey Katzenberg, Roy Disney, Stan Kinsey and Ed Hansen, January 7, 1985, Ed Hansen Collection, Walt Disney Archives.

731   Notes from meeting attended by Michael Eisner, Jeffrey Katzenberg, Roy Disney, Stan Kinsey and Ed Hansen, January 7, 1985, Ed Hansen Collection, Walt Disney Archives.

732   James C. Taylor, "Part of Their World," *The Orlando Sentinel*, April 11, 2010, F12.

733   "Linda Ronstadt: Biography, Music & News," *Billboard*, https://www.billboard.com/artist/linda-ronstadt/.

734   "An American Tail," Box Office Mojo, www.boxofficemojo.com/title/tt0090633/.

735   "The Great Mouse Detective," Box Office Mojo, www.boxofficemojo.com/title/tt0091149/.

736   "Domestic Box Office for 1987," Box Office Mojo, https://www.boxofficemojo.com/year/1987/.

737   "Domestic Box Office for 1988," Box Office Mojo, https://www.boxofficemojo.com/year/1988/.

738   "Domestic Box Office for 1989," Box Office Mojo, https://www.boxofficemojo.com/year/1989/.

739   "Domestic Box Office for 1991," *Box Office Mojo*, https://www.boxofficemojo.com/year/1991/.

740   "Domestic Box Office for 1992," Box Office Mojo, https://www.boxofficemojo.com/year/1992/.

741   "Domestic Box Office for 1994," Box Office Mojo, https://www.boxofficemojo.com/year/1994/.

742   CDC/National Center for Health Statistics, "Total Fertility Rates and Birth Rates, by Age of Mother and Race: United States, 1940–2003," *Vital Statistics of the United States: 1980–2003*, National Center for Health Statistics, https://www.cdc.gov/nchs/data/statab/natfinal2003.annvol1_07.pdf.

743   "Brands (US & Canada)," Box Office Mojo, https://www.boxofficemojo.com/brand/.

744   "Brands (US & Canada)," Box Office Mojo, https://www.boxofficemojo.com/brand/.

745   *TODAY*, season 1985, episode July 18, 1985, NBC News, July 18, 1985.

746   Catherine Hinman, "French Theme Park Troubles Hurt Disney's Income; For the Year, Disney Revenue Was Up 4%," *The Orlando Sentinel*, November 11, 1993, A-1, A-14.

747   Raymond L. Watson, "Planning and Developing the New Town of Irvine, California, 1960-2003: Irvine Company President, 1973-1977; Walt Disney Company Chairman, 1983-1984," an oral history conducted in

2003 by Ann Lage, Regional Oral History Office, The Bancroft Library, University of California, Berkeley, 2005.

748   Joshua A. Luna, "The Toxic Effects of Branding Your Workplace a 'Family,'" *Harvard Business Journal*, October 27, 2021, https://hbr.org/2021/10/the-toxic-effects-of-branding-your-workplace-a-family.

749   "Employee Tenure in 2022," Bureau of Labor Statistics, Department of Labor, September 22, 2022, https://www.bls.gov/news.release/pdf/tenure.pdf.

750   "Top Lifetime Grosses," Box Office Mojo, www.boxofficemojo.com/chart/ww_top_lifetime_gross/.

751   Minal Zaheer, "30 Highest-Grossing Media Franchises of All Time," *Yahoo! Finance*, February 15, 2024, https://finance.yahoo.com/news/30-highest-grossing-media-franchises-133420902.html.

752   "Geneva Dinner Menu," November 20, 1985, folder Geneva Dinner Box, box OA 13779, Linda Faulkner Files, Ronald Reagan Library.

753   Diane Haithman, "Disney Gives $25 Million to Downtown Concert Hall," *The Los Angeles Times*, December 2, 1997, https://www.latimes.com/archives/la-xpm-1997-dec-02-mn-59753-story.html.

754   Mike Boehm, "A Rocky Road, Step by Step," *The Los Angeles Times*, September 14, 2003, https://www.latimes.com/archives/la-xpm-2003-sep-14-ca-boehm14-story.html.

755   "10 Buildings that Changed America," WTTW, https://interactive.wttw.com/ten/buildings.

756   Roy E. Disney, letter of resignation to Michael D. Eisner, November 30, 2003, www.sec.gov/Archives/edgar/data/1001039/000119312503090215/dex991.htm.

757   James Bates, "Disney Daughter Says Eisner Should Leave," *The Los Angeles Times*, March 10, 2004, A1, A20.

758   Ana Leal, "Sunday Memorial Held for Walt Disney's Nephew Roy E. Disney," *Chip and Company*, January 11, 2010, https://chipandco.com/sunday-memorial-held-for-walt-disneys-nephew-roy-e-disney-5632/.

759   Christine N. Ziemba, "Remembering CalArts Trustee Roy E. Disney," CalArts (blog), January 12, 2010, https://blog.calarts.edu/2010/01/12/remembering-calarts-trustee-roy-e-disney/.

760   "Remembering Ron Miller," The Walt Disney Company, February 10, 2019, thewaltdisneycompany.com/remembering-ron-miller/.

761   Michael Eisner (@Michael_Eisner), Tweet, February 10, 2019, https://twitter.com/Michael_Eisner/status/1094625921955434496/.

762   "The Walt Disney Company 2019 Fiscal Year Annual Report," The Walt Disney Company, 2019, https://thewaltdisneycompany.com/app/uploads/2020/01/2019-Annual-Report.pdf.

763 Alex Sherman, "Disney's Wildest Ride: Iger, Chapek and the Making of an Epic Succession Mess," CNBC, October 19, 2023, https://www.cnbc.com/2023/09/06/disney-succession-mess-iger-chapek.html.

764 Patricia Battle, "Nelson Peltz Gets a Vote of Confidence from Elon Musk in Battle Against Disney," *The Street*, April 4, 2024, https://www.thestreet.com/investing/nelson-peltz-had-a-controversial-ally-in-disney-proxy-battle.

765 Andrew Ross Sorkin, "Why Nelson Peltz Wants P.&G. to See Him as a 'Constructivist,'" *The New York Times*, July 17, 2017, https://www.nytimes.com/2017/07/17/business/dealbook/nelson-peltzs-play-for-pampg-honorable-intentions.html.

766 Alex Sherman, Rohan Goswami, and Sarah Witten, "Disney Wins Proxy Fight Against Activist Investor Nelson Peltz, as Shareholders Reelect Full Board," CNBC, April 3, 2024, https://www.cnbc.com/2024/04/03/disney-annual-meeting-shareholders-vote-on-nelson-peltz-and-bob-iger.html.

767 "Major Disney Shareholders and Influential Business Figures Support CEO Bob Iger and The Walt Disney Company's Board of Directors," The Walt Disney Company, March 25, 2024, https://thewaltdisneycompany.com/major-disney-shareholders-and-influential-business-figures-support-ceo-bob-iger-and-the-walt-disney-companys-board-of-directors/.

768 "Major Disney Shareholders."

769 "Major Disney Shareholders."

770 Alex Weprin, "Disney Declares Victory in Proxy Fight as Nelson Peltz Fails to Win Board Seat," *The Hollywood Reporter*, April 3, 2024, https://www.hollywoodreporter.com/business/business-news/disney-proxy-fight-result-bob-iger-nelson-peltz-1235863896/

Author's Note

I first embarked on this journey in 2008. It was the golden summer of the DVD era, and it seemed Hollywood had pulled back the curtain on nearly every movie in existence. Films that were previously unavailable for much of my youth were now presented as jeweled artifacts, ripe for discovery. Filmmakers who were not typically in the spotlight were thrust in front of the camera, telling their stories for the first time. These behind-the-scenes recollections occasionally proved more interesting than the movie itself. In that spirit, I set out to discover more about a childhood curiosity, *The Black Cauldron*.

I remain grateful that in those early stages, a handful of key contributors were willing to share their stories with me—including Ron Miller and Joe Hale. Joe and his wife Beverly invited me and my then-fiancée to visit their home in California. His walls were adorned with work from artists who had passed through Disney at various points during his thirty plus year career. The talent on display fundamentally changed my understanding of the artistry required for animation.

Disney animation has been a key part of my life since I first encountered animator Ruben Aquino as a child. He had traveled across the country to speak at an animation gallery in Woodbridge, New Jersey, in the late 1980s. He showed the assembled group his pencil animation of his new character in the upcoming film *The Little Mermaid*. He introduced us to a half-octopus villain named Ursula as she "wasted away to practically nothing." I was at an age when animation seemed like a childish thing to be put away, but this was exhilarating. What I didn't know was that this encounter would be an early entry into what would become known as the Disney renaissance. Getting to interview Ruben Aquino for the book was particularly special. To shake his hand at a screening of 2023's *Once Upon a Studio*, featuring new animation of Ursula, was a full-circle moment for me.

This book is in large part an oral history of Disney Animation. One of the joys of my journey was getting to speak with people whose work I had long admired—whether I originally knew their names or not. Among them: Tony Anselmo, Ralph Bakshi, Esther Barr, Nancy Beiman, David Block, Hendel Butoy, Randy Cartwright, Michael Cedeno, Lorna Cook, Sue DiCicco, Rick Farmiloe, Andy Gaskill, Gary Goldman, Ed Goral, Steve Gordon, Carolyn Guske, Don Hahn, Dan Haskett, Mark Henn, Steve Hulett, Ron Husband, Glen Keane, Jorgen Klubien, Doug Lefler, Phil Nibbelink, Floyd Norman, John Pomeroy, Ruben Procopio, Dave Pruiksma, Saskia Raevouri, Jerry Rees, Rebecca Rees, Lenord Robinson, Henry Selick, Peter Schneider, George Scribner, Mel Shaw, Dave Smith, Tad Stones, Donald Towns, Gary Trousdale, Darrell Van Citters, and Cyndee Whitney. Not all of them have quotes featured in the final book, but each conversation was a vital building block in assembling my story. A special thanks to Mike Gabriel, who decided to answer my questions with written responses so he could put more thought into his replies. He returned with over a hundred pages. Don't meet your childhood heroes unless they are animators.

My gratitude extends to the children of key figures who were no longer alive to share their stories: Walter Elias Disney Miller, Bruce Reitherman, Ted Thomas, Joan Webster, Susan Reep, and Cathy Nourafshan. In that same vein, my thanks to Anthony Ladesich for turning me on to "Riff Charles" Embree—a figure worth rediscovering—as well as Jennie Livingston and Kemie Nix for sharing stories of their beloved friend Lloyd Alexander. Thanks also to the participating members of *The Black Cauldron*'s voice cast—John Byner (Gurgi and Doli), Susan Sheridan (Eilonwy), Phil Fondacaro (Creeper), Grant Bardsley (Taran), and Grant's mother, Pennie. Also, Cynthia Millar, who performed the ondes Martenot for the film's score.

A note on sourcing: In the many instances where interview subjects agreed to speak with me—in person, via phone or other devices—I transcribed the conversations and they are included in the book without additional citation. Likewise, some information comes from email correspondences with these subjects. These interviews and emails span the course of 2008-2024. Tim Burton's quotes are from a press gaggle held for the opening of his MoMA show which I attended.

Special thanks to Disney historian Didier Ghez, who helped me kickstart the project again in 2020 after it spent several years in the proverbial wilderness. His generosity and guidance were invaluable. Thanks to a varied assortment of other helpful personalities, including Katherine Barrett and Rich Greene, Michael Barrier, Hal Barwood, Michael Huebler, Audrey Kamb-Studdard, Roger Kim, Al Lowe, Ron Magliozzi, Dave Mattingly, Genevieve Maxwell, Jenni Matz, Kent Ramsey, Janet Reilly, Rebecca Wilson, John Taylor, and Jeannette Walls. Taylor's *Storming the Magic Kingdom* remains the definitive account of the greenmail attempt of 1984, even more so as key participants are no longer with us. I extend my gratitude for his permission to use his reporting. Please seek out a copy of his book for more of the story. Additional thanks to the teams at Brigham Young University, Boston University, Nixon Library (Elizabeth Macias, Carla Braswell, Ryan Pettigrew), and CalArts (president Ravi Rajan, Kiara Brown, Cynthia Villasenor, Susan Lowenberg, Lucy Griffin, Blake Jacobsen) for their research assistance.

This book would have remained an unrealized dream without those who helped get it out of my head and onto the page. Among them, Andrew Arenge, Nate Garneau, Ron Barbagallo, my literary agents at Screenland LA Paula Allen and Barbara Marcus, and my editors at Post Hill Press Adriana Senior, Aleigha Koss, and Kate Post. Also thanks to David Paul Kirkpatrick and Story Summit. Finally, my thanks to my family and friends who offered unwavering support and patience over the last sixteen years.

About the Author

Photo by Darius Nichols/DNPhotographyNYC

Neil O'Brien is an award-winning journalist and producer who has worked at NBC News for more than two decades. He has produced hundreds of hours of television over the course of his career and his work with NBC News Specials has been honored with four Emmy Awards, a Peabody, and an Edward R. Murrow Award.

Neil has spent more than a decade researching and conducting interviews for this book. He also serves on the Advisory Committee of the Berkshire International Film Festival. He graduated from the College of the Holy Cross in Worcester, MA. He lives in New Jersey with his wife and two children.